Export Practice and Documentation

A. G. Walker

Dip. Econ., F.I.Ex., M.Inst.M.

Formerly Principal Lecturer and Director of Marketing Studies,
Buckinghamshire College of Higher Education

Principal, Export Practice Associates

BUTTERWORTHS
London   Boston   Durban   Singapore   Sydney   Toronto   Wellington

First published 1970
Second edition 1977
   Reprinted 1978, 1980
Third edition 1987

© A. G. Walker 1987

British Library Cataloguing in Publication Data

Walker, A.G. (Alexander George)
   Export practice and documentation.—3rd ed.
   1. Export marketing—Great Britain
   I. Title
   658.8'48'0941   HF3506
   ISBN 0-408-02800-9

Library of Congress Cataloging in Publication Data

Walker, A. G. (Alexander George)
   Export practice and documentation.

   Bibliography: p.
   Includes index.
   1. Export sales.   2. Export marketing.   I. Title.
   HF1009.5.W34   1987   658.8'48   86-29945
   ISBN 0-408-02800-9

Phototypeset by Scribe Design, Gillingham, Kent
Printed and bound in Great Britain by Robert Hartnoll (1985) Ltd, Bodmin, Cornwall

Preface

It is a privilege to offer this third edition as a modest contribution towards the immense effort that has been made by exporters, professional bodies and government departments to bring about a high degree of expertise in the realm of international trade administration. My ambition is that the book will continue to be on the bookshelf of the busy practitioner as well as the student preparing for the wide range of professional and academic qualifications that today include this subject matter in their curricula.

To this end, and in keeping with the Institute of Export's wise development of the total export concept, I have added chapters on international marketing and physical distribution.

Due to the expansion of trading areas and growing harmonization between countries in their export and import procedures, it has been possible to give this edition a wider international application, although naturally some chapters will have a degree of United Kingdom orientation. This has been considerably facilitated by various projects carried out with my colleagues in UNCTAD/GATT.

As always, it is difficult to acknowledge adequately all the help and encouragement received in the preparation of this work, as any book must of necessity be the result of working with many companies, institutions and colleagues. I should like to express my gratitude to Dennis Brewster, Charles Coyne, Patrick Parsons and Simon Horsington, Barrister-at-Law, Midland Bank International. The regular contributors to the *Institute of Export Journal*, too, receive my thanks for, as busy practitioners dealing with current export situations, they are always a great source of inspiration. Special mention must also go to Mrs Elsie Hinkes who has so cheerfully and efficiently undertaken the task of typing the manuscript.

My final dedication is to all those engaged in international trade whose work not only enhances the material welfare and prosperity of their own countries, but also fosters a growing harmony and understanding between nations.

A.G.W.

To Billie and the girls

Contents

1 International marketing

There are many definitions of marketing, all of them of importance, but a useful starting point might be the definition:

Marketing is the process of providing

the right product
in the right place
at the right price
at the right time

And to this we could add: to achieve the appropriate objective (such as profit, growth etc.), and to meet the corporate target of the seller.

When we apply the above to international marketing it is obvious that although all the principles set out above remain equally valid, they must by their very nature take place against a more complex background.

Products may have to be 'right' for many different countries and in the 'right place' in markets perhaps long distances away against the background of different climates, political and cultural conditions. There will also be a more complex pattern of transportation methods required to move the products into the 'right place' at the right time: therefore patterns of shipment by sea, air, road, roll-on/roll-off, with their attendant costs and complications, will be encountered.

Decisions as to the 'right price' will be influenced by many factors such as transportation costs, foreign exchanges and, to a greater degree in the international scene, by overseas governments and institutions.

Essentially, the international marketing operation will be one of recognizing a pattern of variable factors and responding to and adjusting these in order to achieve the correct balance. This pattern is normally referred to as the 'international marketing mix', as illustrated in *Figure 1.1*. The first and most vital point of the marketing mix is to highlight the relative *degree* of importance

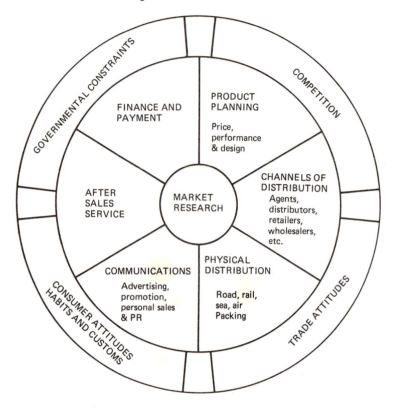

Figure 1.1 International marketing mix

to the exporter of the various segments. It must be stressed that although all the variables are important, their degree of importance will vary from exporter to exporter and market to market, depending upon the type of industry and product involved.

To an exporter of basic chemicals, bulky and low cost, the segment of physical distribution will be a key area of marketing in order to achieve the most economical transportation, storage and packing costs. Such a company may have little power to influence the price which may be virtually a market price level to which the seller must conform.

On the other hand, an exporter of high-technology scientific instruments may place greater importance on the back-up after-sales segment and product performance and design, whereas price may be less relevant and transport costs perhaps form only a very small fraction of the overall selling price.

An exciting aspect of the marketing mix, particularly internationally, is that these variables also have to be viewed against a sometimes rapidly-changing background of international events. The periphery of the marketing mix diagram stresses aspects such as government constraints and legislation, changing degrees of competition, and customer and social attitudes.

The starting point for all good overseas marketing should of course, be market *or* marketing research. The distinction between the two (sometimes a little blurred) is that the former envisages more of a quantitative measurement of the likely size and volume of sales, population figures and growth, etc., whereas the latter extends the process into researching other factors such as distribution channel analysis, promotion methods, terms of sale and payment, etc.

Some degree of research must be undertaken, but the degree will itself depend very much upon the size and resources of a company. It can vary from very precise research carried out in a most sophisticated manner by specialized departments, to very much *ad hoc* work carried out by a harrassed export manager.

Essentially, the research is going to consist of:

BASIC DESK RESEARCH
  Referring to various published
  sources of information

RESEARCH IN THE COUNTRY
  Conducted by visits, forms of survey and
  analysis into the market/industry itself

A surprising amount of information can be assembled by an exporter utilizing government, banking and trade association sources and studying appropriate trade publications. In the United Kingdom for example, the exporter is well supported by such organizations as the British Overseas Trade Board (BOTB) with its many specialized departments and operations. All UK banks regularly publish detailed profiles of individual countries. Chambers of commerce at local level represent a powerful force in focusing attention on particular marketing problems for specific countries. At a more international level the International Chamber of Commerce (ICC) maintains relationships with its membership of over 160 countries.

When 'focusing the microscope' in more detail, methods of surveying markets overseas will be developed and investigation and analytical techniques developed. For example, in the industrial sector much use can be made of correlation techniques; that is, relating the anticipated demand for the exporter's product with other back-up data on, say, industrial projects, statistics of industrial growth and output, etc. In the consumer and consumer durable fields attention must be paid to methods of surveys and motivation research, i.e. what is really influencing the customer to make his purchase; is it price, name, colour, or some other psychological factor?

Attendance at or visits to an industrial exhibition or trade fair can by itself be a very effective step along the road of market research. *Figure 1.2* illustrates a framework of market research,

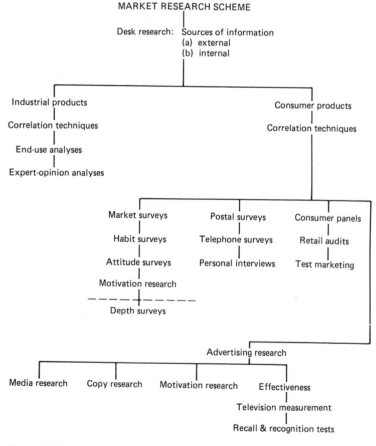

Figure 1.2 Market research scheme

and although this looks complex it must again be stressed that if a systematic approach is made then useful research results can be obtained with quite limited resources.

Essentially, therefore, the object of the research has been to discover:

(1) Whether there is in fact a market of the appropriate volume and price for our product in its present form.
(2) Whether a market potential does exist, provided that some product modification or price adjustment is made.
(3) Have we in fact discovered a demand for some quite new product which it is within our resources, experience and capacity to supply?
(4) If the marketing mix variables can be adjusted to bring about a successful sales and marketing operation.
(5) To what extent there is any domestic or other competition.

Some of the marketing mix variables should now be considered in greater depth.

Product

This should be considered under three main headings:

Product design

Suitable and efficient for its purpose
Necessary safety factors and reliability
Conforms with any regulations in the overseas market
Necessity of attractive appearance

Production adaptation

Degree of change, if necessary, to meet customer/market's preference
Change of operation, e.g. from hand- to power-operated (or vice versa)
Size or measurement change – to metric, for example
Suitability for different regulations – health, safety and environmental regulations vary from country to country
Packaging of product in different sizes or volumes.

Product presentation

To catch customer's attention
To provide a brand 'image'
To identify the company that made the product
To identify the product and quantity.

With regard to product design and adaptation in international marketing it will be vital to be aware of any particular specifications and standards that may be laid down by particular organizations. These may well be legally required and therefore mandatory to the design of the product. Over the years there has been a progressive move towards various degrees of harmonization but the starting point will usually be the considerations of a particular country's own set of standards.

In the United Kingdom a prime source of standards and codes is the British Standards Institution (BSI). It will be necessary, however, to view this matter internationally and therefore in international trade, reference will constantly need to be made to other sets of standards. In France, for example, there is the Association Française de Normalisation (AFNOR), in Germany DIN Specifications (Deutsches Institut für Normung) are frequently encountered.

It should be appreciated that the various national standards' authorities will often recognize and co-operate with other industrial bodies and associations. The Verband Deutscher Elektrotechniker, or VDE (Association of German Electrical Engineers), plays a large part, and in the USA, in addition to the American Standards Institute, there are currently more than 400 organizations actively involved in the preparation of standards and codes.

There is both a growing degree of international standards and at the same time an emergence of more nationally-adopted pratices. We might find, for example, that one country, say Algeria, will tend to adopt French standards whereas in Australia and New Zealand there is a move away from British standards to writing their own to meet their *own* requirements. Iran is a country where there have been moves towards adopting 'home-grown' specifications.

A powerful tool in the hands of UK exporters is to be found in the institution Technical Help for Exporter (THE) based at Milton Keynes. This body offers a wide range of services which help to identify and relate various international requirements and standard specifications.

Appreciation of possible technical specification requirements should therefore play a large part in the design or adaptation of a particular product for a specific market. It should also be borne in mind that the interpretation and application of standards can sometimes be employed as a 'non-tariff barrier' and therefore may represent one of the many obstacles to be overcome when penetrating an overseas market.

It should not be overlooked that apart from actual technical standards, requirement may also apply to such items as pre-packaging, net weights and labelling of foodstuffs. Just to give an example, recent French requirements (Dec, 1984) published in *Journal Officiel* applied to:

Pasta and pasta products
Coffee, chicory and coffee substitutes
Ingredient labelling
Manufacture date and batch markings
Quantity labelling and exempt products
Milk: net volume for retail sale

The above will give some idea of the detail into which a manufacturer may proceed when considering the product's suitability for a specific overseas market.

The relative degree of importance of product planning will vary enormously from product to product, e.g. consumer products or industrial products. It must be remembered that there is no hard-and-fast rule; an industrial power tool could succeed or fail in the market according to whether its design, colour and shape are either better than or not so attractive as a competitor's, even though the mechanical functions of both are identical.

With product presentation, even a name can be vital. This is particularly important in overseas marketing when there is often the problem of translation into a different language. There are many recorded cases of where a name has lacked appeal or even proved to be downright offensive. It is interesting to bear in mind the difficult decisions that sometimes have to be made in this field. On the one hand the projection of a specifically-named product globally means a greater international image and draws strength from overall promotion. On the other hand, it may be necessary to formulate, for the same product, a series of names suitable for different countries.

Pricing

Pricing is easily understood and manipulated whereas quality, customer reaction, visual appeal, etc., are more difficult to assess.

Flexibility in pricing is regarded as important in the economic theory of a free-enterprise state system.

Economists tend to give less weight to non-price variables than to price as tools in stimulating/matching demand.

The phenomenon described as 'negative price-elasticity of demand' could, in many cases, be labelled 'positive promotion-budget elasticity of demand'.

A higher degree of competition in marketing occurs in non-price areas.

Circumstances in which pricing is important (or more so)

1 New product pricing
2 Cost changes
3 Increasing demand → inflation
4 Stagnating/declining demand → deflation
5 Competitors' changes in marketing mix
6 Changes in interrelated product prices
7 Submitting for important (large) orders.

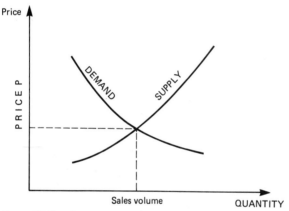

Figure 1.3 Supply and demand curves – standard economic model. The supply/demand function will influence sales volume and selling price ratios

Assumptions associated with the model (*Figure 1.3*):

(1) The curves are generally used in connection with either of two implied objectives: profit maximization or revenue maximization – both generally short run.
(2) Information received is likely to be biased towards current market structures – the only customers specifically considered are actual and potential ones on the present basis. The opportunity to change this drastically is not implied.
(3) It assumes that prices are independent of cost levels of other marketing variables.
(4) Assumes that the demand curve is accurate and invariable in the short term.

Some marketing objectives with pricing implications

– and additional to maximization of profit and revenue.

Market penetration

Used when

1 Market is either growing or susceptible to growth stimulation.
2 Market is relatively highly positive price elastic.
3 Production and distribution economies of scale exist.
4 Low price discourages actual and potential competitors.

Market skimming

Used when

1 Some market segments have relatively inelastic demand.
2 Diseconomies of scale are not excessive.
3 There is little danger of encouraging rivals to 'cream off' the same market. This fear would be counteracted by patent, high technology, long lead time, high promotion costs, etc.

Early cash recovery

Used when

1 Rapid positive cash flow is the overriding need.
2 The future appears uncertain – the market may be declining or random-variable.

Although pricing is rarely carried out purely on either a cost basis or a demand basis, it is nevertheless useful to look at these two basic models:

Cost-oriented pricing

1 'Mark-up' pricing
A percentage is added to cost, and this varies from product to product
2 'Cost-plus' pricing
A percentage is added to cost, constant throughout the range of products
3 'Target' pricing
An estimate of sales volume is used to derive price – it being accepted that price influences turnover

Profit, costs, revenue, and turnover are also simultaneously targeted and are incorporated into budget.

Generally:

PRO: (a) Easy and accurate to apply,
      (b) Socially equitable, provided that the percentage is not too high,
      (c) Tends to avoid price wars.

CON: (a) May fail to extract high profits
      (b) Reduce competitive ability *vis-à-vis* price cutters
      (c) During periods of inflation it will lead to either declining profits or frequent price readjustment.

Demand-oriented pricing

Price discrimination – an item is sold at two or more prices

(a) *on a customer basis,*
    – depends upon (i) Volume taken
                (ii) Bargaining power/ability
                (iii) Economic strength
                (iv) Relative importance
                (v) Lack of communication between customers

(b) *on a version basis,*
The provision, for example, of 'extras' or luxury features – which are charged to a greater extent than their cost would imply. Also, of course, simplified versions can be offered.

(c) *on a place basis*
    – theatre seats
    – regional and geographical price differences
    – different shopping areas in the same town
    – different outlets

(d) *on a time basis*
    – so as to even out usage fluctuations
    – so as to extract more cash from an inelastic situation

Competition-oriented pricing

(a) Going-rate pricing – either charge the same rate as competitors or, by some process of assessment, price according to the relative merits and/or marketing effort of your competitors.

(b) Bidding.

Channels of distribution

Chapter 2 deals with many of the administrative aspects of the employment of agents, etc., and the impact upon the operation of export transactions. At this juncture it is necessary to consider the question of channel selection as a part of marketing strategy. Broadly speaking we can distinguish three main sectors of channel utilization, namely:

Outside the market

The use by an exporter, in the company's *own country*, of specialized export merchants, buying houses or confirming houses. In practice, therefore, a manufacturer could sell its products overseas but be based domestically.

Selling into the market

At this stage the alternatives multiply into the choices of agents, distributors or setting up the exporter's own company in the overseas market. Joint ventures, assembly arrangements, and even licensing agreements, can come into this category.

Operating with the market

Depending upon the type of product there will be the question of the channels of selling within the country itself in the possible employment of a wholesaler/retailer chain (particularly for consumer products) and the use of stockists and authorized dealers.

Much of course, will depend upon the nature of the actual end-user who could literally be the man or woman in the street or, at the other end of the scale, a state purchasing organization or large corporation. Some exporters will be selling to a small number of industrial companies but some could find themselves selling to a very large number of individual companies.

It should also be borne in mind that the channel selection may also have a bearing upon another marketing mix segment, namely 'after-sales service'. Clearly, the use of stockist and authorized dealers will play a large part in the maintenance of spare-part availability and repair services so very essential for a sustained and growing export marketing effort. It has been said in the past that UK exporters tended to neglect this aspect of export marketing. It is obvious that for many types of products the ultimate user must have confidence in a back-up service and it is often suggested that

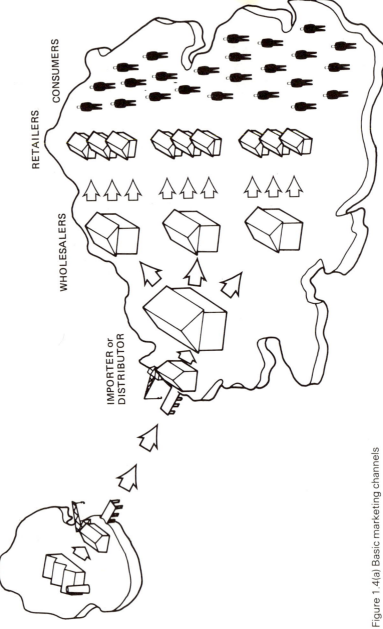

Figure 1.4(a) Basic marketing channels

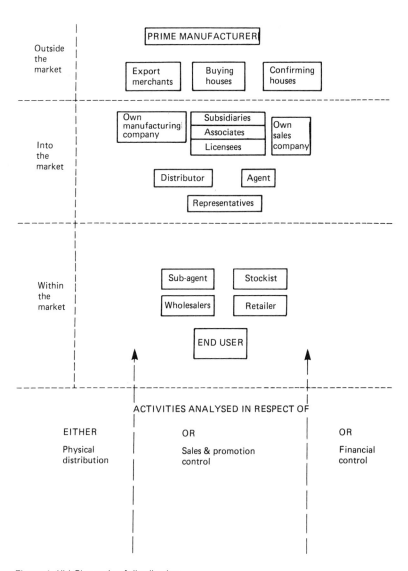

Figure 1.4(b) Channels of distribution

laying down the firm foundation of a back-up after-sales service should really come first in the overall export offensive.

Figures 1.4(a) and *1.4(b)* illustrate some of the patterns of channels of distribution in more detail. It should be stressed, however, that the use of channels should not lead the exporter to abdicate from his responsibility of being involved with the effective buyer. In *Figure 1.4(a)*, for example, the seller could easily regard the importer/distributor as being the 'cut-off point', but in practice he should really also be carrying out research into the consumer 'end point'.

Marketing communications

Under this heading of the 'mix' the concept of actually being in touch one way or another with the actual purchaser should be considered in the widest context. Here, the actual promotion of the product is taking place together with the selling element. Very rarely can a product be expected to sell itself, although there will be varying degrees of effort needed depending upon various background circumstances. Even in hard times there will be fortunate exporters who may find themselves in a seller's market. At the other end of the scale the majority of manufacturers are more likely to operate in highly competitive conditions where the selling and promotion efforts have to be at their peak. Even if a seller's market was in fact available, times change; therefore, there is never any real justification for complacency.

Basically the promotional effort can be seen to encompass the following elements:

(1) Making a potential buyer aware of the product's existence.
(2) Placing the product in a favourable light compared with any competition which might exist.
(3) Creating a desire to purchase on behalf of the buyer.
(4) Obtaining an actual order and finalizing all the various sales contract terms.
(5) Ensuring a continuous relationship with the market to ensure further business.

The overseas sales and promotional operations will make use of a variety of methods to achieve the selected objectives. *Figure 1.5* illustrates a spectrum of such means that are available and may be used in various combinations. It must be borne in mind that the employment of the various approaches and indeed their very viability will depend heavily upon the nature of the product and

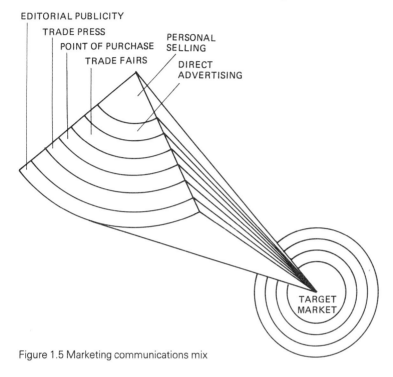

EDITORIAL PUBLICITY
TRADE PRESS
POINT OF PURCHASE
TRADE FAIRS
PERSONAL SELLING
DIRECT ADVERTISING
TARGET MARKET

Figure 1.5 Marketing communications mix

the market itself. There will be quite a difference between the marketing of say heavy capital equipment and high-volume consumer products. Similarly, the selling into a market of a centrally-planned economy country where state industrial prog-rammes and state buying organizations are the order of the day will present many different problems compared with operating in a highly-developed market economy such as in the USA or West Germany.

Nevertheless, the differences should not be exaggerated and the underlying principles of an export promotion effort remain valid for a wide range of different international marketing operations.

It is probably true to say that the most direct form of communication and promotion will always be the actual personal selling effort expended by a sales executive or sales force in one way or another. It has already been seen that the actual employment of overseas channels could possibly involve, say, the employment of an agent who may be charged with, amongst other things, the responsibilty of carrying out direct selling effort on behalf of the exporting company.

On the other hand, another approach for the exporting company might be to employ a national residing in the target market country. This could be compared with the exporter sending overseas the company's own personnel on selling missions.

Naturally the various choices will depend heavily upon many variables such as volume of business, relative costs and the basic personnel resources available to the exporting company.

As an aid to considering the various permutations the following aspects should be considered in the formula:

$$S - P - L$$

Where S = Selling/negotiating skill
      P = Product knowledge
      L = Linguistic ability.

The above selling mix should assist in relating to the various proportions of skill required for different types of product and market conditions.

Selling/negotiating skill

Here we consider the importance in a particular product/market relationship of the ability to discuss with a potential buyer the proposed sale and to succeed in actually obtaining a concrete order. In sales training parlance we really have in mind the ability to 'close' a sale. In selling a simple basic raw material, for example where, by and large, market prices and conditions prevail and are well known to the potential buyer, much may depend upon the sales executive's personality, determination and ability to succeed in ensuring that the buyer actually places the order accordingly.

Alternatively, complex negotiations with, say, a state trading purchasing organization, might call for a high degree of background knowledge of personalities, political conditions and bureaucratic procedures to ensure a smooth series of negotiations and ultimate success in obtaining the contract.

These skills will not only call for a considerable degree of training but will also tend to put a premium on actual experience in the field. Success will depend a lot upon the executive becoming well known, respected and accepted in the appropriate circles. The need for personal contacts, knowledge of sources of information and other background details will be vital.

Product knowledge

A knowledge of the product as such is of course essential to all export sales personnel whether they are selling a simple range of textile goods or a multimillion-pound aerospace project. The question is, how easy or otherwise is it to acquire this knowledge and how vital is it as a part of a sales presentation? Selling paper sacks, for example, might mean that it is fairly easy to obtain product knowledge quickly and that given basic quality, sales discussions might not place as much emphasis on the technical nature of the sack as opposed to price or delivery position. Automobile engine filters may not be too difficult in themselves but their application might call for a high degree of 'product application' knowledge, i.e. what particular versions of a car utilize which particular filter. Any misunderstanding in the latter aspect could be very serious.

At the other end of the scale it might be that very precise technical knowledge is required to present a product to a potential buyer/user necessitating considerable technical or scientific qualifications. In some cases the sales and negotiating processes may involve technical aspects so complex that a 'team approach' has to be adopted to include specialists in the product itself and personnel more skilled in selling and negotiating.

It will be seen therefore that there are varying degrees of relativity of the need for knowledge of the product itself and/or knowledge of the application and use of that product. This product factor, therefore, plays a vital part in the assessment of the marketing mix in general and the selling mix in particular.

Linguistic ability

There can be little argument as to the desirability to be able to sell overseas in the language of the market itself. Clearly, however, the average exporting company is generally going to sell to a large number of overseas markets and a considerable number of languages could be involved. Unless a company possesses a large and specialized field sales force, compromises will generally have to be made.

There are, of course, bound to be certain languages which can be regarded as 'keys' in the sense that for historical and political reasons they have come to be in widespread use outside their originating countries. We can, perhaps, identify French as providing a key to many African and Middle East countries. German can be a very widely useful language for dealing with, say, the Eastern European markets. Spanish is of inestimable value for certain South American countries. English is naturally likely to be in wide use because of the Commonwealth and North American connections.

From the export executive's point of view, therefore, there will be the desire, naturally, to speak the overseas language, or at least to be able to cope by using a mutual key language. There will be the need, however, to identify the markets where this may be either relatively easy or in some cases downright impossible, and the feeling may be that any business conducted must be in the overseas language. If this language is highly specialized then it may lead to reliance upon either the indigenous overseas agent or the employment by the company of an overseas national.

Naturally the ideal situation would always be where an export sales executive combines all the three above-mentioned factors perfectly with an abundance of expertise in all three fields. This will not however be a state of affairs easily achieved and therefore the marketing effort will generally have to cope with various combinations and compromises. It is felt that the above-mentioned features should be seriously considered when planning a sales effort of any sort. There can be very little doubt that if export markets are to be taken seriously then there must be a considerable investment in sales personnel because to succeed there must at some time be a marked degree of face-to-face contact in the promotional operation.

Even if the exporter is in fact operating through various channels such as agents or distributors, etc., there will always exist the need for the manufacturer to exert some sort of initiative in the personal selling effort.

The above will also assist the exporter in systematically awarding degrees of priority of selling initiative to his growing pattern of export markets.

Before leaving the personal selling aspect it should be borne in mind that on top of all the factors indicated export personnel need natural resourcefulness, self-reliance and an ability to operate in different climates and surroundings and, in most cases, to exercise their own initiative particularly where communications with the parent company may be difficult.

Within the marketing communications mix, of course, the personal selling aspect will take place against a background of other promotional factors. On page 14 five factors of the promotional effort were mentioned. The export sales executive can in a sense span all these aspects in his sales calls, but naturally they will be backed by recourse to media and other promotional tools.

Media

Factors (1)–(3) given above could be supported by the employment of advertising through technical journals and other forms of trade press. National or regional newspapers could carry the message. If a television network is available then this would be a powerful instrument, particularly in the form of consumer goods or services. Naturally these promotional tools are likely to be expensive and they must normally be carried out on a reasonable scale to make them effective. The suitability of such means will naturally vary between the type of product, i.e. consumer, consumer durable or industrial goods, and indeed how large a budget is available for this type of advertising. Careful planning can sometimes achieve a reasonable promotional effort at modest expense. In selling, say scientific instruments with new or improved applications, much can be achieved on a modest budget by linking selected adverts with editorial publicity. Correct timing can be a vital attribute in this type of situation.

Sales literature

This is obviously going to be of importance in international sales and will almost always represent an essential form of marketing communication. The sequence will usually be as follows:

Fairly simple basic leaflets or booklets with sufficient text/illustrations to awaken interest.

More detailed catalogues with sufficient detail to provide information to enable a potential buyer to make decisions.

Back-up literature to accompany the products to cover operations, utilization or installation.

Literature to cover point of sale outlets, etc.

Designing good sales literature is an art in itself and of course in international trade such matters as translation of the text, use of names, and even colour, can be of vital importance. Today, if one studies sales literature it is surprising to find incorrectly-translated text emanating even from exporting countries such as Japan and Italy which otherwise exhibit high standards of promotional material.

Again, decisions will have to made as to whether specific languages can be catered for, although this could be difficult in the case of very specialized languages. In most cases the use simultaneously of a number of key languages can be employed to enable a wider range of countries to be catered for and yet still allow a fairly standardized form of literature to be produced.

A certain amount of literature distribution can be achieved by the use of 'mail shots' despatched directly to addresses obtained from such sources as the *Kompass Registers* or accumulated data obtained from government sources using their various overseas embassies and consulates. In the UK the BOTB and various sources of export intelligence can provide a considerable amount of valuable data.

Naturally the viability of such methods will vary enormously with the type of product/market situation. It may be simple if a particular overseas market consists of a relatively limited number of industrial users for, say, material handling equipment compared with sales of high-volume consumer goods needing the penetration of sophisticated dealer/wholesaler/retailer outlets requiring point of sale merchandising material.

Unless this type of promotional material is of a very high standard it is probably wiser not to employ it at all since such material can, by inference, reflect an impression of the quality image of the exporter's products and indeed his standing as a worthwhile supplier.

It may even be possible at times with products of particular classes to combine a certain amount of market research with the promotion itself. Literature combining questionnaires can be quite effective as a means of actively involving a potential customer and indeed alerting their interest.

Trade fairs, exhibitions and missions

Another category of marketing communication of importance to the exporter will be some form of collective involvement in an overseas market. An extremely effective activity is participation in a trade fair or specialized form of exhibition where stand space can be hired and products physically exhibited to stir the interest of potential buyers. Here, under one roof it is possible to rub shoulders with large numbers of potentially interested companies or individuals (and even competitors). Valuable contacts can be established and much useful market research data including addresses, can be accumulated as a result of the many conversations that can take place during even a week or fortnight.

There are many specialized companies who can help with the administrative planning and shell construction, etc., and translation services are normally readily available if required. Care must be taken to observe all the regulations and use the appropriate paperwork, such as carnets, to satisfy the various customs requirements as products will have to be shipped abroad to the host country and perhaps returned when the fair or exhibition is over.

Generally speaking information is normally easily available from government or trade association sources as to forthcoming calendars for various exhibitions covering many specialized needs. In many countries some form of government financial and promotional assistance is available. In the United Kingdom the BOTB can, through its fairs and promotion branch provide such assistance for certain designated markets. Indeed, under this heading there may also be the possibility of support for outward missions. Under this scheme a number of companies can organize together a group visit to certain designated target market areas overseas. This may sometimes operate on a geographical basis, i.e. a number of different types of companies from a local area perhaps operating in conjunction with a local chamber of commerce. Other approaches may be on a more industrial basis, i.e. companies sharing similar types of, say, industrial customers.

It will be seen, therefore, that for most exporters there can be a wide range of choices relating to active *communication* with their potential markets, and the point to stress is that even on a modest scale with quite a limited budget much can be achieved by positive planning and a thorough grasp of the various approaches that do exist.

An essential component part of planning the various forms of promotion is for the exporter to be selective and discriminating with regard to market selection. It is no use just considering the whole world as the object of export marketing in blanket terms. Key market selection should be the theme by which a company examines, selects and operates a short list of markets appearing to have the best potential, and *concentrates* resources on these key areas. Spreading the promotional effort too widely and thinly could mean that no real success is achieved anywhere. Some of the great export success stories attributed to such countries as Japan and West Germany can usually find their roots in a careful assessment and concentration in depth on selected key markets.

Physical distribution

The art of ensuring correct packing, handling, storage and transportation of the goods overseas, plus correct accompanying paperwork, is now firmly established as a vital discipline by itself, and later chapters will deal with various aspects of this operation in more detail.

After-sales service

In order to sustain an on-going success in export marketing the provision of a reliable back-up service is of vital importance in almost every category of product. This means that the supplier must maintain repair and spare part facilities and also be able to give technical and sales services to his customers or through the appropriate distribution channels. We have seen that this concept will in most cases be linked with the channels of distribution employed.

The finest quality product and the most competitive price may easily count for very little if the consumer lacks confidence in having his complaints or queries, spare parts or repairs, attended to promptly and efficiently. In the case of automobiles, as a classic example, a vital component part of the marketing mix in the buyer's mind will be reliability plus after-sales attention. Many users of products can accept the fact that things can go wrong and that breakdowns can occur with even the best model, but their final judgement is usually based on the speed and efficiency with which problems can be solved. As mentioned earlier, in some cases the creation of a suitable after-sales operation may actually *precede* the promotional effort of launching a product into an overseas market. It is useless regarding this as an afterthought and relying upon the outcome of events.

Finance and payment

Again, aspects of payment terms and export finance will be covered in other chapters in more administrative detail, but suffice at this juncture to say that the overall corporate marketing objective must envisage the receipt of money for goods supplied with the least possible delay and maximum reliability. An element of profitability for one's export effort is required in all cases, even where in the case of planned economy countries other objectives may be paramount.

To the export manager of today the question of granting credit terms, access to lines of credit, or the knowledge of various development fund sources such as the European Development Fund, is a vital tool in the marketing approach. In some cases there may be little difficulty in locating customers only too willing and anxious to purchase the exporter's product but the main problem lies in obtaining the necessary funds. In these cases the skill of the export marketer might well depend upon the ability to stage-manage available sources of money and therefore play a part in helping buyers to be able to pay for the goods within reasonable periods of time.

In looking back over this chapter the wisdom of the Institute of Export in placing increasing emphasis upon the Total Export Concept (TEC) can be readily appreciated. Good market research, correct product planning and development, plus efficient packing and transportation, leading to satisfactory receipt by the buyer of the goods and rewarded by correct profitable payment all lead to a successful and continuous export trade.

2 Export management administration

Functions of the export department

This book is concerned mainly with the handling of export documentation and the procedures involved. It will therefore be necessary to consider the export office in the light of these requirements.

A manufacturing organization will often be chosen as an example, although this does not imply any limitation of the analysis – it can be applied equally to purely commercial or service firms.

It is customary to regard an industrial organization as having three basic functions, namely (i) finance, (ii) production, and (iii) sales. Although this is an over-simplification, it does offer a suitable starting-point. We have seen in the previous chapter the importance of the marketing concept, meaning that all the diverse activities of the firm are directed towards the objective of meeting the customer's needs and should therefore be regarded as an integrated exercise of business activity.

Accurate export administration is essential to enable goods to move safely overseas, whether by air, sea or road/rail; to enable the customer to receive quick and trouble-free delivery; and to enable the exporter to obtain full and satisfactory payment for the transaction.

An indication of the importance of some aspects of the need for documentary accuracy can be gained from a 1984 Midland Bank/SITPRO survey. This estimated that the delay and expense due to inaccurate documents presented to banks against letters of credit alone cost UK exporters an annual total of about £50m. This would not allow for extra warehousing, etc., charges which may be incurred in the importing country through late or inaccurate documentation.

The export office acts as a link between the finance, production and sales operations. It will support the sales function in providing data on methods of payment, building up the cost elements to provide an accurate quotation and advising upon and arranging the methods of packing and transportation. The export administration manager will work closely with the works and production managers in order to harmonize the production and delivery schedules as far as booking shipping space and transportation, etc. are concerned. With regard to the financial aspects, the export office will co-operate with the accounts department in varying degrees with respect to letters of credit, bills of exchange, credit status checks and final invoicing.

The precise shape and responsibilities of the export department

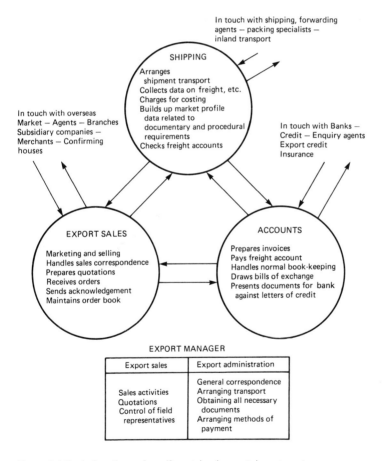

In touch with shipping, forwarding agents — packing specialists — inland transport

SHIPPING

Arranges
   shipment transport
Collects data on freight, etc.
Charges for costing
Builds up market profile
   data related to
   documentary and procedural
   requirements
Checks freight accounts

In touch with overseas
Market — Agents — Branches
Subsidiary companies —
Merchants — Confirming
houses

In touch with Banks —
Credit — Enquiry agents
Export credit
Insurance

EXPORT SALES

Marketing and selling
Handles sales correspondence
Prepares quotations
Receives orders
Sends acknowledgement
Maintains order book

ACCOUNTS

Prepares invoices
Pays freight account
Handles normal book-keeping
Draws bills of exchange
Presents documents for bank
   against letters of credit

EXPORT MANAGER

Export sales	Export administration
Sales activities Quotations Control of field representatives	General correspondence Arranging transport Obtaining all necessary documents Arranging methods of payment

Figure 2.1 Basic functions of a self-contained export department

will vary considerably. Some principal determinants are size of company, nature and spread of markets, types of selling organization, complexity of product and, quite often, the stage of evolution reached by the company itself. All too frequently, unfortunately, the export side of a business is the result of haphazard growth, but there is now a trend towards a much closer study of export organization and the induction and training of appropriate personnel.

Bearing in mind the various determining factors that will underly the organization of the export activities of a company, one can identify certain basic functions (*Figure 2.1*). There is first of all the export sales element under the direction of an export sales director or manager. The task of this department will be to handle the selling activities necessary for the various overseas markets. This executive will often concentrate mainly on controlling the sales force, corresponding with customers, preparing quotations and price lists, receiving orders and sending out suitable acknowledgements. Sometimes an organization will tend to divide these activities into two main areas, giving rise to an export sales manager and an export office manager.

A basic task facing any manager is that of maintaining efficient communications. In no sphere of commerce is this more important than in the field of export. Although the world is shrinking year by year as transport and communication systems improve, it is nevertheless neither economical nor practical to use the telephone/telex for many overseas markets and carefully constructed correspondence is essential. In many cases, letters have to be addressed to overseas buyers who use a different language and employ different units of measurements. The ability to correspond in a foreign language is daily becoming more and more necessary for any export department which prides itself on its professionalism. Needless to say, the use of a foreign language must be of a high standard; otherwise more harm than good could be done, particularly if technical and commercial terms with very precise meanings are used. For example, interpretations of the word 'agent' can vary enormously.

Equally, it should be borne in mind that many overseas countries use more than one language, sometimes concentrated in different geographical areas. The use of French for certain Canadian markets, or Flemish in Belgium, are examples, and Switzerland, of course, uses French, German and Italian. Also a language itself may vary, as in the case of Spanish as spoken in Colombia differing somewhat from the Spanish of Argentina.

The employment of units of measurement or currencies in

correspondence, quotations and orders must be precise, and any possiblity of misunderstanding, such as with the American short ton of 2000 lb or English long ton of 2240 lb, must be avoided. Naturally, with the adoption of the metric system and wide international usage there is much more standardization. Nevertheless, some variations may still be encountered in the use of units of measurement by some very specialized industries. Similarly, with currencies the use of the dollar, for example, must make clear reference to the particular nationality of that currency, e.g. US, Canadian, Australian, Singaporean, dollars, etc.

Within the export organization in general will function the shipping and transport sections. These are of paramount importance in international trade because of the range and complexity of transport facilities available to carry the exporter's goods to an overseas market. It is becoming more and more apparent that a scientific approach to physical distribution is now a vital part of marketing. Nowadays, total physical distribution costs, i.e. packing, insurance, warehousing and transportation, can amount on average to between 15 and 40 per cent of the selling price. The shipping manager of today, therefore, has many complex decisions to make when choosing methods of transportation and comparing their overall costs. Air freight might mean a higher freight cost but it reduces the time period during which money is tied up in stocks. Packing costs can often be reduced by utilizing different means of transport. So important has this concept of physical distribution become over the years that this subject will be covered in more detail in a following chapter.

One of the key activities of the shipping department will be the negotiation of freight and carriage charges. The export sales department, when calculating the selling price, will need accurate freight rates, costs of insurance premiums, packing costs and various other incidental charges. Many of these are constantly fluctuating and a professional shipping manager has to work very hard to keep completely up-to-date and obtain the best rates consistent with good and reliable service. A miscalculation which over-estimates carriage charges could mean that the sales department might lose a potential order at the quotation stage. Similarly, a mistake in the other direction could seriously reduce, or even at times eliminate the profit margin.

Any commercial organization must, of necessity, see the objective of all its activities as a satisfactory profit margin. Marketing strategy may at times dictate that overseas business carries a lower profit margin or even sometimes be operated at cost in order to break into a difficult market. In the long term, however, overseas business can only be carried on satisfactorily with a reasonable profit margin and a satisfactory settlement of overseas payment. Consequently, only when the proceeds of an export sale have been safely received can the transaction be considered successful. Thus, the invoicing function and accounting activities have to be dovetailed with the export sales and transport activities.

Types of export organization

It is extraordinary that there appears to be a lack of uniformity in export organization and that two companies of similar size, selling almost identical products to similar markets, will organize themselves quite differently. Some will establish a completely separate and independent export department which will look after all the costing, transportation, invoicing and payments for every export transaction. Other organizations may distribute the export activities throughout the various specialist departments. For

---

Vertical organization

  1 Correspondence
  2 Credit status enquiries
  3 Order processing
  4 Preparing packing specification details
  5 Negotiating freight rates, booking shipping space
  6 Preparing bills of lading/air waybills, etc.
  7 Checking freight accounts
  8 Invoicing
  9 Preparing bills of exchange
10 Handling letters of credit
11 Sending statements
12 Checking overdue accounts
13 Filing
14 Recording

Horizontal organization

EEC Countries	South America	USA/Canada	East Africa
Dept 1	Dept 2	Dept 3	Dept 4

While each of the four departments would handle an export order as an organic whole, they would specialize in different geographical areas as shown for examples.

Figure 2.2 Two principal types of export-order organization

example, the export order will be split up into its various component parts, i.e. invoicing, transportation and payment, and the invoicing department of the company will handle the export invoice alongside its activities for invoicing home market orders. Similarly, the transport department will handle shipment and air freight, together with road transport operations for the home market.

Again, different approaches are to be found in the division of the parts of the export order itself. There are many systems in use, varying in degree between the two extremes which, for the sake of simplicity, will be referred to as the 'horizontal' and 'vertical' (*Figure 2.2*).

(a) *Horizontal*: Here the approach is to parcel out whole orders to individuals or departments so that an export order is treated as an organic whole. The specialization here will usually be geographical. Personnel will handle the total order and look after the processing from receipt to final invoicing, but will be allocated specific market areas. For example, groups of personnel will handle, say, South America, or Europe, both areas which may be subdivided; for instance, Europe into FTA or the EEC.

(b) *Vertical*: The company divides the order itself into the various parts of the spectrum, i.e. receipt of order, acknowledgement, processing, despatch, correspondence and final invoicing. A department, or perhaps even an individual, will look after one particular segment and will consequently become a specialist in, say, order acknowledgements or booking shipping space, and looking after consular documentation or invoicing. Under such a system, personnel will become accustomed to handling in depth small parts of the order process.

Between these two extremes there will, of course, be many permutations, conditioned by market and product categories and the historical development of the organization.

It is always presumptuous to be dogmatic about the superiority of one method over any others, as such factors as economy, availability of staff and existing personnel patterns will determine the issue. There is also no doubt that the growing use of computer systems and internal documentation structures call for much more specialization. There seems to be little doubt, however, that, wherever possible, the creation of a separate export department should be the ultimate objective and will increase efficiency in the long run. The morale of export personnel must also be considered. Operation of the 'vertical' system, for example, will certainly promote simplified documentation and lend itself to increasing mechanization but, on the other hand, may turn much of the order processing into a large number of fairly irksome tasks where no-one experiences the pride of handling an export order in its entirety. Consequently, there may be a lack of job identification. In this case, however, it may be akin to automation where much of the repetitive work will be removed from human hands, and a complex mechanized system will be controlled and operated by a small number of highly-skilled 'documentary technologists'.

The export order

When considering the structure and operations of any export organization, it might be profitable at this stage to take an analytical look at the export order itself, that is, from documentary and procedural points of view. Basically, an export order can be divided into four main parts, namely transport, methods of payment, risk element and regulations.

Transport

The exporter will be using either sea or air, or combinations of road/rail, or perhaps post. The appropriate documents will therefore be bills of lading, air waybills, consignment notes or postal receipts.

Methods of payment

Four main methods are employed; cash with order, open account, documentary bills and documentary credits. These procedures will necessitate bills of exchange, invoices and various types of letters of credit, as well as calling for credit status enquiries.

Risk element

By this is meant the covering of special risks in export business, e.g. marine insurance, export credits guarantee cover, foreign exchange variations, insurance policies, certificates and cover notes.

Regulations

This is perhaps the most difficult aspect from the exporter's point of view, as there are so many varieties of documents encountered in this field. The heading can be sub-divided into two. First of all, the regulations encountered internally, i.e. in the exporter's own country. In the case of the United Kingdom this might mean encountering such documents as export licences, forms and various types of customs entry declarations. Externally, the documentary requirements will vary from country to country. Some countries may require consular invoices, others special invoices or certificates of origin such as EUR 1 for EEC/FTA agreements. Other countries may require special wording and markings on packing or bills of lading. When considering this particular aspect of the order, the exporter will always check the background regulations of a market whilst negotiating an order with his customer. Some country's regulations may specify for example that all shipments must be made against freight payable in their own country. This could lead to, say, bills of lading being marked 'freight forward' and, of course, would influence the type of price quoted in the sales contract.

The four headings above are not absolutely self-contained and there will, of course, be a good deal of interaction. The 'regulations' heading will often condition the 'methods of payment'. Similarly, a letter of credit will determine the type of documentation required, e.g. by insisting upon certain types of bills of lading. The usefulness of such a method of analysis is to provide a framework of reference against which can be judged the formation and structure of an export department and the allocation of the various tasks to the personnel involved in these activities.

Channels of export selling

Any approach to export procedure must of necessity primarily take into account the methods an organization employs to conduct its export business, which will be called the 'channel of selling'. An exporter may use any one or a combination of the following:

(1) Export houses
(2) Agents
(3) Distributors
(4) His own selling machinery, completely under his control
(5) Branch offices
(6) Subsidiary companies

Table 2.1 Channels of exporting

Exporter	Export merchant	Overseas customer
Gets business which he may not have realized exists	Uses specialized mktg knowledge	Manufacturer's products are brought to his attention, but he may not be able to bring enough influence to bear on manufacturer
Saves trouble – reduces many transactions to almost home orders	Brings products to customer's attention	
Can save specialized staff	Acts as principal	
May not establish identity and image	Takes credit risk	
Difficulty perhaps of keeping abreast of mkt needs and linking product/design with mkt growth		
May fail to detect a declining mkt and finish up over-producing		
Sales forecasting difficult		

Exporter	Confirming house	Overseas customer
Often a source of business because credit being supplied through confg house		A powerful and often traditional link, particularly with Commonwealth and developing countries
Confirming houses often offer specialized shipping and packing facilities, which can simplify the transaction		
Most of the same advantages and disadvantages as with export merchants, except that it is often easier to make and maintain contact with ultimate customer and there is greater possibility of establishing image		Can often obtain credit facilities

Note: Crown Agents for the overseas govts and admin in many ways provide the same effective link for the exporter as confg houses.

Exporter	Overseas agent	Overseas customer
Can look to agent to hold stocks (a), or underwrite certain bad debts (b)	Examples: (a) Consignment (b) Del credere (c) Exclusive (d) Commission	Can deal with somebody in his own country
Care necessary when drawing up agency agreements to ensure energetic promotion by agent	Intimate knowledge of mkt, language, etc.	After-sales service

Exporter	Overseas agent	Overseas customer
Must take a large part in the export transaction, i.e. despatching, invoicing, administration, etc.		

Exporter	Distributor	Overseas customer
Can look to distributor to take title to goods	A degree of exclusivity	Usually, more points of contact
Deal with only one entity	Greater control over sales, etc., operation	Greater degree of back-up in his own country
Expect distributor to be very involved in mktg policy and operations	Closer identity with manufacturer	Brings contacts more closely to resemble dealing in own domestic mkt
	Greater possibility of exercising policy initiation	

Exporter	Overseas customer
Full force of company's own promotion put into the mkt	If mkt is sophisticated/large and complex, this type of customer will expect to be approached direct
Intimate knowledge and feedback of mkt information	
Complete company image and identity	
Exporter takes whole responsibility of export transaction (he can of course avail himself of ancillary services) and needs knowledge of overseas regulations, duties, shipping, etc. Needs fully-sophisticated export dept sales force and administration	

Exporter	Branch office	Overseas customer
Can look to branch to clear many awkward problems on site	More durable and effective extension to exporter's activities	Obtains more personal contact by dealing with branch office
	Can simplify debt collection and credit control, and provide information obtained on the spot re taxes, duties, regulations, etc.	
Extra cost – sometimes legal difficulties such as percentage of nationals to be employed, etc.	Gives company domestic appearance	

Exporter	Subsidiary co	Overseas customer
Possible tax concessions	Perhaps associated with overseas factory	Main basic overall gain should be lower price and superior after sales service etc.
Avoidance of tariff barriers	Vulnerable to overseas politics	
Avoidance of import quotas	Assembly KD (knocked down) CKD (completely knocked down)	
More comprehensive representation and promotion		
Large capital outlay generally required with perhaps slow return		
Legal problems – controlling interest may have to be vested in nationals		

Note: As a variation of some of the above channels, companies may export through associating with a group of similar companies in order to join forces and share promotion costs; they may also combine in the shape of export groups of particular industries. Basically, however, most of the points set out above apply in principle just the same.

It is not intended to consider the above in all the technical, marketing and legal detail that will be found in the specialized text books on these subjects, but rather to identify them and to see how they shape and influence documentary responsibilities and procedures. The main points are set out below and in Table 2.1.

Export houses

(a) *Export merchants*
The export merchant acts as a principal in his own right. His classic contribution is to locate an overseas demand and to satisfy this by finding a suitable source of supply in the United Kingdom. The merchant, who himself will usually have extensive experience in shipping, insurance and arranging exports, will often place the order and look after packing and shipping. This will enable a UK manufacturer to treat the business almost on the same basis as a home order. The merchant will make payment in his own name and consequently take upon himself the overseas credit risk. It is often the merchant who first introduces a manufacturer's products to the overseas market. His skill and expertise may often make it more convenient for the UK company to continue this relationship.

Much will depend on the nature of the product, the size and growth rate of the manufacturer and the exploitation of the merchant's image and identity.

(b) *Confirming houses*
This type of organization has historically grown up along the lines of acting as agent for the overseas buyer. Whilst at one time they tended to decline, they are once more very much in evidence. Nowadays, they are perhaps more active in the provision of credit for the overseas buyer. Orders from confirming houses are usually placed with the manufacturer on an *indent* basis. If the indent is closed, it means that the buyer has specified a particular UK manufacturer. On the other hand, an open indent enables the confirming house to seek sources of supply and to evaluate them on the basis of competitive price, quality and availability. Again, confirming houses will often be assembling orders from a number of UK companies and may group them together for packing, shipping and transport in order to achieve economies in space and freight rates.

The above two categories represent the most important type of operation to the exporter/manufacturer so far as export houses are concerned. Organizations such as these are represented by the British Export Houses Association, who can provide considerable assistance to manufacturers seeking help in their overseas market. It must also be made quite clear that (a) and (b) above refer to *functions* and that these functions can often be represented in different combinations. For example, classically, a merchant operates legally as principal but, in some cases, might conduct a transaction more in the capacity of an agent. Similarly, a confirming house in some cases will place orders and confirm them in its own name. The basis of remuneration will vary. The manufacturer must be prepared at times to look after packing and shipment, even when handling business through institutions such as these. The most important thing is that flexibility in outlook can be maintained and it is possible to identify the actual function of the particular transaction. The combined efforts of the export houses make a powerful contribution to the United Kingdom's overseas earnings.

Agents and distributors

Use of the services of these operators is, of course, very widespread amongst exporters. It must be borne in mind that the employment of these terms is by no means clear-cut, and confusion can arise owing to different forms of interpretation. If in doubt, legal advice should be sought. From the strictly legal outlook there is a clear distinction between agent and distributor inasmuch that the former is only really taking orders on behalf of his principal, i.e. the exporter. This would mean that in many cases the credit risk of non-payment by customers will be the responsibility of the seller. However, this may be qualified in the case of del credere agents who assume a degree of credit risk involvement in exchange for a higher commission.

The distributor is really taking orders *on his own account*, having already taken title to the goods, and subject only to the limitations in his agreement with the principal.

The actual size and nature of the *territory* covered does not necessarily vary with the nature of the appointment. However, there is a general tendency for distributors to have larger territories, within which they may even themselves employ agents, etc.

It will be seen, therefore, that the essential difference is a contractual one concerning the ownership and financial responsibility for goods and services. An example of the blending of these can be seen by the consideration of the consignment agent. Here, stocks can be held by the agent and therefore good follow-on and after-sales services provided. However, in contrast to the distributor the goods are being held on behalf of the exporter and not being paid for until subsequent sale.

When using agents or distributors, exporters will normally expect to be responsible for handling the transaction completely as far as documentation is concerned. The agent/distributor, however, can often help by advising upon Customs formalities, duties and taxes. Great care is necessary when drawing up agreements and the questions of responsibilities and basis of remuneration should be covered fully. It is also very important to be familiar with the laws relating to agencies in the overseas territory, as these can vary from country to country.

Sales by UK exporter direct to overseas market

This, of course, entails more involvement with the overseas market, as the exporter will need sufficient skill and knowledge to plan and execute the whole transaction and consignment. He will, therefore, handle all the documentation and procedure.

Branch offices

An expansion of the manufacturer's overseas marketing may call for the opening of a branch office. The aim will usually be to use this mainly as an administrative and selling foothold, but such an office can be of great assistance in dealing with documentary problems, e.g. with overseas Customs, clearance and import duties. By studying freight rates and inland transportation costs, the branch office can assist the UK exporter in finalizing his costing and quotations. It can also play a useful part in the collection and transmission of proceeds.

Subsidiary companies

These play a large part in modern exporting. Nowadays, the exporter often finds that it is essential to extend his company overseas and this process is frequently associated with assembly, shipping on a knocked-down basis and manufacture abroad under licence. This process has been greatly accelerated by the desire of companies to set up subsidiaries in some countries to avoid tariff barriers. This pattern often enables large-scale shipments and consignments to be carried out and reduces the burden of the individual shipment/consignment routine. The problem of payments is on many occasions reduced to the equivalent of inter-departmental book-keeping transactions, consistent with exchange control regulations.

Ancillary services

Other factors that exert an influence upon the procedural pattern are those that may result from the employment of various ancillary services which are at times available to the exporter. Any practitioner will therefore need to have some knowledge of the various types of organization which will assist him with the export transaction. At the outset, a distinction should be drawn between the services that will be used *directly* and those that will be of *indirect* assistance. The types of aid can also be classified, i.e. whether they are 'advice' or 'guidance' or 'practical, functional' help. Having identified these functions, it will be possible to relate them to particular institutions. For example, a bank could give an exporter some general background information and marketing intelligence for a particular country, and thereby act in an advisory capacity. Alternatively, the bank might function directly at the exporter's bidding by arranging a specific payment transaction, or carrying out a precise financial investigation into the credit-worthiness of the customer.

Equally, a shipping and forwarding agent will work directly for the exporter by arranging a particular shipment and making a Customs entry. He might also function in an indirect manner by obtaining for the exporter some freight rates or advising on a particular shipping route. The specialized services of the British Overseas Trade Board provide a very wide range of advisory services and to an increasing extent carry out functional activities for the UK exporter.

During the course of this work, the reader will be referred from time to time to various organizations which come within the category of ancillary services. At this stage it might prove useful to set out in tabulated form the main types of institution involved:

Organization	Service performed
Shipping and forwarding agents, shipowners/ loading brokers, air freight agents	Arranging shipment/air/road, rail transport. Entering goods at Customs. Might pay freight. Can arrange insurance. Provide information re sailings, routes, frequency, freight rates; can sometimes provide services in country of destination and, in the case particularly of air forwarders, can carry these services right up to a COD basis.
Packing specialists	For highly-specialized products, i.e. aircraft, machinery, extra-heavy, bulky or unwieldy loads. Such companies generally incorporate in their services the collection of goods from the manufacturer, packing and subsequent delivery to docks or airport.
Clearing banks	Provide information on markets, regulations, currency, credit, status checks. Arrange payment methods, transfer of money. Deal in foreign exchange, lend or advance money. Discount or advance against bills.
Merchant bankers, discount and acceptance houses	Provide acceptance credit facilities; discount and accept bank bills, long-term loans. Participate in international transactions and loans. Provide financial consultancy.

Organization	Service performed
HM Customs and Excise via Head Office and various branches and offices at docks and airports – in many cases a highly personal contact with individual officers necessary for detailed problems	Functional in the sense of the need for the exporter to make Customs entries; obtain drawback in certain cases and conform to Customs regulations regarding exchange control, export licensing, etc.
British Overseas Trade Board: Head Office, London; various regional offices. Number of departments, e.g. export licensing branch, export services and promotions division	Provides a wealth of information on markets, overseas regulations, payment restrictions; details of overseas Customs duties; taxes. Participates in schemes for improving and simplifying documentation.
Lloyd's of London, insurance companies, brokers	Main interest to exporter is to cover marine and other forms of insurance for overseas shipments. From this section will be obtained insurance policies and certificates; information related to types of cover; nature of risks and costs of premiums.
Export Credits Guarantee Dept: Head Office, London; various regional and branch offices throughout the UK	Provides various types of risk cover not normally available from the commercial insurance houses. Exporter will negotiate type of policy applicable to his business, arrange limits of individual cover. There will be a constant interchange of information and monthly returns.
Chambers of commerce, London and provincial offices	Sources of information. It is also from these offices that the exporter normally obtains certificates of origin and has invoices verified and countersigned. Membership of a chamber is often a great advantage to exporter.

Organization	Service performed
Overseas embassies and consulates	Provide information on current regulations and requirements of the particular country. Exporter obtains, where necessary, consular invoices, invoice legalization, etc.
Professional bodies: Institute of Export, Society of Shipping Executives	Maintain libraries and other sources of information, data on export education; active in the whole field of export practice. Offer examinations and professional membership.
Export organizations and associations for various trades and industries	Can be very useful, as such associations often provide information in depth about individual products or industries. Examples: Building Material Export Group; British Food Export Council; London Fur Fashion Export Group.
Simplification of International Trade Procedures Board	Main objective to guide and assist the rationalization of international trade procedures and documentation. Provides many booklets, reports and check lists.

The exporter has a whole range of institutions and services at his disposal which the skilled practitioner will know how best to employ to assist him with his transactions. However, the professional exporter will never wish to abdicate his responsibilities; although, for example, he may employ a shipping and forwarding agent to prepare Customs entries and arrange shipment, it is still incumbent upon him to have a knowledge of the mechanics of the procedures involved. In the first place this will be necessary to enable an exporter to pass clear and concise instructions; in the second instance, to take appropriate and swift action if anything should go amiss with the transaction.

3 Export sales quotations

Export sales terminology

When the exporter negotiates an order with the overseas buyer, decisions have to be made as to the use of a particular sales clause such as FOB or CIF, etc. This is a vital element in the export transaction and determines the procedural and documentary responsibilities of the export department. The sales clause is, of course, important in all commercial transactions. In overseas trade, with its complex overseas transportation and specialized insurance and payment requirements, a thorough understanding of export sales terminology is vital for efficient export sales office management.

For example, a chemical manufacturer in Manchester quotes his customer as follows:

200 × 100 kilo cartons of Carbon Black Mk 11-A @ 60p per kilo ex works Manchester

From the seller's and buyer's points of view this implies the following:

(1) That the price per kilo covers the cost of the Carbon Black packed in cartons as it stands at the seller's works or warehouse.

(2) That the buyer will have to arrange collection of the goods and bear all costs of transferring them to his own premises. These costs will be additional to the 60p per kilo.

(3) That the seller need only provide the packing mentioned in the quotation which will enable the buyer to carry out a satisfactory collection. Should any additional protective packing for transit be required, it would be for the account of the buyer.

Two points emerge:

(a) The Manchester manufacturer has a minimum costing problem, virtually nothing more than assessing the cost of the finished product, allowing a profit margin and adding a cost for packing.

(b) From the viewpoint of the buyer the 60p per kilo price leaves him with a whole range of unknown expenses. The total ex-works price can be calculated, amounting to £12 000 per 200 cartons. In addition to this, however, will be collection and transport charges, and, if the goods are being bought by an overseas buyer, then packing, freight, insurance, import duties and taxes and final transportation costs will all have to be added to the primary ex-works quotation. Only then will the importer be able to see what his final price will be, thus enabling him to calculate his own mark-up, or see how much the charges will affect his cost of production, depending on whether he is importing the material for resale or for use in manufacturing a finished product.

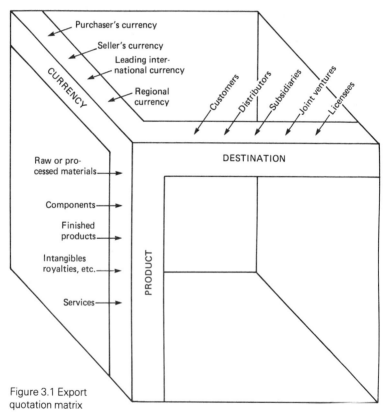

Figure 3.1 Export quotation matrix

See *Figure 3.1*.

It will be seen that the ex-works quotation might mean very little to a potential overseas customer and at this stage it would be profitable to examine another type of quotation representing the other extreme, namely delivered 'duty/taxes paid'. In this case, the quotation might read as follows:

> 200 × 100 kilo cartons of Carbon Black Mk 11-A @ 75p per kilo delivered tax paid Paris (it is assumed here that as an EEC partner no duty is applicable; there might, however, be a value added tax)
>
> (a total of £15 000 for the whole consigment as compared with £12 000 ex-works)

This time, the position has been virtually reversed. The buyer in Paris can look at a quotation and know that the sum of £15 000 represents the whole amount which will have to be paid for the 200 cartons. The 'delivered' price includes all the charges involved right up to delivery at the appropriate address in Paris. The quoted price can be compared at a glance with other possible competitive prices, and the buyer need not fear the many variations in charges which there might be in packing, transport and *tax*, etc.

It will follow that the Manchester exporter is now involved in a complex sequence of costing items, and his export department will need to have all the necessary expertise to identify and calculate the various expenses involved. A simplified breakdown of the 'delivered duty/tax paid' price structure could appear as follows:

200 × 100 kilo cartons Carbon Black @ 75p per kilo ex-works total	£12 000.00
Extra packing/strapping for shipment	£ 600.00
Loading onto lorry and transport to docks	£ 150.00
Wharfage/porterage, dock dues, loading on to ship	£ 150.00
Sea freight charge London-Le Havre	£ 1 200.00
Landing charges at Le Havre, plus French added value taxes, etc.	£ 600.00
Loading onto lorries, handling and delivery charges Le Havre-Paris	£ 225.00
Marine insurance premium plus warehouse-to warehouse clause	£ 75.00
Total	£15 000.00

Total £15 000 delivered tax paid Paris.

The above two types of quotation can best be summed up in the following manner:

	Exporter	*Importer*
Ex works	Easy to calculate, involves a minimum of responsibilities.	Leaves many unknown factors. Not conducive to placing an order on this basis. May find it difficult to compare with other quotations.
Delivered duty paid	Places considerable responsibility on export department. Calls for many calculations. Numerous variable factors – changes in freight rates, etc., may reduce profit margin once quotation has been accepted. However, there is an advantage, inasmuch that the exporter can exercise a greater degree of control over the complete process of the transaction.	Enables him to see at a glance the full cost of product. Knows that any unexpected changes in freight or duty, etc. charges will have to be borne by exporter.

It should be borne in mind that the above type of price structure is based very much on a conventional type of sea shipment, hence the itemization of the various cost elements. It will be seen in later chapters that the modern developments of transportation such as containers, through road transport and combined transport operations have revolutionized shipping practice. This has had a considerable impact upon quotations and pricing and costing. For example, in many cases a container operator, etc. will be able to give an exporter a 'through delivered freight rate' and to telescope together the various freight elements.

Types of quotation

The main types of export sales quotation can now be examined.

Ex works (might be ex warehouse, ex mill, ex factory, etc.)

Sometimes referred to as 'loco prices'. Care must be taken to show clearly a geographical place name such as 'ex works, Liverpool'. It may be, for example, that a manufacturer selling to an export merchant in Kent, and quoting from his London office, may be using a storage warehouse in Birmingham. In the absence of any specific location being mentioned in the quotation, the merchant might assume that the goods are ex works, London, and a big haulage charge discrepancy could result. Similary, it may be necessary, to avoid misunderstanding, to clarify the position pertaining to packing. Although 'ex works'implies only primary packing, it might well be preferable, if selling to a buyer who is going to export the goods, to indicate that export packing is extra. To comply with an ex-works contract, the manufacturer must have the goods available at the correct place, provide suitable primary packing and notify the customer when available for collection.

FOL – Free On Loading (seller's works)

This a slight embellishment to ex-works quotes used often with container traffic. Essentially this caters for the cost and effort involved in actually loading the goods into a container.

FOT (Free On Truck), FOR (Free On Rail)

In practice these terms are encountered mainly in connection with railway transportation. There may need to be a distinction between, say, loading goods on a railway vehicle at the seller's works (FOR) or the seller delivering, and loading the goods onto a rail wagon at a public railhead. This distinction may be important, for example to determine the question of insurance liability.

FAS (Free Alongside Ship + departure port, e.g. FAS London; sometimes FAS + name of vessel)

The responsibility in this case extends to transporting the goods to the docks and normally to a dock or wharf designated by the buyer. The seller should ensure that the buyer is notified accordingly and should also obtain, if required, appropriate dock receipt or wharfinger's receipt. In this quotation, care should be taken with regard to the geography of the particular port. The FAS quotation might on occasions mean transporting the goods by lighter and laying them physically alongside the vessel.

FOB (Free On Board + departure port, e.g. FOB Liverpool)

A widely-used type of quotation in export trading. In this instance, the exporter is responsible for all risks, responsibilities and expenses involved in having the consignment of goods placed over the ship's rail. At this point it is essential that the buyer be advised that the goods are in an FOB position so that steps can be taken to effect insurance and make all necessary arrangements to receive the consignment when it arrives at the destination port.

Although basically a clear-cut type of definition, the term FOB needs careful analysis in respect of certain points of detail. In the United Kingdom the definition of FOB varies slightly from port to port. There are small differences in relation to whether port rates, dock dues, customs entries, etc., are for account of seller or buyer.

Some of the borderline responsibilities can be of vital importance, for example the question of obtaining an export licence. In practice, it will usually be the FOB seller who will take steps to obtain the necessary action to apply for, and obtain, a suitable licence. A strict legal interpretation of FOB, however, might place the responsibility on the shoulders of the buyer, assuming that nothing to the contrary was either stated or implied in the contract of sale. This could be of vital importance to a seller in a case of the sudden imposition of an export licensing scheme engendered perhaps by the outbreak of war or sudden change in governmental economic policy. The incoterms definition referred to later in this chapter clarifies in the FOB definition the duty of the seller to procure any necessary export licence.

It is also important to bear in mind that many FOB transactions are carried out on a 'mixed contract' basis. In this case, an exporter would base his quotation and costing on an FOB basis but in addition act on behalf of his customer in arranging shipment, procuring the bill of lading and perhaps on occasion also arranging insurance.

FOB + departure (e.g. FOB Heathrow)

The exporter, here, will undertake to prepare, pack and deliver the goods to the appropriate *air carrier* i.e. British Airways, Lufthansa etc. The sender may, or may not make the necessary air freight shipping arrangements, (see page 48, incoterms)

CIF (Cost, Insurance, Freight + destination port, e.g. CIF Calcutta)

This is perhaps still the most classic export sales clause used in international trade and around it have crystallized all the traditional methods and procedures pertaining to bills of lading, tendering of documents, transferring of ownership and methods of payment. The responsibilities of the CIF seller involve the supplying of the goods suitably packed, delivering them to the docks, arranging shipping space, obtaining a bill of lading, arranging the correct type of marine insurance applicable to the goods and finally handing over to the buyer a bill of lading, insurance policy, invoice of the appropriate type and other peripheral documents that may be necessary to enable the buyer to take safe delivery at the port of destination, e.g. a certificate of origin.

CFR (Cost and Freight + destination port, e.g. CFR Lagos)

This will involve most of the obligations as set out above under CIF. Obviously the exception will be that the exporter does not arrange insurance and therefore will not include the premium in his price and not have to be responsible for procuring the insurance certificate/policy. This type of clause may be mandatory in some overseas markets. For example, currently in Nigeria the sales terms are normally CFR.

Several other terms may be encountered such as 'delivered frontier', 'ex quay' and 'ex ship', etc. Equally a degree of flexibility is necessary, for example 'delivered duty paid' is often expressed internationally as 'franco domicile' and indeed some companies use a simple 'door-to-door' expression.

Implications of different types of quotation

It will be seen therefore that, dependent upon the type of export sales clause employed, the exporter will be involving himself in varying degrees with no less than three contracts, namely

(1) The normal contract of sale
(2) Contract of affreightment
(3) Contract of marine insurance

For example, in an ex-works sale the exporter has only the sales contract to consider. With CFR he would be involved additionally with a contract of carriage. A CIF seller would engage in all three contractual relationships.

Normally, the CIF contract will be discharged when the seller hands over the appropriate set of documents to the buyer, thus enabling the latter to arrange customs clearance and payment of duty, and to obtain the goods from the shipping company. It is important to distinguish the right of the buyer to reject documents when tendered, as opposed to the right to reject the goods. A buyer would accept the appropriate set of documents on condition that the goods would subsequently be found to accord fully with the terms of the contract. Similarly, acceptance of the goods by the buyer would not preclude the seller from taking action against the buyer if it were subsequently found that the documents were in some way inaccurate. As will be seen when considering methods of payment, the tendering of documents against bills of exchange or letters of credit calls for considerable precision in the terminology of the contract.

There are several variations of the basic CIF clause, such as 'CIFL', which would include landing charges, and 'CIFL Duty Paid', which would entail the seller in covering the cost of the appropriate import duty. Beyond this stage a seller would reach the 'franco domicile' quotation which has already been considered above.

When employing any particular export sales clause, the exporter must be flexible in outlook and try to be aware of the varying interpretations which can be encountered in different countries. For example, in the United States of America it is usual to employ the term 'FAS' to mean basically the same as 'FOB' in this country. A French customer may use 'CAF' (Coût, Assurance, Fret) but this would, of course, be equal to our CIF.

Considerable care must be taken to avoid misunderstandings, especially those which could easily have serious repercussions. It is to assist international traders in circumstances such as this that the International Chamber of Commerce has done such important work in achieving a greater degree of uniform understanding amongst a large number of countries. The ICC, which was formed as long ago as 1919, has formulated (amongst many other important documents) 'Incoterms'. This document defines all the main export sales clauses from ex works to franco and sets out the responsibilities of both buyer and seller, thus providing a single point of reference. An exporter could, for example, define his quotation 'CIF Calcutta (Incoterms)' and this would enable the buyer to have a much clearer understanding of what each party had in mind.

A good example of the use of these terms is found perhaps when considering an FOB airport sale. On strictly legal definitions this could be held to mean that the buyer is going to specify and arrange the carriage contract with the air carrier. Incoterms, however, defines the right to arrange carriage as being that of the exporter *unless* the buyer stipulates otherwise. Clearly, this is a help towards speedy despatch arrangements. The current ICC Publications Incoterms is dated 1980 and is from time to time up-dated. The quotation can also be qualified in other ways. When quoting an export merchant on an ex-works basis, it might be an advantage to quote 'ex-works (export packing extra)' just in case the merchant might assume that, because he is going to ship the goods, the manufacturer is prepared to pack for shipment, whereas the clause may include only primary packing. See Appendix A. (There is also a set of German delivery terms known as 'Combiterms' which are particularly adapted to International Groupage Traffic.)

Once the customer has been quoted with a particular sales clause and an order has been received, then basically the price has to remain firm. Care must be exercised if it is wished to retain some flexibility with regard to price alterations, in the event of any unexpected increased cost such as in freight rates or insurance premiums. An exporter might wish to insert a clause into the contract to cover a freight increase and consequently may state in the conditions of sales, for example, 'The price CIF Calcutta is calculated on the basis of a freight rate of $2.60 per cubic metre, any variations in this rate for buyer's account.' It may be that an exporter's price is subject to variations in the price of basic raw materials such as steel or hydrocarbon oils. It is often quite customary in such cases for appropriate clauses to be inserted into a contract during the negotiation stage.

There will be a marketing element involved in the decision pertaining to the insertion of any variation clauses. Obviously, it is safer for an exporter to retain as much right as possible to alter a price or condition of an order. If, for example, freight costs represent a high proportion of the selling price and the rates are very unstable, or if the contract is one spanning a lengthy period of time, then such clauses may be imperative. Equally, however, the customer will always prefer precise and definite prices and conditions.

Practical marketing aspects of quotations

When considering the question of type and structure of his quotation, the exporter should bear in mind the following points:

(1) The competitive and sophisticated markets, e.g. USA, Germany, France and Canada represent areas where precise and comprehensive quotations are essential. Often it will be desirable to advance the quotation to the franco stage.

(2) The background of exporter's business should be borne in mind, e.g. the stability of raw material prices and the predictability of freight rates or insurance premiums, etc.

(3) The duration of the contract. With orders extending over a period of some years, it might be very difficult to quote firm prices.

(4) The type of market. How stable is it economically and politically? What are the business ethics of the customer?

(5) The extent of profit margins. If they are slender, they will be very sensitive to slight changes in, for example, freight and insurance, etc. charges.

Quite apart from the cost element incorporated in the quotation, there is also the question of performance obligation. This factor places upon the shoulders of both sellers and buyers certain obligations and responsibilities. For example, the ex-works quotation literally interpreted means that the customer would have to call at the seller's works or warehouse and physically collect the goods in question. The seller's responsibilities would be to ensure that the goods were ready and notify the customer when they were available for collection at the particular warehouse or works in question.

Similarly the franco quotation would mean that the export department of the seller would have to arrange and carry out the packing, shipment, payment of overseas import duty, customs clearance and final delivery charges to the customer's final address (plus, of course, all necessary insurance costs.

Equally, it is important to consider the importer's view. It may well be that he has extensive international commitments, in which case, he probably has advantageous connections in the fields of shipping, transportation and insurance. Consequently, he may prefer to arrange his own shipping and insurance and therefore require an FOB quotation.

Another vital factor is the regulations that apply to a particular market area. It is always possible that a country may wish to develop and expand its shipping and insurance facilities. Consequently, importers in these countries may be obliged by law to place orders on an FOB basis only. This is also affected by a nation's ability to find necessary foreign currency to pay for shipping and insurance services.

Equally, it is important for the professional exporter to keep himself informed with regard to the way overseas markets assess duty payments or grant currency allocations or import licences. It may well be the case, for example, that a particular country grants an import licence or provides foreign currency on an FOB basis. In this case the exporter should ensure that when he submits a quotation, it shows clearly the various component parts of the price structure. The quotation could be on a CIF basis but care should be taken to show also the FOB cost so that the customer's authorities can make the necessary calculations. A typical illustration of such a breakdown might be considered as follows:

1 Mk II heavy-duty compressor 200/250 V, 50 Hz, ac, complete with extension cable @ ex works Birmingham	£250.00
Cost of export packing-loading on a lorry and delivery to docks and other incidental charges	£ 50.00
FOB London	£551.00
Cost of ocean freight, etc., charges	£40.00
CFR Calcutta	£591.00
Cost of Marine insurance premium and charges	£ 5.75
CIF Calcutta	£596.75

Such a quotation would ensure that both the potential customer and his authorities would be able to identify the main component parts of the price structure. So long as the main elements are identified, there is so often no need for excessive detailed information.

Subsequent chapters will examine in more detail the various aspects of charges encountered in an export transaction, particularly in respect of freight and insurance costings, but it is useful at this stage to refer to the invoice shown in *Figure 3.2*, which illustrates certain detailed items. This particular invoice is an example of one which might be received from a shipping and forwarding agent who has handled a shipment on behalf of an exporter, to whom this invoice would be sent, together with the appropriate shipping documents which in this case would be the necessary number of copies of the bill of lading, together with an insurance certificate. In this particular instance the sum of £531.00 would in fact represent the amount that an exporter would have to add to his ex-works (plus export packing) price to convert it into a CIF figure. As was explained in Chapter 2, the export department of a company might well itself carry out many of these tasks, such as insurance, the consignment and arranging shipment.

Having identified the *cost* and *performance* obligations involved in some of the main export clauses, it is important to bear in mind

TO

TALBOT PAINTS (SALES) LTD.,

19, CANNON STREET,

LONDON, E.C.4.

INVOICE

DATE   30/11/86

YOUR REF   EX 05052

OUR REF   TAL/154 D.

EDWARDS SHIPPING & TRANSPORT CO. LTD.
CORONATION HOUSE
4 LLOYDS AVENUE
LONDON E.C.3.   TELEPHONE 01-481 2497/8
                      TELEGRAMS EDSHIPCO LONDON

VESSEL	FROM
s.s. 'BENVENUE'	LONDON

TO   PORT SWETTENHAM

MARKS AND NUMBERS	NUMBER AND KIND OF PACKAGES	DESCRIPTION OF GOODS	GROSS WEIGHT
INDUSTRIAL PAINTS EX - 05052 PORT SWETTENHAM	THIRTY (30) CASES LABORATORY APPARATUS (Hard Drying Time Recorders)		1.2 tonnes 13.5 cubic m

URGENT ENCLOSURES			
TWO	BS/LADING ORIGINAL(S)	SUPPLY CASES ☐ EXPORT PACKING ☐	
TWO	BS/LADING COPIES	CARTAGE INCLUDING WAITING TIME	
	CERTIFICATE OF ORIGIN	F.O.B. CHARGES	
	CERTIFICATE OF SHIPMENT	PORT RATES AND PREPARATION OF ENTRY	12.75
	COMMERCIAL INVOICES	DOCK DUES	17.50
	CONSULAR INVOICES	CUSTOMS ENTRY	7.50
	EXPORT LICENCE	PRODUCING TO CUSTOMS FOR EXAMINATION	
ONE	INSURANCE CERTIFICATES	INSURANCE £7500 @ £0.60 POLICY AND ARRANGING	45.00
	PACKING SPECIFICATION	BILLS OF LADING per cent	5.50
	THROUGH B/L ORIGINAL(S)	FREIGHT 13.5 cu.m. @ £35.00 W/M	430.00
	THROUGH B/L COPIES	less 9½% rebate	
		CONSULAR DOCUMENTS AND FEES	
		CERTIFICATE OF ORIGIN ☐ CERTIFICATE OF SHIPMENT ☐	
		E.O.D.	
		C.O.D. COLLECTION CHARGES	
		TELEPHONE POSTAGE CASH CABLES TELEX.	12.75
		SUPERVISION AND HANDLING OU R SERVICE FEE	

TOTAL TO
YOUR DEBIT £   531.00

Figure 3.2 Forwarding agents invoice

that in a large number of cases the sale is handled on a 'mixed-contract' basis. This is, in effect, a useful compromise in which the exporter for example quotes an FOB price and enters into that type of contract but undertakes to arrange all, say, shipping and insurance for his customer and invoice him at cost. It could be said that the normal operation of an FOB Airport sale is in effect usually on a mixed-contract basis, as the exporter will usually arrange and pay for the freight and then debit the charges additionally to the customer.

Legal aspects of quotations

To view the problem in perspective, it might be useful to consider very briefly the background to a normal contract of sale. Such a contract contains the component parts of 'offer', 'acceptance', 'performance' and 'consideration'. Such contracts may well be concluded verbally, by implication, as well as by a formal contract or quotation. In any form of commercial correspondence pertaining to buying and selling, there are bound to be time-lags; this is very noticeable in overseas trading. Basically, therefore, the first task of the export manager will be to consider just how far he is going to commit his company, and for how long, once a quotation is submitted to a potential buyer.

Generally speaking, the ideal situation is for a quotation to be considered as an 'invitation to make an offer'. Consequently, should an order result from the quotation, the seller is in a position to consider the order as an 'offer' and is therefore free either to accept or reject. This is, of course, all very well, but in commerce, particularly with overseas markets, it is natural that the customer himself requires some degree of stability. For example, in quite a number of countries the overseas buyer, once he receives a quotation from the exporter, has then to apply for an import licence or currency permit before he can proceed. It would be extremely frustrating if, having obtained the necessary permit, it was then found that the price had been raised. The exporter will 'accept' the order when an appropriate acknowledgement letter or form is sent to the buyer.

When evolving an appropriate strategy for quotation procedure, therefore, the exporter will have to take into account the length of time involved between quotation and order and the number of variable factors involved in a price structure such as materials, labour and physical distribution costs. Equally he will have to distinguish between the general type of quotation and the more specific. Usually the more general type will be represented by the price list and catalogue. Here it is normal procedure to incorporate a clause indicating that the company reserves the right to change the price or specification, etc. of the product in question.Usually such lists give basic ex works or perhaps FOB quotations. More detailed quotations are given upon request.

On the other hand, if the enquiry and resulting quotation cover a very specific situation, it would be good policy to indicate that the price and conditions would remain firm for a prescribed period in order to enable the potential buyer to make the necessary preliminary arrangements, e.g. obtaining an import licence. In situations such as these it is often customary to submit a quotation in the shape of a 'pro forma' invoice. This document may be required by an importer's authority when he applies for any appropriate licence or permit. This type of invoice, as distinct from the normal commercial or trading invoice, does not pass through the ledger system. Consequently, if an order does not materialize, there is no need for a credit note to be issued. When an order does result from a pro forma, then a 'definite' commercial invoice is subsequently sent to the customer.

Particular care has to be taken when submitting 'tenders'. Here the potential buyer, often a government department or very large organization, puts out tenders which really represent an invitation to the seller to put forward for acceptance a form of quotation. Normally, such transactions should involve the most careful scrutiny of the conditions surrounding such potential orders, as the obligations and requirements are generally very precise and most exacting. Sometimes manufacturers may be called upon to provide 'Tender Guarantees', which may mean paying a sum of money if their tender is accepted, and yet they cannot fulfil the tender obligations.

Bearing in mind the complex pattern of costs and responsibilities in the overseas transactions, it will be seen that it is of crucial importance for the export department to ensure that its routine procedures involved in quoting potential customers and processing subsequent orders are clear-cut and free from ambiguities. Normally a company is in touch with a circle of potential buyers through the medium of:

(1) Circularizing price lists and catalogues.
(2) Responding to individual enquires by means of quotations and pro forma invoices.
(3) Submitting tenders.

The export manager will have the responsibility of ensuring that the methods employed by his department will provide maximum satisfaction for his overseas buyers. At the same time, he must make sure that his company is not taking upon itself any unnecessary risks of price variations which might make inroads upon profit margins. He must ensure that should any problems arise, there will be no possibility of misunderstanding with regard to the price or performance obligations.

Conditions of sale

All that has been considered so far pertains to the quotation and order stages. The next step will be when the exporter, having received an order, responds by sending an appropriate acknowledgement. This acknowledgement will in fact represent the seller's official acceptance of the order, and it is most essential that the 'conditions of sale', as envisaged when the quotation was made, are clearly understood by both parties. Details must be checked carefully against the order as, very often, the buyer will include certain 'conditions of purchase' and if any of these are not in line with the seller's wishes then this point must be clarified before the contract proceeds further.

Naturally, the exporter will seek legal advice when initially drawing up terms and conditions of contract which he will have printed on his quotation and order forms. Such conditions will have to be drafted to meet the particular requirements of his product category and markets. A typical set of conditions which cater for the main points at issue could well be as follows:

(1) Our aim is to provide you with good service and a first-class job in accordance with this quotation.

(2) Unless otherwise stated in the quotation or varied by written agreement, the terms of payment on which this quotation is based are as follows:

FOB Shipments. Payments in cash against delivery of goods to nominated vessel.
CIF Shipments. Payment terms to be agreed. The price is based on a London Banker's Confirmed Irrevocable Letter of Credit, or Documents against Payment under Documentary Bills of Exchange. Any variations in the method of payment may render an amendment of price necessary.

(3) Dimensions, descriptions and weights supplied by the company for the purpose of shipping or transport requirements are approximate only and shall not form part of the contract.

(4) The purchaser will be responsible for obtaining import licences, currency permits or any other necessary documents of this nature, and for complying with all regulations governing the admission of any goods into the country of destination for payment of all Customs duties, port dues and other changes arising therefrom.

(5) Delivery dates are given in good faith, but are subject to the movement of transport and may be amended by us due to strikes, lock-outs and other causes beyond our control.

(6) The quotation is based on the present cost of materials, transport and labour. If any of these costs decrease or increase our price may be amended accordingly.

(7) Our liability under this quotation for any damage or loss is limited to making good any defects in our contract work which may arise directly from any failure of our design material or workmanship and of which we have received notice in writing within six calendar months of the practical completion of our contract work.

(8) The contract shall be interpreted in accordance with English Law including Statue Law.

It must be emphasized that the above would not suit every type of business and would, of course, depend upon the framework of the particular export sales clause that was being used. Nevertheless, the items set out indicate the main points of emphasis.

The exporter may very well find that there is available some standard model contract form that has been drawn up by a particular trade association such as London Corn Trade Association or the Timber Trade Federation of the United Kingdom. The United Nations Economic Commission for Europe has sponsored model contracts for various categories of products including cereals, citrus fruit, potatoes and steel products.

4 Licensing and export control

International Customs controls

International trade involves the complex flow of goods and services between many countries who in most cases will all possess organised Customs services to monitor and control this flow. This will be necessary to implement tariff and trading agreements between individual or groups of countries (such as the EEC). There will be the need at times, to levy duty or tax and to administer possible quotas or other trading agreements. Owing to the gradual formation of trading groups and agreements there has been a move towards greater standardization of procedures. To the exporter these controls will impinge upon his operations in two ways:

(1) The observance of certain types of procedure and documentation to satisfy his own country's Customs requirements.

(2) The necessity of being aware of possible import licensing or currency exchange controls or other tariff requirements in the countries to which the goods are being exported.

In this chapter we are mainly concerned with the permutation of procedures and ensuing documentation that may be encountered by the exporter when sending goods out of the United Kingdom.

Before arranging a contract and the subsequent overseas transaction, it will be the exporter's responsibility to ensure that full attention is paid to any official requirements that may affect his particular sphere of activity. In Chapter 2, when an analysis was made of the export order, it was seen that the fourth heading covered regulations encountered both in the United Kingdom and in the various overseas countries. The task of this chapter is to consider the possible types of regulation that the exporter might have to face in the United Kingdom.

At the present time there is the minimum number of obstacles placed in the exporter's path. On the contrary, every emphasis is placed upon assisting him in exporting his goods and extending his overseas markets.

Nevertheless,there are bound to be some occasions when a particular restriction might be encountered due to the nature of the product, the market to which the goods are being consigned or some financial aspect such as remission of duty or value added tax. In practice, such problems are likely to be encountered under the following headings.

(1) *Export licensing* – making it necessary for application to be made for types of export licences and for the necessary documentary procedure to be carried out when shipping the consignment from the United Kingdom.
(2) *Customs entries* – certain formalities are necessary and will call for the completion of Customs entry forms and for these to be produced to HM Customs and Excise at port or airport, or to provide certain declaration forms at the Post Office.

The type of Customs entry and form and procedure will vary according to whether the goods are, in fact, subject to export licence or perhaps some other specialized factor such as agricultural products linked with the Common Agricultural Policy (CAP) of the EEC. There will, however, be one common factor in all types of entry and that will be *classificatory*. This will mean providing a certain input of statistical data concerning the type of goods exported, the FOB value and certain other transport, etc., information. From this, HM Customs will be able to build up the balance of trade and ultimately the balance of payment figures so essential for monitoring the economy.

Types of export licence

Logically, the first category that will be dealt with when considering a potential export order will be the question of *export licensing*. The United Kingdom authorities will naturally wish to avoid, wherever possible, placing any restrictions upon the exporter, but circumstances may make some control inevitable. In the field of international trade a number of basic factors will influence the attitude of a government when considering export licensing operations.

Sometimes, and this is of paramount importance to exporters, there is the possibility that their products may have some military or strategic character and therefore be subject to export control. Most countries are now becoming increasingly sensitive to the export of cultural and historical objects which, together with antiques, often need export licences. Another reason may be the sudden appearance of a political problem leading to one country imposing economic sanction against another. In circumstances such as these it may well be the case that all exports to a particular country may overnight become subject to control and consequently require licence application.

With the above factors in mind, therefore, it will always be the task of the exporter to acquaint himself with the current prevailing requirements, so that he can fulfil the necessary procedures relevant to his range of products and markets. The appropriate source material will emanate from the Department of Trade, Export Licensing Branch, in the shape of the current Export of Goods (Control) Order. Subsequent modifications or amendments should be watched carefully in such publications as *British Business* and other similar export reference books.

Basically, the Order in question will set out a Schedule 1 (sometimes known as the 'Prohibition List') which gives a wide range of items arranged into groups. In the 1981 Order these are as follows:

Schedule 1, Part I

Group A	Certain goods specified by reference to EEC Common Customs Tariff.
Group B	Photographic material, antiques, collectors' items, etc.

Schedule 1, Part II

Group 1	Aircraft, arms, ammunition, military stores and paramilitary equipment, etc.
Group 2A	Atomic energy minerals, materials and appliances.
Group 2B	Nuclear facilities, equipment and appliances.
Group 3	Certain strategic goods not specified in Groups 1 and 2 (see page 62).
Group 3A	Metal-working machinery and associated equipment.
Group 3B	Chemical and petroleum equipment.
Group 3C	Electrical and power-generating equipment.
Group 3D	General industrial equipment.
Group 3E	Compasses, gyroscopes and marine equipment, etc.

Group 3F   Electronic equipment including radar.
Group 3G   Scientific instruments and apparatus.
Group 3H   Metals, minerals and their manufactures.
Group 3I   Chemicals, metalloids and petroleum products.
Group 3J   Synthetic film and synthetic rubber.

By studying the current Export of Goods (Control) Order, the exporter will be able to see whether his product falls within any of various groups and therefore whether or not an export licence is required. This will very often depend upon the country to which the goods are being exported. An indication of this is given by code letters that appear beside the particular description. For example, the letter 'A' indicates that a licence is needed for export to any country, and 'E' indicates that a licence is needed for export to any country outside the EEC.

To illustrate the operation of this system, a computer manufacturer studying the list would find that computers designed for use in aircraft are marked with an 'A' (licences required for all destinations), whereas certain other types of computer are marked with a 'C' to indicate that licences are not required for certain countries, e.g. the United States.

The term 'open general licence' (OGL) is encountered in the Export Control Order and, applied to a particular commodity category, means that at the particular time there is no need to apply for a 'specific licence'. The OGL may, of course, be limited in application to certain countries.

The exporter should, therefore, be in a position to check the various sources of reference pertaining to export licensing and, if appropriate, to take steps to apply for a specific licence. In most cases the application form needed will be Form A. Part I of this is the actual application which has to be completed; Part II, after validation, will be returned as the actual export licence. In addition to the form, two carbon copies on plain paper should be sent with the application. See *Figure 4.1*.

It is necessary for the value of the goods to be shown as FOB and, most important, precise units of quantity and measurements as per the current export list to be given. For example, tons, cwts, or gallons, etc. should be stated and not ambiguous descriptions such as cartons, barrels or bags. Applications should always show a reference number to be used in all subsequent correspondence. The status of the signatory should be given and should be the party directly interested in the transaction as consignor. Signatures by forwarding agents or other similar persons are not acceptable. No export licences are transferable and obviously no unauthorized

APPLICATION FOR AN EXPORT LICENCE

Return to:
Department of Trade and Industry
Export Licensing Branch
Millbank Tower
Millbank
London SW1P 4QU
Tel: 01-211 3000

FORM A   PART I

No:

Your ref. — quote in correspondence:

Telex   8811074 DT HQG
8811075

Consignor, name and address

Consignee, name and address

Ultimate consignee if different, name and address

Please supply two carbon or photocopies of this sheet.

For certain goods, notably arms, atomic energy related goods and other strategic goods applications must be supported with detailed specifications unless

— these have been provided with a previous application, *and*
— there has been no significant modification to the specification.

If in doubt see Schedule 1, Export of Goods (Control) Order obtainable from H.M. Stationery Office or consult Export Licensing Branch, Department of Trade and Industry.

If you have made a previous application to export similar goods, state Department of Trade & Industry's reference . . . .

No.

If you have any of the following give its reference
— UK international import certificate . . . .
— import licence . . . .
— certificate of essentiality . . . .
— approval by other government department . . . .

Department

Reference

What is the proposed date of shipment? . . . .

Date

Read the notes on page 4, then sign in final box below.

WARNING

Penalties may be imposed for false statements in connection with applications for export licences.

DECLARATION

I am habitually resident in the United Kingdom or Isle of Man.
I am aware that the exporter or shipper must, if so required, provide to Customs and Excise, within the time they allow, proof to their satisfaction that the goods covered by this licence were delivered at the ultimate destination. The goods to be exported are the property of the consignor.

Other signatories than those shown below may be authorised upon written application to the Department of Trade and Industry

Consignor's telephone number

Official number of authorised signatory

Date

Status: owner* proprietor* partner* director* company secretary*

Signature

* Delete those which do not apply

Figure 4.1 Application form for an export licence

amendments are allowed. Any changes in destination must receive the consent of the Export Licensing Branch, Department of Trade.

In addition to the above-mentioned OGL and specific licence the exporter may encounter a type known as 'general' or 'bulk'. Whereas the 'specific licence' normally refers to goods shipped in one consignment, the 'general' covers goods despatched over a certain specified period. The validity period of the licences is usually 12 months from date of issue.

There may arise the need for a 'transhipment licence' if a United Kingdom company wished to import goods of a nature that, if they were produced in the UK, would need an export licence. If the intention was merely to bring them into a British port for the purpose of transhipment to an overseas destination, then a transhipment licence would be required. The application form needs rather more detailed information, such as proposed method of payment and purpose for which goods are required. The value is required CIF United Kingdom port.

Transport arrangements, either for exports direct from a UK port or for transhipment, should not be made until the appropriate licence has been obtained. Penalties for offences against export licence regulations are heavy, including forfeiture of goods. Neither must it be overlooked that the existence of an export licence does not by itself relieve the exporter of the responsibility of ensuring that his customer has complied with all regulations and obtained any appropriate import licences or currency permits. The export licence is concerned strictly with actually shipping the consignment from the UK and not with entry of goods into the destination country.

Strategic goods

Running closely parallel to export licensing, is the control exercised over 'strategic' goods. This is operated through the Strategic Goods Control Order 1978. Essentially, this is an external type of control which is aimed at certain classes of goods being bought from outside the UK and being disposed of by a UK resident company to a specific list of countries. The Strategic Goods Control Order provides one schedule which covers the categories of goods and another which lists the countries subject to the embargo. Strategic goods imported into the UK may be brought under official control, and sometimes the UK importer/ exporter may encounter import certificates or 'waiver licences'. The exporter involved in transactions with these types of product must also be careful to ascertain whether any transit authorization or delivery verification certificates may be needed if the goods are crossing the frontiers of different countries.

Customs entries

Having considered some of the factors involved in the need for customs control, we are now in a position to identify some of the different types of documents and outline procedures involved. Remember, when we mention 'customs entry', we are in this context thinking of the exporter preparing some form of document and lodging it with HM Customs and Excise in a particular fashion.

For Customs purposes, the term 'exporter' includes the shipper of the goods and any person performing in the case of an air consignment functions similar in an aircraft to those of a shipper. If an exporter is normally in the course of his business utilizing the services of a shipping and forwarding agent, it is quite permissible to appoint the agent to conduct Customs business on his behalf. In such a case, an authorization is lodged with the Customs authorities with appropriate specimen signature.

It should be borne in mind at this stage that the permutation of Customs entries can be quite complex and it is essential to build up a working familiarity with the excellent Customs Notices that are available for different situations. An essential one for all exporters is the basic Notice No. 275/A which covers all the revised procedures introduced in 1981 to conform to EEC Directives for Customs procedure harmonization.

The first task is to identify the various types of Customs entry, how they relate to different circumstances and what differences arise with regard to the appropriate forms and procedures. Customs entries can be divided broadly into two categories, namely 'pre-entry' and 'entry'.

Pre-entry

With pre-entry it is essential for the particular entry form, together with any other necessary documentation, to be made available at the Custom House at the particular port of exportation in time for it to be passed and presented to the Officer of Customs and Excise at the ship's side for clearance before shipment. Similarly, of course, it would have to be available in the same way before goods were consigned by air. The type of pre-entry form used for consignments subject to export licence, for example, is the C.63A.

Some examples where pre-entry procedures would be mandatory are:

(1) Goods subject to specific export licences.
(2) Shipment drawn from bonded warehouses.

(3) Goods on which relief from import duty has been claimed
(4) CAP goods

For more details and further examples, reference should be made to Customs Notice No. 275/A.

Post-entry

The other method, or entry, which can better be distinguished by referring to it as 'post-entry', allows for the lodging of the Customs entry at any time within 14 days after the clearance of the carrying vessel or aircraft. This is a very simple type of entry and falls into the category described above as 'classificatory.' The sole purpose is to provide HM Customs with details and value of the consignment plus certain statistical information. The main type of entry form encountered is this category is the C.273.

It will be seen that there are situations where, although pre-entry is not mandatory, it may be employed with the C.273 type of entry form, because, in certain circumstances the shipper/exporter may find it more convenient. The procedure would be for the exporter to complete the C.273, usually in duplicate, and forward it with say a shipping note or equivalent document, with the goods when going forward to the dock, container depot or airport etc.

Completion of C.273 (*Figure 4.2(a)*)

Boxes 2, 5, 6 and 13 would indicate exporter or forwarding agent and any particular reference numbers.

Boxes 22, 24, 25, 26 and 27 would refer to the tariff/trade code numbers and the units of quantity to be employed and the FOB value.

The information in these boxes is very important and refers to the classification of the particular product according to our HM Customs Tariff Description List. This is based on the internationally-used Customs Co-operation Council Nomenclature (CCCN). See page 141, Chapter 7. We are usually looking for an eight-digit figure, and a typical Customs classification could be: Domestic spin dryers = 84.18 0006.

The classification list (usually obtained through HM Stationery Office) will specify also the unit of quantity to be used. This might be metric tons, kilos, packages, pairs or just a single unit. Sometimes more than one unit of quantity may be required.

EX ORIGINAL

C 273 (1)

3a. Status of goods (See Note 6)	

1. Number of Forms C 273 (CS) attached	2. Exporter (name and address)	3. Customs reference (if appropriate)

6. Exporter's reference

5. F/Agent's reference

EXPORT DECLARATION

STATISTICAL COPY

1

HM Customs and Excise

FOR STATISTICAL OFFICE USE

13. Forwarding Agent (name and address)	Insert codes here ▶	7. COUD	8. FZ	9. Cntnr.	10. ToT	11. Flag	12. Port

14. Country of ultimate destination

15. Date of Sailing/Flight etc.	16. Dock/Wharf/Station

17. Ship/Flight etc.	18. Port/Airport of export

19. Port/Airport of discharge

FOR OFFICIAL USE
Date of acceptance

20. Marks and numbers	21. No. and kind of packages; description of goods	22. Tariff/Trade code number

23. CAC

24. Quantity 2	26. Quantity 1 (net weight)	27. Value (fob) (nearest £)

25. Quantity 3

NOTES

1. Further instructions on the completion and use of this form will be found in the Customs and Excise Tariff and in Notice 275.
2. Where lodgement of the duplicate is also required the address panel thereon must be completed.
3. This form may be used as a pre-entry only for goods which are not relieved from any U.K. duty nor subject to an export licence, apart from certain free zone goods.
4. Only one Tariff/Trade item may be included on this form. For consignments of more than one item, attach Form(s) C 273 (CS) or use Form C 273(2) or C 273(4).

5. When used as a pre-entry this document **MUST** accompany any Community transit or ATR document for the goods described hereon when that is presented to Customs for authentication.
6. Status of goods — Boxes 3a and 21.
   Box 3a need be completed only on pre-entries and in respect of goods sent to or via another member state of the European Community or to the Channel Islands. The status (T1, T2 etc.) of the goods entered on this form and on any continuation sheets must be shown in this box (see Notice 750). Where goods of more than one status are included, insert "T1 and T2" and indicate the status of the goods in red in the extreme right of box 21 against each item, including those items on any continuation sheets.

WARNING: There are heavy penalties for making false declarations

DECLARATION

I, the authorised signatory declare that:

(a) all the particulars given on this form and any continuation sheets attached are true and complete;

(b) exportation of the goods does not contravene export restrictions.

28. Signatory's company and telephone No.

29. Date

30. Signature

830

C 273 (1) (1986)   F 3680 (October 1986)   Printed in UK for HMSO Dd 8051452 2000M SETS S&K 10/86

Figure 4.2(a) Form C 273 (1)

Boxes 20 and 21 cover the description, packing and marks and numbers of the goods involved in the consignment and the use of say, a C.273(1) would indicate that only one type of product classification could be used. A C.273(CS) continuation sheet could be employed where, say, a consignment of several different classifications is involved.

Box 23 CAC Customs Additional Codes: This makes provision for the insertion of certain code numbers relevant to some specialized type of situation. An example could be Code 80 where certain products of particular classifications are being exported for military use abroad.

Boxes 15–19   In certain cases, when the C.273 is being used as a *pre-entry*, these may be left uncompleted if the information is not available at the time. Similarly with boxes 11 and 12.

Boxes 7–10 seek code numbers and letters relating to the ultimate destination country (COUD) and certain transport and Inland Clearance Depot (ICD) information if appropriate.

Reference to Code Nos. and letters should be related to Customs Notices 37 and 276, *Coding Lists Used in Completion of Customs Documents*.

Let us now consider the alternative usage of the C.273 if the post-entry system is being used. This can be operated under the Simplified Clearance Procedure (SCP) whereby the goods could in fact be shipped, the C.273 completed and forwarded to HM Customs within 14 days after shipment. The key factor in employing SCP is the exsistence of a Customs Registered Number (CRN) plus another number which pinpoints the actual consignment. Collectively these two numbers form the Export Consignment Identifier (ECI). This number will appear something like *Figure 4.2(b)* and it is used in box 3 of the C.273 and also appears on the other documents, usually shipping notes, etc.

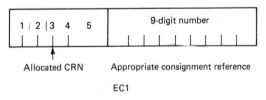

Figure 4.2(b) Export consignment identifier (ECI)

It will be appreciated that the allocated CRN will remain constant, identifying the party *responsible* for the entry. Exporters themselves might apply to HM Customs for allocation of a number or, as in many cases, they may operate under the umbrella of their forwarding agent's number, whichever is applicable. Whichever technique is being employed the important point is that when goods go forward for shipment they should either be covered by the C.273 (pre-entry) or reference to the ECI should be made on the appropriate covering documents (post-entry). Again, it must be stressed that these possibilities of post-entry will not apply to those operations where pre-entry is mandatory, i.e. export licensing, etc.

Customs relief

An important Customs procedure is that known as 'Inward Processing Relief' (IPR) which, in effect means that in certain circumstances manufacturers may claim remission or reimbursement from any import duty they may pay on, say, raw materials or

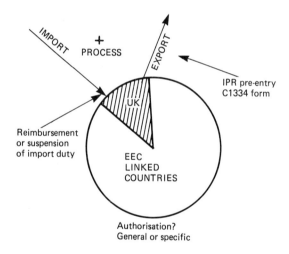

Figure 4.3 Basic outline of Inward Processing Relief (IPR)

components which they import from overseas and utilize in the production of items which they subsequently export. *Figure 4.3* shows a basic outline of this operation. Apart from certain special procedures involved at the time of importation the exporter will normally 'pre-enter' his shipments and employ, instead of a C.273, a special C.1334 form which will link the exportation to the relief received.

Bonded goods

A bonded warehouse is one which is licensed to accept imported goods for storage before payment of Customs duty, revenue duty or VAT. This can be of considerable benefit to importers and exporters covering goods which are perhaps not required immediately for home use or where there is a chance of re-exportation.

We have already seen that goods ex bond will normally need pre-entry and that specific types of shipping bills will be required to effect the entry. The new shipping bills and warrants are the OW60 and WW60 (for wet goods) ex bonded warehouse. The shipping bill, together with a bond form, should be sent to the Custom House for passing before being sent to the bonded warehouse where the goods are held. Reference should be made to HM Customs to check the particular bond form which is required as there are a number of types. Care must also be taken to ensure that the correct categories of principal and surety are employed. The bond office at Custom House issues notes of general guidance covering this point.

Developments in Customs' procedure

When considering HM Customs' procedures, the exporter must bear in mind that considerable development is taking place in the streamlining and simplifying of Customs entry and documentation. In many cases the C.273 type of entry lodgement can be replaced by computer statistical scheduling, information on magnetic tape and other forms of data transfer.

One of the most significant changes which is gradually being phased into operation is that of Local Export Control (LEC). The facility will become increasingly available for approved exporters, groupage operators and forwarders. In essence it will mean that export clearance can take place at the trader's premises, based mainly on controls exercised by a Customs and Excise Office which will normally be dealing with customs matters in the locality of the exporter's premises. This will be known as the 'control office'.

Normally, approved traders will be those exporting goods in Full Container Loads (FCLs), pallets and other similar unitization. Some of the main conditions for approval by HM Customs for LEC will be:

(a) Suitable facilities at the exporter's premises;
(b) The maintenance of a high standard of entry preparation, record keeping and documentation;
(c) Sufficient volume of export activity.

This can be of immense benefit, particularly to a large exporter, because it means virtually that all the necessary procedural paperwork can be handled on the premises, and the goods go forward to airports, seaports, container depots, etc., normally covered by a C44A form. On their arrival there they can expect to be loaded and despatched with minimum delay.

When considering Customs procedures in general the exporter must bear in mind that there are many variations, special provisions and developments to be encountered. Reference should always be made to their various Notices and other publications, and if in any doubt the appropriate Customs officers should be consulted.

5 Export distribution and packing

The efficient and economic ways of international trading today demand that we understand fully the various methods of moving goods. There is no need these days to emphasize the word 'economic' since we must find the appropriate mode of freighting our products if the distribution element in our costings is indeed to be the right one; that is to say, is our price the most competitive and advantageous possible? The nature of our products, the time factor and routes, with service frequency, restrict our choice, but these considerations must never limit the search for, and constant appraisal of, what makes good sense for us.

It is very important to realize the vital place physical distribution has in international trading mangement. In recent years it has become obvious that we could not continue looking at each transport method seperately, and now we integrate these methods into a *total distribution concept*, involving sea, road, rail, air and inland waterway – not forgetting the postal services. For each movement more than one method will be used.

Just as marketing and sales are complementary, so distribution and marketing are close partners in our efforts to move goods onto the market. No one function can exist and operate properly without co-ordination and cohesion with its peers in our organization. Demands of modern marketing, speed of traffic movement and the ever-increasing tempo of communications urge us to make sure we do have the correct answers to our distribution problems. Physical distribution is satisfying demand, marketing is creating demand.

The pillars are materials handling, warehousing and storage, packaging and unitization, and transport. Good planning is the basic requirement, and this covers forecasting, space utilization, inventory control, damage during handling/transit/storage, protective packaging, security, documentation and order processing. A constant aim must be the reduction of the lead time – start to finish of order. A useful instrument is a flow chart, to show chain links, strengths and weaknesses. *Figure 5.1.*

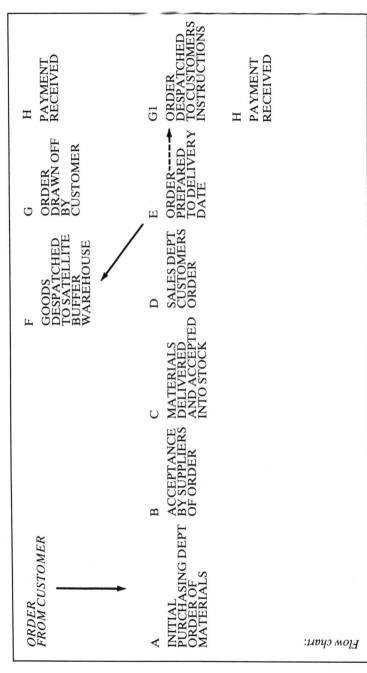

Flow chart:

ORDER
FROM CUSTOMER

A
INITIAL
PURCHASING DEPT
ORDER OF
MATERIALS

B
ACCEPTANCE
BY SUPPLIERS
OF ORDER

C
MATERIALS
DELIVERED
AND ACCEPTED
INTO STOCK

D
SALES DEPT
CUSTOMERS
ORDER

F
GOODS
DESPATCHED
TO SATELLITE
BUFFER
WAREHOUSE

G
ORDER
DRAWN OFF
BY
CUSTOMER

H
PAYMENT
RECEIVED

E
ORDER---
PREPARED
TO DELIVERY
DATE

G1
ORDER
DESPATCHED
TO CUSTOMERS
INSTRUCTIONS

H
PAYMENT
RECEIVED

Figure 5.1 Physical distribution flow chart

International transport methods

(a) *Sea* – many variations available from small coaster/Rhine vessel, through to large container ship, including LASH (Lighter Aboard Ship) and BACAT (Barge Aboard Catamaran), conventional cargo liners, roll on/roll off ferries

(b) *Inland waterways* – variety of craft available: dumb barge, powered barge, shallow-draught coaster

(c) *Road* – most vehicles carrying goods abroad subject to TIR regulations, and include rigid vehicles, semi-trailer and road trains – Transport Internationaux Routiers – CMR (see below)

(d) *Rail* – wagons hired from British Rail, private wagons or used in joint groupage arrangements through agents – CIM (see below)

(e) *Air* – scheduled or charter flights available. Regulating body is the International Air Transport Association (IATA)

(f) *Post*

International agreements

(a) The convention on the carriage of goods by sea – Hague Rules

(b) The convention on the international carriage of goods by road – Convention de Marchandises par Route (CMR)

(c) The convention on the international carriage of goods by rail – Convention Internationale Concernant le Transport des Marchandises par Chemin de Fer (CIM)

(d) The convention on the carriage of goods by air – Warsaw Rules

Some of these conventions and agreements will be referred to in more detail in Chapter 6 as to their impact upon documents and procedures such as bills of lading, consignment notes, waybills and carnets.

Costing

Constant monitoring and assessment are carried out by differential cost analysis, e.g. order sizes, transport methods, packaging uses; and these days computer comparisons of differential costs give us answers quickly and help to identify most economic patterns. Fundamentally, costs include

a in-factory movement and storage
b factory to depot of transit
c depot work: materials handling, storage and overheads
d depot to customer
e inventory control
f selection of goods to meet order
g packaging
h documentation
i insurance
j securing payment from overseas customer, through bank or other agencies
k transportation charges – dock/rail/airport delivery – freight, port charges
l duties
m foreign distribution charges – franco domicile terms of sale – Incoterms
n interest on transit capital

• *Direct costs*, or variables, relate directly to particular goods or projects, such as, raw materials, assembly, production wages, direct energy/power costs for running machines
• *Indirect costs*, or invariables, fixed, overheads, embrace rents, rates, lighting, heating, repairs/maintenance; each product or project must contribute to costs such as purchasing, factory office, inspection, progress chasing, quality control, accounts, personnel, advertising, sales, research and development

Direct + indirect + profit mark-up = ex works

Materials handling

This is the fastest-changing and developing part of distribution and it is essential to keep up with new techniques and means of handling goods, if costs are to be controlled effectively.

From small pallet truck through to heavy-lift trucks there is a wide variety of equipment available to speed the work of goods handling, whether it is of raw materials entering the production unit or manufactured articles leaving to meet an order.

For every type of operation there is an appropriate machine, and to cope with the demand of users for specialist handling more and more varied aids are introduced.

A simple way of thinking of materials handling is to consider a large factory layout – there are fork-lift trucks, mobile cranes to load vehicles arriving at and leaving the facility, overhead conveyor systems and goods holding areas.

Warehousing and storage

In any distribution system, *Figure 5.1*, there are warehouses at many points which are essential to the free flow of goods to the market. Some are used as assembly points, perhaps near a port or airport, others are at the factory site, whilst others again serve as buffer stock reserve stores, particularly in times of economic stringency and uncertain international financial conditions. To build and equip a modern, efficient warehouse requires the outlay of a substantial capital sum, so very careful planning is needed to fix the correct position and to identify the uses – will it be automated or labour controlled?

It will be seen, therefore, that PDM (Physical Distribution Management) takes its full and proper place in the Marketing Mix. The choices made, and patterns selected will in turn shape the procedures and documentation necessary to support the appropriate distribution and transport mode.

Consulting the simple flow chart, *Figure 5.1*, the all-important lead time of any order can be traced. First, an order from the customer is processed at D. Materials, however, need to be allocated – A, B and C. The necessary planning therefore is: initial purchasing department order to suppliers, acceptance into stock, thence to production and despatch.

It is likely that finished goods will move to satellite buffer warehouses regionally and nationally convenient to customers – a good example is trading within the EEC, where member states' companies organize such operations – among others, foodstuffs and auto component and spares.

The length of time taken from acceptance of customer's order to final delivery *and* payment is a measure of the overall efficiency of a physical distribution system.

Packaging and unitization

The three main purposes of packaging are protection, containment and identification. The right balance is required between too costly material and the false economy of using inferior material, but we are bound by considerations of the nature of our goods, fragility, dangerous state, contamination, dampness, ease of pilferage and perishability. Other restraints are the duration of transit, type of transport mode and government regulations.

If for no other reason than economy, the past decade has forced urgent adaptation of freight methods which bulk smaller consignments with others to make convenient unit loads, perhaps by use of a pallet or a shipping container, or specialist product pack, i.e. groupage and consolidation.

Although, of course, the whole concept of unitization in the shape of standard ISO (International Standards Organization) 20 ft and 40 ft container, plus palletization, has revolutionized the whole process of packing there are still many basic packing and packaging problems associated both with unitized and conventional load movement of goods internationally. These factors will have a bearing on both the marketing and transit aspects of the operation.

Packing units

First of all, there are certain basic elements of packing which will face any manufacturer wishing to send his products from his works to a buyer, whether in the home or overseas market. The broad concept of packaging and packing can be split into two fundamental parts, namely:

(a) *Retail unit pack*. This is closely allied to the selling and marketing function and is itself a highly-specialized study. It embraces many aspects such as the psychological, functional, point-of-sale, display, etc. The choice of the correct type of packaging can be a considerable influence for consumer acceptance. The costs can be correspondingly high, particularly on such products as cosmetics and jewellery. In this respect, therefore, the unit pack has a marked bearing upon cost/price relationship and consequently upon profit margins.

(b) *Transit pack*. Here the concern is with providing a suitable pack to enable the goods to move from the manufacturer's works to his ultimate customer. A customer is interested in receiving goods in perfect condition and is *not* interested merely in collecting insurance claims. Therefore, packing will have to be provided which will hold and protect adequately. At the same time the choice must represent a compromise between maximum protection, relative cost of packing and the impact of the packing itself upon the form of transportation being utilized.

When we apply these two aspects of the packing concept more particularly to exporting, it will be seen that the special problems encountered overseas with the retail unit pack might be:

(a) In most cases, a wide range of markets in a number of countries has to be catered for, and might call for a number of different retail packs.
(b) On the other hand, decisions have to be made as to whether an international image is to be created or whether single or multiple brand images are to be exploited.
(c) There is almost certain to be a range of different legal requirements regarding weights, sizes and labelling.
(d) Various overseas consumer protection bodies are constantly reviewing and influencing unit pack requirements.
(e) Different markets may have very different preferences regarding shape and colour of packs. Various religious or social customs may entail prohibitions of the use of certain colours or wording. (See Chapter 1, p.7).

There is considerable scope for creative marketing in the sphere of designing unit packs for specific markets.

The transit pack is the one with which this book is mainly concerned. The special overseas problems become more acute because of the distances involved, the different types of climatic conditions and the varieties of handling that the goods will receive.

Let the classic concept of an overseas transaction be considered as follows:

1	2	3	4	5	6
Works packing/ loading	Docks/ airport handling/ stowing	Sea journey/ flight	Docks/ airport handling/ unloading, Customs inspection	Inland journey, various methods of transport	Customer's warehouse receiving/ unloading, opening

Every one of the six stages will to some extent influence the exporter in his choice of type of packing. The following criteria can be distinguished:

(1) Actual method of transportation.

(2) Characteristics of the product.
(3) Climatic conditions likely to be encountered during journey.
(4) Any specific requirements of customers with regard to the type of package that will be acceptable.
(5) Any specific regulations or legislation pertaining to the packing encountered, either in the exporting country or country of destination.

Choosing the method of transportation is always likely to be one of the first considerations. First of all, it must be realized that carriers, such as ship-owners for example, will themselves call for certain standards of packing. The Carriage of Goods by Sea Act 1971 excludes the carrier from any responsibility for damage due to insufficiency of packing. Freight rates will often be based upon specified packing for particular commodity characteristics.

Air transportation, by its very nature, does not call for heavy packing. Nevertheless, the latter must be sufficient to protect the goods and to enable them to be handled satisfactorily. The nature of the method employed will also indicate how much handling and unloading will be encountered. Will there be transhipment problems or breaks in the journey which call for warehousing and storage? What type of inland transport will be encountered in the importing country? It could be extremely primitive such as mule transport and therefore we might envisage a journey that commences with the latest type of twentieth century jet air-freighter and finishes on a 2000 BC ox-train. Higher freight costs can sometimes be offset by use of cheaper packing, as in the case of light, cardboard metal-tape-bound cartons by air transport, whereas heavy wooden cases or crates might be necessary by ship; the nature of the whole journey must be borne in mind. It will be readily appreciated how vast an impact the new types of container and road transport systems will have on packing; the number of stages represented in our table will be radically reduced.

The characteristics of the product itself will also influence packing specification and design. The size and shape, the degree of fragility, the number of units being packed together, and the possibility of shifting and movement will all have to be borne in mind.

If freight is being charged on cubic capacity over a large number of units, there could be a considerable amount of wasted freight space. Sometimes this wasted freight space can present problems. Consider the case of a product such as an electric fire which is mounted on legs (*Figure 5.2*). In many cases the problems can be overcome by the packing influencing product design as, for example, the electric fires being designed with detachable legs which can be reassembled at the point of destination.

Another method in the case of our product example might be for the exporter to pack the wasted space area with other allied products, e.g. spare electric elements. When mixed units are being included in the same pack, care must be taken to ensure that the different units are not rated at different freight categories. Equally, of course, hazardous goods must not be included with products being shipped as general cargo. This might well happen where perhaps mixed chemicals are shipped together but have different flash points or other dangerous characteristics.

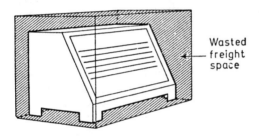

Wasted freight space

Figure 5.2 Economical packing needs forethought

Very often a compromise or calculated risk will have to be taken. Let us suppose the shipment is a consignment of electric light bulbs. These are very fragile and to be on the safe side would probably require cardboard cartons within sound wooden crates. Such products, however, are keenly competitive and such packing might amount to about 30 per cent on retail price. The strategy, based upon experience over a period of time, might be to use only carton packing, to accept a percentage breakage and to devise a system whereby the receiving customers, such as retailers, are advised to check immediately upon receipt and return broken bulbs for replacement. This action might, in the long run, be more economical than continually using heavy and expensive packing for every consignment.

International trade means that in a number of consignments goods may pass through several sets of climatic conditions before reaching their destination; therefore the packing must be designed accordingly. There is always the possibility of the exposure of goods to a corrosive atmosphere (e.g. by being opened for Customs examination on a quayside). The popular use of plastics wrapping material can sometimes exacerbate the condition known as 'sweating' unless suitable openings or air holes are provided. Internal wrapping such as waxed paper, etc., can often play a very useful part in catering for climatic conditions.

The possible *tactical uses* of the packing must not be overlooked. In some cases, whatever the exporter's thoughts are on packing, his customer may have fixed ideas on what type of packing he wants. Sometimes, as with wooden cases in countries where timber is short, the cases may have a re-sale value which is of considerable importance. Equally, the packing itself may be required for storage of the goods.

Another factor which will influence packing design and materials is the risk of pilferage. How easy is it going to be for the contents to be observed and, if desirable, to be broken open? The pilferage factor will, of course, in many cases go hand-in-hand with the method of transportation, the length of journey and how often the goods are handled and warehoused before reaching their final destination.

Regulations pertaining to packing can be considerable and they generally fall into two classes, i.e. the outside packing from the point of view of safety, and the contents of internal packing material. The former case is exemplified by the Merchant Shipping Dangerous Goods Rules and the *Blue Book* which sets out recommendations covering packing, marking and stowage of certain classes of dangerous products such as poisonous substances, corrosives and those having low flash points, etc.

The other class, which mainly relates to internal packing, often springs from health and allied requirements, particularly in predominantly agricultural or livestock breeding countries. Many of these countries prohibit the use of straw as a packing material, e.g. the Republic of Ireland, will return to sender any consignments packed with such materials. The Netherlands is another example of a country which prohibits this type of packing. In these and similar cases alternatives such as wood wool should be employed. South Africa, in addition to similar restrictions, goes further and requires that statements be provided certifying that any timber used in packing is free of certain diseases. New Zealand also comes in this category and the following is a specimen of the type of certificate an exporter would be expected to provide for the destination port:

A. N. Exporter Ltd.

Declaration by Exporter for wood packing

To: The Customs Authorities
....
....
I, ... of .... , hereby
declare that all timber used for packing the goods listed
below has been inspected by me and was to the best of my
knowledge free from bark and from visible signs of insect
and fungal attack when the goods were shipped to New
Zealand.

....
....
(Signed & dated)

Class of goods   Shipping marks   Port of discharge,

No. of cases

Categories of export packing

Sometimes countries permit the use of materials such as straw, hay
or moss for packing, provided that it is certified disinfected.
Canada, which is one such country, also prohibits the use of
second-hand bags or sacks.

The choice of packing material is nowadays very extensive and,
as always, the exporter will be balancing cost against protection
and customer requirements. The following is a list of some of the
more usual categories encountered in export packing:

(a) *Retail unit packs*: cardboard cartons, cellophane bags,
    plastics containers, polystyrene mouldings, tin cans, bottles,
    etc.
(b) *Internal packing materials*: wood wool, wood shavings,
    straw, chaff, waxed paper, sheets of cellophane film,
    multi-wall paper bags, plastics or paper linings.

(c) *Outer transit packs*: hessian sacks, special multi-wall paper bags, steel drums and cans, wooden crates, trusses, wooden cases, sometimes battened, or wire-bound. Plywood cases – occasionally metal-edged. Barrels, fibreboard packing cases and plastic or polystyrene containers which can be very strong and yet light and easily handled.

It should not be forgotten that ship-owners and air-freight operators are by the very nature of their business extremely experienced in the characteristics of packing and can often be a rich source of information for the exporter as they can give him the benefit of their experience of shipping different commodities in various types of containers.

Below is a brief classification of some of the relevant types of packing for exportable goods.

(1) *Bulky raw materials – carbon black, cement, fertilizers, etc.* plywood drums, multi-wall bags/sacks.

(2) *Machinery and capital goods*: wooden cases, plywood cases sometimes crated, sometimes on flats covered with polythene sheeting as when despatched by air. Care must be taken to see that the items cannot move about inside crates or cases.

(3) *Furniture*: wooden cases, fibreboard cartons, crates, protective polythene and paper wrapping; often shipping on a 'knocked down' (KD) basis. 'Completely knocked down' (CKD) is where the whole article is disassembled in order to save freight space and sometimes assembly costs.

(4) *Kitchen and sanitary equipment*: can often be nested, using straw extensively, and then packed in wire-bound crates.

(5) *Liquids*: casks, metal drums, carboys (particularly for acids) suitably encased in straw wrapping.

(6) *Instruments – electrical apparatus, radious, etc.*: cases or cartons, great care being taken with the internal packing.

Marking practice

Of equal important is the marking of the packages themselves. This is vital in order to make possible speedy identification of the consignment and also to comply with any regulations in force with regard to hazardous or dangerous cargo. Overseas territories, also, sometimes enforce certain regulations pertaining to marking of export cases. Equally, the marks should include wording or symbols that will enable the personnel handling the cargo to exercise any special care that may be required.

Identification of the consignment

Basically, the golden rule is to keep case marking as simple as possible. A simple example might well be as shown in *Figure 5.3*. In such a case, the UFP might well indicate the initials of the importing company, 397 the customer's order number, 1/6 Up indicating that this particular case is case No. 1 of a consignment of 6 cases. The second case would be 2/6, the third 3/6 and so on throughout the consignment. The port of destination, Copenhagen, should, of course, figure prominently in the set of markings. Such markings would enable the ship owners and dockers, etc., to sort out the consignment and to link up the cases with the bill of lading, thus enabling the customer or his agent to effect prompt collection. The Carriage of Goods by Sea Act 1924/1971 relieves the carrier from responsibility for delay, loss or damage due to 'insufficiency or inadequacy of marks'.

No. 1/6 UP
COPENHAGEN   Figure 5.3 Shipping marks

Of course, it is not always possible to keep the markings simple. On occasion, an importer may call for a number of additional project or serial numbers. This can be of great importance, particularly when shipping components for large capital projects, as the indicator numbers may well have to serve as a form of guidance to assembly engineers. Certain centralized economies, particularly in Eastern Europe, might call for fairly detailed serial number markings which link up with the various official buying organizations.

Hazardous or dangerous cargo

Mention has already been made of the *Blue Book*, which advises that, in certain cases, the nature of the hazardous cargo should be indicated by stencilling or labelling as shown, for example, in *Figure 5.4*.

Figure 5.4 Poisonous substance label

Sea

In addition to the UK Department of Trade's *Blue Book*, reference should be made internationally to the IMDG (International Maritime Dangerous Goods) Code Book. This will enable the exporter to identify the various code classifications and to link up with the possible use of the appropriate United Nations Number which is in fact a commodity reference number.

Air

The IATA *Dangerous Goods Regulations* cover a comprehensive list of packing, marking and handling requirements and employ a 'dangerous goods' classification along the lines of the *Blue Book*/IMDG. Shippers by air, therefore, are legally responsible for complying with the appropriate requirements and the ICAO (Internation Civil Aviation Organisation) *Technical Instructions for the Safe Carriage of Dangerous Goods*.

Road/rail

The European Agreement for the International Carriage of Goods by Road (ADR), which came into force in July 1969, prescribes regulations for the packing, marking and loading of goods into road transport vehicles which themselves must conform to stipulated standards. Annex 1 (RID) to the International Carriage of Goods by Rail (CIM) covers the regulations for dangerous goods by this mode of transportation.

It will be borne in mind, therefore, that in order to comply with the above, in addition to the actual packing and marking there will be the need for certain data and classification numbers to be inserted in the appropriate documentation such as shipping notes (see Chapter 6 page 122), consignment notes and air waybills, etc.

An important point to remember is that even apparently quite innocent products can often exhibit hazardous or dangerous effects; e.g. aerosols, instruments containing mercury, certain protective greases and even magnetic items which could serious interfere with, say, an aircraft's instrumentation and controls.

A factor to bear in mind is that quite apart from any potential danger aspects, goods may have to be marked with special stowage requirements such as 'Below deck shipment' or 'Stow away from boilers'.

Overseas regulations

When shipping to any overseas territory, care should be taken to find whether or not there are any requirements pertaining to marking. Western Germany has no general regulations for marking cases but packaged foodstuffs must bear an indication of the country of origin. India requires the gross weight to be stencilled on two sides of each pack or piece. In South Africa, the SA Railways and Harbours Administration accepts goods only if name and address of consignee, destination and port of entry appear on packing cases. Cases weighing over 3000 lb must have the actual weight clearly indicated as part of the shipping mark.

Marks giving handling guidance

Where fragile goods are being transported, it is sound practice to indicate this by marking the cases 'Fragile', or for bags of raw material to bear the notice 'Use no Hooks', or where appropriate for other materials, 'Keep Dry'. It is important to bear in mind that the goods may be handled at a port where literacy might be of a low level, and therefore, symbols such as a broken wine glass or an umbrella give the necessary clues as to the nature of the contents. In fact, since symbols overcome language barriers as well they are replacing a number of the older types of wording. See Figure 5.5.

Figure 5.5 'Fragile' marking

When using second-hand containers, care must be taken to remove or obliterate old markings and stencils. Waterproof paint or ink should be employed wherever possible, and the actual positioning of the marks on the cases should also be borne in mind to ensure that they are visible when the cases are stacked.

The general principles set out above are amplified in greater detail in the British Standard Packaging Code (BS 1133) prepared by the British Standards Institution. The code was drawn up with the co-operation of various Ministries and official bodies and covers the everyday practice of export packing and marking.

Packing can also be of considerable importance since in some instances duty might be assessed on the basis of the weight of the cases themselves. This type of duty is known as a 'specific duty' and would depend very much on the nature of the commodity, being encountered more often in the case of certain bulky raw materials. Naturally, this is a vital marketing aspect because, if the duty is assessed on *gross weight*, then it is of the utmost importance to ensure that as light a form of packing as practical is employed. Remember that:

Gross   = weight of product + weight of packing cases, etc.
Nett   = weight of product without packing
Tare   = weight of packing itself
Nett, nett = weight of product without either internal wrapping
             or outer transit packing.

It will also be important to ensure that the packing cases or containers are marked very clearly with the various weights and, of course, the metric system should be employed wherever applicable, certainly throughout Europe.

Free ports and Customs zones

A vital factor gaining importance in the physical distribution process has been the evolution of certain geographical zones free of normal Customs and duties procedures. These can greatly facilitate the shipping, transportation and handling of goods in international trade. Such international free trade zones as for example Margarita Island off Venezuela and Mersin in Turkey play a part, particularly in entrepôt trade.

In the UK, for example, six free zones or ports were opened in the last quarter of 1984 at Belfast, Birmingham, Cardiff, Liverpool, Prestwick and Southampton. After a pilot and guidance period has passed other areas may be authorized.

A free port is an area into which goods may move without paying duty to Customs or similar import charges, including value added tax, charged at importation in the normal way of goods entry. There are no special reliefs in the zones or ports such as company taxes, Excise duties, and local rates. Users are subject to normal domestic laws within the zones or ports, for employment, health and safety and the environment on the same basis as outside the areas. Before listing eligible activity and benefits, it should be noted that Customs and Excise will not permit retail trade to be carried on, other than catering for staff canteens, or employee facilities.

Free-port eligibility: activities permitted
Loading, unloading and transhipment.
Storage, including stockholding pending quota availability.
Sampling, packing, labelling, and other minor handling for preparation of goods for marketing.
Processing of most third world country goods for export outside the European Community, subject to the 'protective test' applied by EEC legislation.
Destruction of, say, unsaleable or surplus goods.

Free-port benefits
Simplified Customs procedures.
Cash-flow advantages resulting from exemption of duties unless and until goods are released into free circulation.

Secure environment provided by ring fence enclosing area.
Economy of scale from physical concentration of facilities.
Better potential for marketing/sales presentation.
More flexible decision making on quota goods final destinations.

Before considering an application to use a free zone or port it is useful to sum up what is involved. In general, Customs duty and agricultural levies are due only when goods are consumed either within the zone or port, or when they cross the boundary into United Kingdom markets or those of member states of the EEC. Traders VAT registered may import goods into a freeport without accounting for tax on them. Immediately those goods leave the free zone or port for use in the United Kingdom VAT is chargeable. Normal VAT rules still apply to goods and services supplied to or within the zone. Relief from Excise duty will be limited to bonded warehouse arrangements under existing legislation.

The first step towards using a free zone is an application to Customs and Excise responsible for the particular free port, who will grant a letter of authorization. A copy of this authority will be passed to the zone operator, who maintains security by controlling entry and perimeter patrolling. The operator must provide certain import statistics to Customs on goods moving into his zone, which he has obtained from you.

Operators are:

Belfast	Northern Ireland Airports Ltd., Belfast Airport
Birmingham	West Midlands Freeport Ltd., County Hall, Birmingham
Cardiff	Pearce (Wales) Building Contractors, Cardiff
Liverpool	The Mersey Docks and Harbour Co. Pier Head
Prestwick	Freeport Scotland Ltd., Prestwick
Southampton	Southampton Freeport Ltd., Holborn, London

The development of free ports coupled with the growth of local export control facilities (LEC), as outlined in Chapter 4, will play an ever-increasing part in streamlining the flow of international goods and transportation and make a valuable contribution to the total distribution concept. It is very important to observe the development of such professional institutions as the Institute of Physical Distribution and the resultant improvement of professional skills in this particular sphere of activity which is so obviously vital, particularly when applied to international trade.

6 Transport documentation and procedures

In no section of documentation and procedure has there been such widespread growth and modification as in that devoted to international transportation. There is now a very wide spectrum of different types of document that will play their part in monitoring the carriage of goods overseas, facilitate the obtaining of these goods by the importer, and relate various conditions of carriage between shipper, carrier and possibly forwarding agent.

Equally, this category of documentation will naturally play a large part in determining how the physical possession and title of ownership and property will pass from seller to buyer in the international scene. Consequently, the nature of the transport document and its deployment will often have to be related to the terms of payment involved in the export order.

Shipment and bill of lading practice

By far the largest volume of international trade is still carried by sea. Therefore, much of that trade, its commercial, legal and financial systems, revolves around ships and shipping practice.

When considering the shipment of his goods, the exporter will take into account a number of factors. The first point will be whether use is to be made of a shipping and forwarding agent. When making this decision, a company will have to examine its own organization and personnel to see whether it possesses the expertise to carry out the many complex procedures that will be required. The total number of individual consignment shipments over a period of time will also influence the decision. A company with a considerable overseas business, involving a large number of shipments, may often find it preferable to develop its own shipping department, thus enabling it to have more direct control and making it possible to integrate the shipping function more closely with its internal production and despatch schedules. The experienced shipping staff employed by the company will also be charged with the task of studying the freight market and ensuring that wherever possible competitive freight rates and conditions are obtained. Different organizational patterns that may evolve in various companies have already been discussed in a previous chapter.

Shipping and forwarding agents

The services provided by a forwarding agent extend beyond the shipping function. Normally, most agents in the UK work within the framework of the standard trading conditions which are sponsored by the Institute of Freight Forwarders Ltd., the professional organization devoted to this sphere of activity. Some of the points covered by these trading conditions refer to the clarification that such agents are not common carriers, that subject to specific instruction they are free to select routes, entitled to retain all commissions, brokerages, etc., that they would be customarily entitled to receive; also, that all goods and documents held would be subject to a particular and general lien for any unpaid charges, for freight handling, etc. Furthermore, no responsibility is accepted for any lack of accuracy in description of goods, or any fines, duties and taxes that may be levied by any authorities. Insurance cover will not be effected unless express instructions to do so are given. Agreement between the agent involved and his customer are governed by English law and come within the exclusive jurisdiction of the English courts. These conditions should always be carefully studied as they will be of great assistance to an exporter in helping him frame his instructions clearly and concisely when he instructs a shipping and forwarding agent to proceed with a shipment on his behalf. When agents book freight space on behalf of a customer, they are, according to the custom of the London freight market (which has its headquarters at the Baltic Exchange), liable for dead freight should by any chance their customer fail to produce the goods and the ship consequently has to sail with unfilled holds. The agent would normally look for indemnification by his customer.

At the international level there is a growing degree of international harmonization of practice and indeed of layout of certain documents such as bills of lading monitored by an international association known as Fédération Internationale des Associations de Transitaires et Assiniles (FITA). This is in fact a body of international freight forwarders.

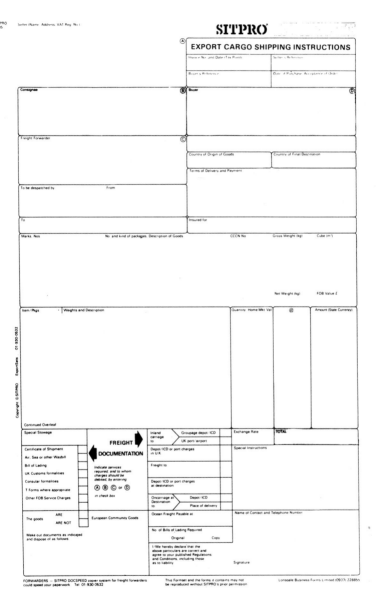

Figure 6.1 Typical export cargo shipping instruction form

To many companies, particularly the small organizations or those new to exporting, shipping and forwarding agents will be of tremendous value. They are experts in their field with an up-to-date and specialized knowledge of all the various methods of transport and relative freight and carriage rates. Their business keeps them in close touch with the constantly-changing conditions at ports and the requirements of Customs authorities. A not insignificant service also offered is the consolidation or groupage of a number of cargoes from different exporters into one consignment, which often makes possible economies of scale in the shape of preferential freight rates or at least the avoidance of minimum freight charges which might otherwise have been encountered on small shipments. Many such agents also operate road transport and can often include in their services the collection of the goods from the exporter's warehouse. Apart from charging their customer any direct costs encountered, such as transport, bills of lading, Customs entry, etc., they will usually levy a service fee based on a percentage of the freight charge.

Most forwarding agents supply a printed form which lays out all the various permutations of instructions that the exporter might wish to give. *Figure 6.1* shows a typical specimen, and it is interesting to note the categories of service that are available, ranging from collection from the exporter and the arranging of insurance right through to customer, i.e. franco domicile. As will be seen from the above-mentioned standard trading conditions, it is essential that the instructions form be completed correctly. This underlines the fact that although an agent may be employed, the exporter must still understand enough of the procedure and requirements involved to word his instructions in a clear and unambiguous manner providing all the relevant information.

Sea freight procedure

Whether the exporter is arranging his shipment directly with shipowners or utilizing the service of an agent, the following procedures will be encountered:

(1) The selection of a vessel and shipping line for the required port of destination.
(2) The procuring of space on board a specific vessel.
(3) The consideration and calculation of the particular freight rates involved.
(4) Payment of freight.

(5) Preparation of the bills of lading.
(6) Despatch of the consignment to the docks.
(7) Utilization of appropriate standard shipping note form.

Shipping space may be booked with the shipping line direct, although it is more often the case that the loading brokers are used as an intermediate link. Basically, the broker in this case advertises dates of sailings, sends out notification or sailing cards, arranges the payment of freight and issues bills of lading. Thus, in short, he sells freight space and carries out the functions of securing enough cargo to fill a ship. The broker's commission will be received from the ship-owner on whose behalf he has been operating.

Examples of publications consulted for sailing details are *Lloyd's Loading List* and the *Handy Shipping Guide*. Both of these publications are issued weekly and enable exporters first of all to find the required port of destination; listed against the port will be found the primary data regarding shipping availability.

A specimen entry is as follows:

BANGKOK, Thailand 13 45N 100E

Vessel	Flag	Gross tons	Loading at	Dock
BENLARIG (m)	BR	8719	London 7/11 Shed	Royal Albert

Receiving	Sailing	Loading Brokers
January 23/31st	February 2nd	Killick Martin & Co Ltd

Booking shipping space

With regard to sailing cards, these will provide more detailed information and an example of a typical card is shown in *Figure 6.2*. It will be necessary to check if there are any restrictions on the despatch of the cargo to the appropriate loading point. Very often it is sufficient to arrange space bookings in an informal manner. In some cases, particularly with high-frequency sailings to the Continent, an exporter will send his consignment to a specific shed and then arrange to notify the ship-owner, taking steps to prepare the appropriate bills of lading. Nevertheless, there may well be cases where prior booking or registration are required.

Sometimes, particularly when ports are congested and shipping lines are finding it difficult to clear cargo, it will be necessary for an intending shipper to provide the ship-owner with a cargo registration form giving full particulars of the consignment. This form generally comprises at least two parts, one of which will

K.S. LINE
KOREA SHIPPING CORPORATION
Regular Container Service to the Far East from UK–Eire–Europe
(A Member of the Far Eastern Freight Conference and ACE Group)

VESSEL	Voy.	FELIXSTOWE				INLAND ICD's		ARRIVAL DATES						
		E.T.A.	E.T.S.	Closing		Closing		Port Kelang	Singapore	Hong Kong	Kaohsiung	Busan	Osaka	Tokyo
				LCL	FCL	LCL	FCL							
KOREAN JACEJIN	28E	11/4	12/4	9/4	10/4	3/4	9/4	9/5	7/5	11/5	12/5	19/5	17/5	16/5
TRANSWORLD BRIDGE	24E	18/4	19/4	16/4	17/4	12/4	16/4	16/5	14/5	18/5	19/5	22/5	24/5	27/5
CHINA CONTAINER	29E	25/4	26/4	23/4	24/4	19/4	23/4	23/5	21/5	25/5	26/5	29/5	31/5	3/6

CARGO ACCEPTED FOR KEELUNG (VIA KAOHSIUNG), NAGOYA (VIA OSAKA) AND YOKOHAMA (VIA TOKYO)

KOREA SHIPPING (UK) LTD UK GENERAL AGENTS
Bookings will be taken at the following offices:

LONDON
Korea Shipping (UK) Ltd
3rd Floor, Alhambra House
27/31 Charing Cross Road
London WC2N 0AU
Telephone: 01-839 4731
Telex: 883189

FELIXSTOWE
Korea Shipping (UK) Ltd
Telephone: 0394 279201
Telex: 98436

MANCHESTER
Korea Shipping (UK) Ltd
Telephone: 061-747 8134
Telex: 668646

LIVERPOOL
Liner Shipping Agencies Ltd
Telephone: 051-227 4333
Telex: 628177

BIRMINGHAM
Liner Shipping Agencies Ltd
Tel: 021-632 5022
Telex: 337871

BRISTOL (Avonmouth)
Liner Shipping Agencies Ltd
Telephone: 0272 822712
Telex: 449419

GLASGOW
Liner Shipping Agencies Ltd
Telephone: 041-221 3775
Telex: 778992

LEEDS
G. A. Woodcock Freight Ltd
Telephone: 0532-711055

SHEFFIELD
G. A. Woodcock Freight Ltd
Telephone: 0742-449944
Telex: 54375

LCL closing on dates shown above at 10.00 hours inland and 12.00 hours Felixstowe

Receiving FCL/LCL cargo at

		Vehicle Appointments
FELIXSTOWE	East Anglia Freight Terminal	0394-278131
LONDON	Containerbases Ltd	01 595 1121
MANCHESTER	Containerbases Ltd	061 747 6330
LIVERPOOL	Containerbase (Liverpool) Ltd	051 521 5288
LEEDS	Containerbases Ltd	0532 713681 Ext 233
BIRMINGHAM	Containerbases Ltd	021 356 0121
BRISTOL	Marexspeed Ltd. ICD Bristol	0272 293452
GLASGOW (Coatbridge)	Containerbases Ltd	0236 24331

Figure 6.2 Example of a sailing card

eventually be returned to the exporter instructing him as to when he should send the cargo forward. It is known as a 'calling-forward notice'.

Equally, if a cargo is a particularly heavy one or includes unusually-shaped items, such as extra long lengths, special days are set aside when tackle and equipment are made available to handle them; similarly for consignments such as explosives, corrosive materials or goods having low flash points, etc. Great care must be exercised in these circumstances; considerable inconvenience and expense might be incurred if a shipper ignored any of these prior requirements.

Further precautions might have to be taken if the goods in question are of hazardous nature. As we have already seen in the previous chapter on physical distribution, there is considerable legislation relating to dangerous types of goods and special procedures and documentation are required. It will be seen later in this chapter that a special type of shipping note may be encountered. Cargo delivered without the correct description, or without compliance with the rules could result in heavy expenses and costs should any damage be done to property or other cargo due to the fact that the consignment arrives at a time other than that set aside for the reception of hazardous goods.

Ship categories

The prospective shipper will encounter different categories of vessels; for example the fast mail boat where freight rates are high but, of course, advantages of speed are obtained. Tramp steamers do not follow fixed routes or adhere to regular sailing timetables, but often ply according to the supply and demand for cargo space and take advantage of seasonal variations. The liner, on the other hand, sails regularly on advertised and specific routes and maintains a predictable service with fairly steady freight rates.

Attention will also have to paid to the fittings and services offered within a particular type of vessel. Ships serving tropical climatic areas are invariably equipped with refrigerating machinery. From the point of view of product, special facilities will often be available to cater for the shipment of fruit, livestock or chilled meat, etc. One of the most obvious of advanced types of specialization is the oil tanker. Now, in addition, there is a rapid expansion in the construction of ships specially designed to carry containers and pallets. Indeed, today there is a very important differentiation between what are known as conventional 'break bulk' services and the employment of various forms of 'unit loads'. Examples of conventional shipments might be

200 drums of Oxitol Acetate
7 Pieces Wooden cases Roughing Rolls.

Forms of unitization might be:

Pre-slung cargo loads
Pallets
A TIR trailer roll-on roll-off (RO/RO)
A standard 20 ft/40 ft container
Lighter Aboard SHip – (LASH)

As an appropriate guide a 20-ft container can cope with around 800 cu ft ($23 m^3$) and a weight of approximately 19 tonnes.

During the course of examining sailing lists and studying the types of vessels, certain specialized terminology and units of measurement will be encountered. All ships are prefixed with abbreviations related to their method of propulsion, such as 'ss' for steamship and 'mv' for motor vessel. An exporter may meet a type of classification clause associated with a specific ship. Such a clause will be linked with *Lloyd's Register of Shipping*, which book now covers approximately 34 000 vessels. The aim of such a record is to classify ships according to methods of construction, type of propulsion, navigational aids and the condition of general equipment. Symbols are allocated which indicate various characteristics and the term 'A1 at Lloyd's' has become a popular expression for reliability. These classification clauses can be of considerable importance when the question of marine insurance arises, since the risk cover and premium might at times be related to a particular type of classification.

The 'gross tonnage' referred to in ship terminology is obtained from a measurement, in units of 100 cubic feet, of the number of tons enclosed in the total space of the vessel. This can be distinguished from the 'net tonnage' measurement, which excludes from the gross figure such as spaces as are used for machinery, stores and crew. 'Under deck tonnage' is the measurement, in units of 100 cubic feet, of all parts under the main deck. The net tonnage is a very important figure from the ship-owner's point of view because it is the basis for the payment of a variety of shipping dues and charges.

Types of cargo

Varieties of cargo are also met, the most common being 'general cargo', meaning that the vessel carries a variety of consignments of goods or materials, possibly all packed in different types of container. 'Full cargo' relates to the shipment of a similar commodity by a single merchant, or perhaps a number of merchants. Such cargoes are often found in seasonal commodity trading such as grain, cocoa or cotton. In such cases, these commodities may be packed either in some form of container or carried partly in bulk. 'Bulk cargo' applies to shipments of commodities such as coal or iron stowed loose in the ship's hold.

Conference system

We have considered the background factors encountered when seeking shipping space. We may now identify the considerations on which the exporter bases his selection of a particular ship or shipping line.

The basic choice will be made with reference to freight rates to be charged and services offered. A starting point would be the 'conference system' under which shipping companies operating liner services group themselves into associations known as 'freight conferences'. Such associations will normally consist of a group of shipping lines, all operating within more or less the same geographical area. An example would be the United States Atlantic and Gulf Haiti Conference which covers an area between the United States Atlantic and Gulf ports and Haiti and is operated by a number of shipping companies plying their vessels within this range of ports.

Such conferences will maintain regular services, and fix freight rates and general conditions pertaining to the classification and carrying of cargo. The aim of the system is to achieve stability, assisting both the shipper, by providing him with a reasonably predictable system of freight rates and sailing schedules, and the ship-owner, by giving him an assurance that there will be a steady flow of cargo available to fill the holds of his vessels between the various ports.

From the exporter's point of view the most important aspect of this system is the offer by the ship-owners of a rebate or some preferential freight rate in exchange for an assurance that the exporter will use only conference line ships. It is usual to identify two basic types of system, namely the 'contract system' and the 'deferred rebate system'. Under the former, the exporter will sign a formal agreement in advance, for a given period of time during which he will undertake to ship all his consignments by conference lines' vessels. In return, there will be granted either an immediate cash discount, which is deducted from the freight account, or the exporter will be given a lower freight rate than that which would be charged to an exporter who was not a signatory to the agreement. The form of agreement may vary somewhat depending on the conference, but generally speaking most agreements will contain a clause which obliges a shipper to pay as liquidated damages a sum equal to the rebate should he not comply with the agreement by not confining the shipments to conference vessels. As a general rule discounts given under this system will be in the region of 9½ per cent.

Under the deferred system, no such formal advance agreement is undertaken. Instead, a shipper who has confined his shipments to conference vessels for a stated period of time, completes and lodges a claim at the end of the period, usually some three or six months. The benefit is generally about 10 per cent of the net freight paid and is normally payable at the end of a further time period. Naturally there is something of a compromise between an immediate saving of money to an exporter under the contract system on the one hand, and the fact that, under the deferred system, a certain amount of the exporter's capital is tied up. This has to be related to the varying degree of flexibility of choice of ships that exists in the relation to the two systems.

The particular tariff conditions issued by conference associations must be carefully studied by the shipper as they lay down precise details of freight charges and classification of goods, etc., together with packing requirements and regulations for special cargo. An example is given below of an extract from such tariff conditions.

'Where shippers are signatories to the UK Memorandum of Agreement or the XYZ Conference Outward General Cargo Agreement, rates of freight are net without rebate. For shipments made under rebate terms, 10 per cent is added to the freight, with the exception of livestock. With these exceptions a deferred rebate equivalent to the 10 per cent added to the net freight is returned on all shipments made under the terms of the Conference Rebate Declaration. Claims for rebates are made to the lines in two six-monthly periods from 1 January to 30 June and 1 July to 31 December each year, and rebates are payable six months after the end of the rebate period in which a shipment was made. Claims should be made to each line separately and appropriate per cent in full will be paid as interest on the amount of the rebate due.'

Note that with regard to this type of condition there is a differentiation between general and other types of cargo, in this instance livestock. It will be seen that there is also provision in this particular example for an interest payment on the deferred rebate that is eventually given. Also, in this case, both the contract and deferred systems are offered.

Conference terms

The exporter will now have made his fundamental decision as to the employment or otherwise of conference lines. From this point onwards he will be checking with the appropriate shipping companies the actual freight rates offered for his particular export consignment. He may also at this stage be comparing the advantages and disadvantages of possible charter party arrangements. For large and bulky consignments, charter party rates could in many cases offer considerable advantages to the shipper and therefore comparison between charter and tariff rates would be a worthwhile task. There is also much more scope for shopping around as, depending on the season and demand for shipping space, bargain freight costs are often possible. Chartered rates tend to show greater elasticity and can fluctuate from high rates when shipping tonnage is scarce to lower rates during idle tonnage periods.

Charter party agreements

As will be seen, the average exporter will be concerned mainly with normal tariff shipping companies, shipping his goods under a bill of lading which is largely governed by statutory law, binding the shipper and ship-owner together in the contract of affreightment. Charter party agreements are more often governed by the rules of Common Law. We can generally distinguish three main classes of chartering agreement:

(1) *Voyage* An agreement for the carriage of goods from one specific port to another, the ship-owner receiving freight for cargo carried. The freight rate will be a part of the agreement in the terms of charter.

(2) *Time* A contract whereby the vessel is actually hired for an agreed period of time and during this period the charterer usually has a considerable degree of freedom as to how the vessel is employed.

(3) *Demise* In this case the ownership to all intents and purposes changes hands for the period of the contract.

Charter parties can be complicated but generally speaking the core of the agreement, and one which usually has to be defined very accurately when fixing a charter, revolves around the following points:

(a) The ship-owner making the vessel available at the correct place at the agreed time and the vessel being in a seaworthy condition.

(b) Correct agreement on the part of the charterer to provide the specific amount of cargo and the calculation of the appropriate freight rate.

(c) Careful definition of time allowed for loading and unloading, these periods being known as 'lay days'. Also, an agreement for the payment of demurrage on days in excess of the lay days.

(d) Whether the agreement covers a specific commodity and excludes all else or whether there is a more comprehensive range of cargo that can be carried.

The charter can be used in the sense of simple hiring a portion of the vessel, in which case an undertaking is usually made by the shipper to provide a certain quantity of cargo. This might bring into effect the concept of dead-freight, being the difference between the actual freight for the cargo shipped and the total freight originally agreed upon.

There are now certain complications in international shipping which may play a part in limiting the actual choice of vessel selection by an exporter. In the first place of course there are the terms of the contract. Strictly speaking as we have seen, in the case of an FOB contract the choice of selection and port of shipment would really be that of the overseas buyer.

Two other factors may have to be considered: first, that a recent GATT agreement laying down what is known as the '80/20 rule' will place limitations upon the amount of shipping space that can be operated by a shipping company between countries outside the nationality of that company. This could have the effect of giving national shipping lines a greater share of the shipping capacity to and from their own country.

Secondly, the exporter needs to be aware when considering selection of ships, that some markets lay down precise regulations to the effect that the importers of that country have to specify and ensure that their own flag vessels are utilized. In cases where the appropriate flag services are not available certificates of exemption can be issued allowing the exporter to make his own selection. These latter types of requirement change a good deal from time to time and reference should always be made to the appropriate information sources. Croner's reference books and *Lloyd's loading lists* and *Supplements* are of particular importance in this connection.

Freight rates

A proportion of exporters in their everyday practice will be concerned with shipments and freight under the normal bill of lading. We will therefore now consider the question of types of freight rate and the methods of calculation which will be of interest to the shipper when he is contacting companies to arrange the shipment of his consignment.

Three basic freight rates will be encountered, namely:

(1) Weight
(2) Measurement
(3) Ad valorem

Freight based on weight used to be calculated in the UK on the basis of the long ton, this being equal to 2240 lb or 20 cwt. A 'measurement ton' was normally taken as 40 ft^3. Nowadays, of course, most exporters work to the metric system and therefore will be thinking in terms of cubic metres and metric tonnes. The relation between Imperial and metric is as follows:

1 cubic metre = 35.32 cubic feet
1 tonne   = 19.6875 cwt

In practice, most shipping companies calculate freight rates on a weight or measurement basis, e.g. $87.00 per tonne w/m (weight/measurement) ship's option. This usually means that the ship-owner has the option of charging the freight either on the overall measurement of the cargo or on the overall weight, whichever is the *higher*. In practice, by far the larger proportion of freight rates are based upon volume for most types of general cargoes. It should be borne in mind that in many cases the actual freight rate will depend upon and vary with the *type* of commodity. Therefore, shipping freight rates will at times be based upon certain tariff classifications. Freight All Kinds rates (FAK) would be rates irrespective of nature of commodity.

Freight calculations

Specimen freights   sea   *not* container traffic
Automotive parts in cases   UK/Indonesia

Hull/Djakarta-freight rates are for 1000 kilograms or 1 m^3

Measurement

up to 2 × weight = Netherlands guilders, NF, 426 w/m
over 2 × weight =   ”   ”   381 w/m

Less 9½% immediate rebate (for conference signatory) OR
      10% deferred rebate
Bunker surcharge factor = 10.2% (*IGNORE* rebates)

Two consignments moving, the *first* weight gross 4000 kilos
                                    mt   3.75 m^3

		NF	
Freight is 4 × NF 426 =		1704.00
Bunker surcharge		173.81
		———
	NF	1877.81
Converted @ NF 4.70 = £1.00	£	399.53
Less 9½% immediate rebate		34.44
(NF 1704 - 9½%)		———
	£	365.09

the *second* weight gross 4000 kilos
mt   9.25 m³

Freight is 9.25 × NF 381 =	3524.25
Bunker surcharge	359.47
NF	3883.72
Converted	£ 826.32
Less 9½% immediate rebate	71.23
	£ 755.09

Sea freights – containers – (no conference rebates in these trades)

Foodstuffs in cans in cartons   London/Liverpool –
San Francisco

Less than container load = US $ 232 w/m   freight rates
Full container load   216 w/m

Plus 18% currency adjustment factor
Fuel surcharge US $ 12 m or 18.50 wt

Full container consignment shipped, (25 m³ contents)

US $ 216 × 25 m³ =	5400.00
Caf 18%	972.00
Fuel 25 m³ × 12	300.00
US $	6672.00

Foodstuffs in cans in cartons   Tilbury/Sydney
Full container load = £2177.00 minimum 19 m³ OR
£3942.00 30 m³

Currency adjustment factor + bunker surcharge = 36.43%

This last is an alternative freighting method whereby a total cost is charged, either £2177 or £3942, depending upon the utilization of the container – *20 ft.*

Nowadays, the exporter must be very careful when obtaining freight rates to make sure that he has allowed for any freight surcharges that may be in operation. These surcharges are to meet unexpected variable costs and expenses that shipping companies may encounter due to circumstances beyond their control. For example, it was necessary some years ago to levy special surcharges to meet the increased operating costs owing to the closure of the Suez Canal. Currently, the serious delays in discharging or loading cargo in certain ports, particularly those in the Middle East, have led to the levying of congestion surcharges. These charges should be carefully budgeted for because they can repesent very high percentage additions on top of the basic freight rate.

Similarly, movements of exchange rates, particularly in the case where, for example, sterling was 'floating down' quite seriously, will sometimes lead to the inclusion of currency surcharges. Many shipping companies will base their freight rate quotations against a particular currency unit, say the American dollar, and apply this as a ratio when charging freight to shippers in other currency.

The term 'primage' is sometimes seen on freight accounts, generally being in the neighbourhood of 10 per cent. Originally this used to be a separate item added to cover special attention paid to the cargo by the master and was a common surcharge as far back as the eighteenth century. Nowadays, where met, this is usually the sum that is deducted for conference rebate, as mentioned earlier in this chapter.

Measurement of cargoes

It will be clear from our consideration of freight rates that a very important part of the shipping manager's responsibilities is that of packing and bundling his consignments in order to achieve an optimum balance of cubic capacity against weight. Also he will, of course, be responsible for giving to the ship-owner or loading broker the specification of his cargo which will include weights and measurements ultimately to be used for the purpose of freight calculation. Care should be taken to observe the measurement requirements which are laid down by ship-owners. Usually they provide guidance as to how capacity or weight should be calculated with particular reference to rounding up of small dimensions. There are generally accepted methods in shipping circles as shown by 'case cube measurement' by Goodfellow. For example, the rules relating to half inch are: 'Where the dimensions of a package contain fractions of an inch, such fractions are to be rounded off before cubing as follows. Fractions of less than half inch to be disregarded. Fractions of half inch and over to be reckoned as one inch. Where three half inches occur together, the first and third are each to be taken as one inch and the second disregarded. Where two half inches occur together, the half inch in the lesser of the two dimensions to be taken as one inch and the other half inch to be disregarded.'

For continental ports it is, of course, necessary to employ the metric system and this system is in fact now pretty universal. Most UK exporters nowadays will invariably ensure that a metric equivalent is shown on bills of lading. A typical 'rounding off' stipulation would be as follows. 'Where parts of a centimetre occur, such as below 0.5 cm, these are to be ignored. Those parts over 0.5 cm and over are to be rounded off to the centimetre above.'

Shippers should also check to see if any special allowances in freight rates are available from the ship-owner for the use of approved pallets or containers. It should also be borne in mind that often different freight rates will be quoted for various categories of cargo, e.g. machinery, bulk grain or bulk chemicals etc.; this will have bearing upon freight tariff classifications as mentioned earlier.

When it comes to the actual payment of freight by the exporter, there may be several alternative methods operating in practice. Strictly speaking, from a legal standpoint, freight is not really earned by the shipowner until the goods have arrived at the port of destination and he is ready to deliver them to the consignee. However, this rule is invariably qualified by the terms of the contract of affreightment set out in the various clauses on the bill of lading.

Payment of freight

It is usual for most shipping lines to require payment of freight by the shipper before the bills of lading are made available. The exporter, therefore, should be prepared to receive the freight account from the shipping company first; against this he will send a cheque and then take delivery of the bills of lading. Much depends upon the size and continuity of the exporter's business and quite often the freight account will be sent to the shipper accompanied by the bills of lading with a note indicating that the freight must be paid, say, within fourteen days.

Sometimes it is considered worthwhile for a shipper to provide a bond to the shipping line as surety in order to save time and trouble in paying each freight account separately. When employing a shipping and forwarding agent, it is usual for the agent to take care of the freight payment and send the bills of lading to the shipper, accompanied by the freight account, plus the agent's own charges.

Many export contracts require that the cargo should be shipped on a 'freight forward' basis and therefore freight becomes payable at destination by the consignee. In such cases the bills are often claused:

'Freight payable at destination, ship and/or cargo lost or not lost'.

Equally, it is common to find that some form of surcharge is made for collection of freight abroad. A typical example of such a charge would be as follows:

Freight 4 m^3 @ £27.00 per m^3	£108.00
Additional for collection abroad @ 2½%	2.70
Disbursements 50p + 5%	0.53
Total freight charge	£111.23

The normal type of freight forward plussage is 2½ per cent.

Whether the exporter or his consignee actually holds the bill of lading, the shipowner will always possess a lien on the cargo for any unpaid freight, etc. charges. Normally, to satisfy the lien on general goods they must be held for 90 days before being disposed of. Perishable goods obviously come in a different category as they may often have to be sold almost immediately.

The proceeds of such a sale will usually be disposed of as follows:

(a) Settlement of freight.
(b) Payment of any customs duties.
(c) Payment of warehousing charges.
(d) Settlement of any landing costs or dock dues.
(e) Any expenses connected with the sale.

It is possible that bills of lading may contain clauses which permit the lien to be of a 'general' nature. This would mean that the carrier could exercise the lien on goods belonging to the trader other than those which actually incurred the charges.

Back freight: a charge for the return of a cargo which has not been accepted at the port of destination. If a consignee should refuse to take delivery and freight has not been paid, we have seen that a carrier can exercise his lien; but he might return the goods to the shipper; the amount of freight covering the return voyage would be known as 'back freight'. This category might also be applicable where goods have been overstowed or carried beyond the destination because of incorrect marking by the shipper.

Dead freight: payment for space booked but not used.

Lump sum freight: the agreed amount of freight charges for the shipment of goods which are not based upon quantity. The freight is payable irrespective of the amount of cargo delivered. The shipowner can claim freight from the shipper of the goods, the consignee or endorsee of the bill of lading, a seller who stops the goods in transit or, of course, the charterer in the case of charter party agreement.

Minimum freight: the charging of a minimum sum of freight irrespective of the actual weight or dimensions of the consignment.

Pro-rata freight: in certain circumstances this would be a proportion of the freight paid in relation to the part of the voyage accomplished or to the part of the cargo delivered.

Groupage or consolidation rates: here the shipper may receive a beneficial freight rate on the basis of the fact that his cargo is going to be grouped with those of other exporters to make up a block of freight for which the freight forwarder can in a sense receive a quantity discount.

FCL and LCL freight rates: FCL would represent a freight rate based upon the fact that a Full Container Load of freight is being provided,as opposed to a Less than Container Load (LCL) where only a part cargo is being shipped.

Bill of lading and port procedure

So far we have considered the selection of an appropriate vessel or shipping line, the methods of procuring space and the various aspects of freight rates and calculations. The next stage will involve the exporter in the preparation of bills of lading and the actual forwarding of the consignment to the docks with a consideration of some of the documents and procedures involved in this process.

A preliminary outline of the various stages would follow the undermentioned sequence:

(1) The exporter (assuming that he is operating his own shipping department) will obtain blank bill of lading forms from the appropriate shipping company. These will have to be completed with all the information and the required number of originals and copies sent to the ship-owner or loading broker for ultimate signature.

(2) When the consignment is actually forwarded to the docks, it will be accompanied by a 'shipping note'. This will give details of the consignment and usually one copy will serve as a receipt. Nowadays most ports have fairly standard types of forms for this purpose: in the United Kingdom the standard shipping note is used and as this is based on the SITPRO layout it has an international connotation (see *Figure 6.3*).

(3) The goods arrive at the dock and are tallied by tally clerks whose task is to check and list all cargo being stowed in the vessel. They record the shipping marks, port numbers and details and condition of the packages. The specification and weights, etc. may also be checked. All these details are entered on tally cards which go to the port clerks. Here they are compared with the bills of lading, entered on the ship's manifest and form the necessary basis for the preparation of the freight account.

(4) Sometimes at this stage, a 'mate's receipt' may be obtained by the exporter. This is in a sense a preliminary form of receipt given before the bills of lading become available and which, if issued, must be returned to the shipping company by the exporter in exchange for the actual bill of lading.

(5) At this final stage, therefore, the bills of lading are signed on behalf of the master and made available to the shipper against payment of the freight account. A copy of bill, known as the 'master's copy' goes with the ship to the destination port. The exporter will then make available the bill of lading to his customer, who will present this at the destination port and receive in exchange a delivery order enabling him to obtain the goods. The mode of actually transmitting bills of lading to the importer will very largely depend upon the method of payment being used. In the chapter on payment terms it could be seen that such documents as bills of lading could be presented against letters of credit, sent through banks with bills of exchange, etc.

(6) The above sequences are essentially based upon fairly conventional types of shipment but the growth of container ports and inland clearance depots can impose a sequential difference so there has to be a degree of flexibility of interpretation.

Many of the processes outlined above would be taken care of by a shipping and forwarding agent if the exporter did not have his own shipping department but, even so, a practitioner would still

© SITPRO 1981

STANDARD SHIPPING NOTE

IMPORTANT USE THE DANGEROUS GOODS NOTE IF THE GOODS ARE CLASSIFIED AS DANGEROUS ACCORDING TO APPLICABLE REGULATIONS SEE BOX 19A

| Exporter | 1 | Veh. Bkg. Ref. | 2 | Customs Reference/Status | 3 |

Exporter's Reference | 4

Exporter ▸ Freight Forwarder / Other (Name and Address) | Port Charges Payable by * | 5 | Forwarder's Ref. | 6 | SS Co. Bkg. No. | 7

Name of Shipping Line or CTO | 8 | Port Account No.

| Freight Forwarder | 9 | For use of Receiving Authority Only |

Receiving Date(s) | Berth/Dock/Containerbase etc. | 10

The Company preparing this note declares that the goods have been accurately described, their quantities, weights and measurements are correct and at the time of despatch they were in good order and condition; that the goods are not classified as dangerous in any UK, IMCO, ADR, RID or IATA/ICAO regulation applicable to the intended modes of transport. | 10A

Vessel | Port of Loading | 11 | TO THE RECEIVING AUTHORITY — Please receive for shipment the goods described below subject to your published regulations and conditions (including those as to liability).

Port of Discharge | Destination | 12 | Name of Receiving Authority | 13

Marks and Numbers; Number and Kind of Packages; Description of goods | 14 | Receiving Authority Use | Gross Wt (kg) of goods | 15 | Cube (m³) of goods | 16

SYSTEMFORMS LTD. 01 505 6125

SPECIAL STOWAGE * | 17 | For use of shipping company only | Total Gross weight of goods | Total Cube of goods

PREFIX and Container/Trailer Number(s) | 18 | Seal Number(s) | 18A | Container/Trailer Size(s) and Type(s) | 18B | Tare wt (kg) as marked on container | 18C | Weight of container and goods (kg) | 18D

Received the above number of packages/containers/trailers in apparent good order and condition unless stated hereon. RECEIVING AUTHORITY REMARKS | Name of Company preparing this Note | 19

Haulier's Name

Vehicle Reg. No.

Date

DRIVER'S SIGNATURE | SIGNATURE AND DATE | (Indicate name and telephone number of contact)

630 | *Mark X as appropriate. If box 5 is not completed the company preparing this note may be held liable for payment of port charges | PRINTED BY SYSTEMFORMS LTD. 01-505 6125

Figure 6.3 Standard shipping note

want to understand the various stages of operation so that he could provide his agent with accurate instructions. This whole process is a vital one and it is unfortunate that delays in obtaining bills of lading are all too frequent. Accurate completions of bills, careful recording of measurements, marks and specifications and clear instructions will all help to improve the position. This will be achieved by a more professional approach by exporters and co-operation and understanding between shipping and forwarding agents, shipping lines and banks.

Characteristics of the bill of lading

A bill of lading can be considered under three headings, namely:

(1) *Evidence of contract of affreightment.*
(2) *A receipt for goods shipped,* and providing certain details as to the quantity and condition when placed on board.
(3) *A document of title,* without which delivery of the goods cannot normally be obtained.

All three features are important to the exporter but from a practical point of view (3), which relates to the way the bill of lading can convey ownership of the goods, is probably the most important as this will have a crucial bearing on the way the documentary process is linked with methods of payment.

The background of the contract of affreightment in the United Kingdom is the Carriage of Goods by Sea Act 1971. This Act and further developments stemmed internationally from the Hague Rules which, at the International Convention in 1924, were recommended for submission to the Governments of the major maritime nations for adoption and enactment into the law of their respective countries. Amendments and developments have led to the Hague–Visby Rules which, however, have been ratified by only a limited nuber of states. It is important to remember, therefore, that speaking internationally there may be encountered bills of lading with variations in the underlying contractual background. On the back of a bill of lading will be found the *Clause Paramount* which will indicate if the particular Act is applicable. Also on the back will be found a number of clauses clarifying further the relationship between shipper and ship-owner. Broadly speaking, they cover such aspects as payment of freight, handling, stowage and general average provisions, etc.

As our primary concern is the actual completion and use of the bill of lading, we will consider the completion of the necessary details on a specimen such as that shown in *Figure 6.4.*

Shipper		UK Customs Assigned No.	B/L No.
		Shipper's Ref.	
		F/Agent's Ref.	

شركة الملاحة العربية المتحدة (٤.ع)

UNITED ARAB SHIPPING COMPANY (S.A.G.)

Shuweikh,
P.O. Box 3636, Safat
KUWAIT

Consignee (If 'Order' state Notify Party)

Notify Party (ONLY if not stated above: otherwise leave blank)

*Applicable only when document used as a Through B/L.

*Local vessel	*From (place of acceptance or local port of loading)
Ocean vessel	Port of loading
Port of discharge	*Final destination (if on-carriage)

Marks and Nos/Container Nos.	Number and kind of packages. description of goods	Gross Weight	Measurement

ABOVE PARTICULARS DECLARED BY SHIPPER

Freight details, charges, etc.

Shipped either on board the local vessel named above or (if no local vessel be named) on board the ocean vessel at the port of loading thereof (or where this is a through transit bill of lading to which clause 3 (b) overleaf applies RECEIVED at the place of acceptance) in apparent good order and condition (unless otherwise stated herein) the goods above specified for carriage subject to the exceptions, limitations, conditions and liberties hereof to the port of discharge or final destination (as the case may be) and there to be delivered in like order and condition to the consignee or his or their assigns.

The Tariff Conditions of the relevant Conference are (except insofar as they may be inconsistent with the terms and conditions set out herein) deemed to be incorporated in this Bill of Lading. A copy of the said conditions is obtainable from the Carriers.

IN WITNESS whereof the Master or Agent of the ocean vessel has signed the number of Bills of Lading stated above, all of this tenor and date, one of which being accomplished, the others shall stand void.	Number of Pieces or Packages (in words)
Ocean Freight Payable at	Place and date of Issue
Number of Original Bs/L	Signature

For the MASTER

SEE CLAUSES OVERLEAF   Rev 10/80   Printed in England by Rockliff Brothers Ltd., 2 Rumford Street, Liverpool 2

Figure 6.4 Standard bill of lading

The factors which will determine the way the exporter completes the bill of lading will be determined by the following:

(a) Any regulations in force in country of destination,
(b) requirements of customer,
(c) method of payment, and
(d) any regulations in force in exporter's country.

First of all, when beginning the completion of the bill of lading, the number of copies will have to be decided upon. Bills are issued in 'sets', a set consisting of a given number of originals with copies. The point to remember is that each original is by itself valid until one is presented to the ship-owner for the goods. A clause on the bill of lading will clarify this point as follows:

'In witness whereof the agent on behalf of the master of the vessel in which the goods have been or are intended to be loaded and of the several carriers on the route severally and not jointly has signed the number of bills stated above, one of which being accomplished the others shall stand void. One of the bills of lading duly endorsed must be given up to exchange for the goods or delivery order'.

Therefore, when completing the bill of lading, if we insert in the appropriate space, for example: 'Number of original Bs/L = 4', then the shipping company will sign and return four. The number of unsigned copies will depend upon our own internal record system or on what our customer has requested. To avoid confusion, some shipping lines issues original bills in one colour and copies in another. Some stamp bills 'Original' and others 'Non-Negotiable Copy'. The essential difference apart from this is, of course, the fact that all originals can be given in exchange for the goods. If in a particular transaction, the exporter is making the handing over of the goods dependent upon a method of payment (a documentary bill of exchange, for example) then he must obviously ensure that all the originals go through the banking mechanism and that they alone go to the customer when payment has been received by the prescribed method. Although procedure varies somewhat between individuals, we generally find in shipping and forwarding agent circles that the terminology '3/3' would, for example, mean three original bills of lading and three copies. In banking practice however, the tendency would be to interpret this as three originals of a set of three; in other words, '2/3' would mean two originals only out of the set.

The use of the different copies of the bills mean that some can be despatched by air and some by sea in order to minimize the chance of loss. If applicable, an original can always be sent with the carrying vessel in the 'ship's bag' and made available at the port of destination. Although there is no actual limit to the number of original Bs/L the ship's will sign, it is most common to have two or three. Not more than four originals are normally required.

Extensive use can be made of courier services today and one might quote the case of United Kingdom/West African Lines UKWAL who with, say, a 10/11 day sailing period to Nigeria can have the bills of lading transmitted and in Apapa in about five days. Remember, however, all questions of the way in which bills of lading are distributed will in most cases depend upon the methods of payment being employed. The whole concept, however, must be kept firmly in mind as if the goods are arriving at overseas ports ahead of documents and the importer is kept waiting because of delays in bills of lading, then warehousing and demurrage charges will be incurred.

Negotiability of the bill of lading

Mention has already been made of the fact that the bill of lading functions as a document of title, and the manner in which it is completed will determine what is called the *degree of negotiability*. A glance at the bill will show that there are the following entries to be completed:

Shipper

Consignee

Notify party

Against 'Shipper' the exporter will normally fill in his own name. Let us assume an exporter is named K. Contracts Ltd and his customer is Weston Carbons. The bill of lading is completed as follows:

Shipper K. Contracts Ltd.

Consignee Weston Carbons

Notify party International Forwarding Agents Ltd.

In this example, the exporter has made the bill of lading out directly to his customer, Weston Carbons. The shipping company has been requested to notify the forwarding agents at the destination port, i.e. International Forwarding Agents Ltd. In this case the bill can go to the customer without any endorsement by the exporter. Weston Carbons, upon receiving the document, could either present themselves to the shipping company for delivery of the goods, or, as would be more likely, endorse it (i.e. stamp their name on the back of the bill with their signature) and pass it to their agents (International Forwarding Agents Ltd.) who would then arrange to obtain the cargo.

It will be seen that in this case the only party who can negotiate the bills of lading is Weston Carbons or the party to whom they endorse the bills. Assuming that the handing over of the bills of lading was not conditional upon some form of payment, i.e. through a bank, this method would be simple and would mean that such a bill could be sent forward direct to Weston Carbons without having to come back to the exporter for endorsement. This method is most suitable for European countries when the bill of lading can be sent to the customer in the ship's bag, or an agent sends it direct by air mail. Delays often result when it is necessary to send it back to the exporter for his signature. Speed is essential for exporting to Europe when often the vessel may arrive at the destination port in less than 36 hours.

<u>Shipper</u> K. Contracts Ltd.

<u>Consignee</u> To order

<u>Notify party</u> Weston Carbons

In this case, for the bill of lading to be made negotiable, it will have to be endorsed by K. Contracts Ltd, the exporter. This will entail stamping the name of the company on the back of the bill of lading together with an appropriate signature. Weston Carbons would be notified by the shipping company and they would make the necessary arrangements. As will be seen in a later chapter, when methods of payment are considered, this type of negotiability is suitable where the documents are being tendered against documentary bills or credits and where it is necessary for the shipping documents to be used as a form of security. This would be an example of 'to order blank endorsed'.

Another possibility is for a B/L to be made out perhaps to a third party such as a bank. This may apply where, for example, Weston Carbons have received an advance of money and the bank require to have the bills made out to its order to give it some control over the transaction. Thus:

<u>Shipper</u> K. Contracts Ltd.

<u>Consignee</u> To order of Second International Bank Inc.

Notify party Weston Carbons

Here, the bill would need to be endorsed by the bank before ownership could be transferred. As has already been mentioned, care must be taken to observe any special regulations which might have a bearing on the bill of lading. It will be seen that there are headings for 'pre-carriage' and 'final destination' and these will depend on the services offered by the particular shipping line in question. There is now a growing tendency for shipping lines to become more and more involved in arranging inland collection, shipment and delivery to final overseas destination. This is naturally very much the case when container traffic is being operated. In such instances, we meet a 'through bill of lading'. We might postulate the case of an exporter in Birmingham shipping from London to Hamburg for final delivery to a customer in Hanover. In such cases the exporter would fill in the bill as follows:

Pre-carriage by Appropriate Shipping Company

From Birmingham

Port of Loading Terminal London

Port of Discharge Terminal Hamburg

Final Destination (if on-carriage) Hanover

Care should be taken always to check whether appropriate services are offered by the shipping line; the terms of sale must also be borne in mind. If the contract was in fact CIF Hamburg, then any on-carriage arrangements should be cleared with the customer. On the other hand, if it were franco domicile Hanover, then the inland freight component part should have been included in the exporter's price.

When considering the marks and numbers entry of the B/L, accuracy is essential. As the bill of lading is the receipt for the goods, speedy identification between the document and the consignment is vital. Equally, an accurate description of the contents, and type and method of packing is required because the whole basis of the contract of affreightment will rest upon complete disclosure of the type and nature of the consignment which the ship-owner is undertaking to carry. As we have already seen, the weights and dimensions should be completed in the correct units of measurement.

We also have to distinguish those cases where there are prescribed requirements for certain data to be included on the bills of lading in addition to the normal routing information. Chile for example requires the insertion of a Deposit Receipt No. or Registration Certificate No. on bills of lading. These numbers would obviously apply to the importer's currency and import regulations and therefore the exporter would need to ensure that the information had initially been obtained from his buyer. Many countries allow bills of lading to be made out 'to order' but require that the ultimate consignee's number be always shown. Many Middle East countries require the CCCN number on the bill to ensure the application of the correct freight or duty rates. This is obviously important where goods are being shipped freight forward.

Letters of credit are usually fairly precise as to the number of bills and the information to be contained thereon and these requirements must of course be scrupulously observed. The experienced practitioner will also know from experience that certain data, although not mandatory, can often assist the importer in obtaining a smooth trouble-free Customs clearance, and details such as import licence numbers may often be included in the bill of lading data.

Types of bill of lading

It has been stressed that one of the characteristics of a bill of lading is its ability to serve as a receipt, and it is of some importance to consider what type of receipt this in fact represents. The kind of bill of lading which is normally required in commerce and, in fact, is specifically called for in most CIF contracts, is the 'shipped bill', sometimes known as 'on board bills', and usually described in letters of credit as 'shipped on board'. The appropriate clause is shown on the bill and a typical one would be:

Shipped in apparent good order and condition by the vessel first named above.

Thus, the issuing of a shipped bill is an acknowledgement by the ship-owner that the goods are in fact loaded on the vessel.

This can be contrasted with the 'received for shipment' type of bill which might be claused

Received for shipment at the place of receipt the goods mentioned above in apparent good order and condition.

In this case the ship-owner is merely confirming that the goods have been delivered into his custody and might, for example, be stored in a warehouse under his control. The 'received' bill is therefore of a lower order than the 'shipped' type. Nowadays, container lines, who undertake a considerable amount of inland collections, cannot actually issue a shipped bill at the time of collection. Therefore, the received bill is increasingly becoming acceptable. The ship-owner can always arrange later to clause a bill of lading indicating that shipment has been made. A number of shipping lines are now operating bills of lading with both 'shipped' and 'received' clauses in evidence and the appropriate deletion can be made when signature takes place.

Shipping companies always reserve the right to clause the face of a bill of lading giving rise to a 'dirty' or 'claused bill'. Again, this could prove detrimental to the exporter in the case of some contracts, especially if some stringent method of payment such as a letter of credit was involved because, in the main, a 'clean, shipped on board' bill is in most cases the type that is essential. Some typical examples of clauses would be:

Second-hand drums,
Insufficient packing,
Carried on deck without liability for loss or damage, however caused, and
One case short, but if found on board to be delivered.

Such clauses could be of importance in the event of insurance claims so it is incumbent upon the exporter to ensure that there is complete understanding between him and the ship-owner pertaining to descriptions and packing, particularly when he is perhaps employing a new type of packing material which might be perfectly sound but with which the ship-owner is unfamiliar.

As explained earlier, speed is essential in conveying the bill of lading, and therefore the ownership of the goods, to the customer; late arrival of bills is a serious inconvenience. It is often possible that the ship-owner will agree to release the goods without a bill of lading, against the issue of a guaranty for issuance of carriers certificate, and delivery of cargo without surrender of properly-endorsed negotiable bill of lading. The guaranty, countersigned by a bank and produced by either the importer or exporter, is to the effect that the bill of lading will be produced when available and that the shipping company will not be held responsible in any way for releasing the consignment without production of the original B/L.

In the case of bills being lost or destroyed, a similar procedure can be adopted, but usually when it is known that the bill has in fact been lost, the exporter can obtain a duplicate set of documents against indemnity. An undertaking will sometimes be necessary by the exporter to accept the charges for any cable or telex messages to the port of discharge.

Stale bills of lading

Sometimes, owing to delay, bills of lading which may be required for negotiation against letters of credit may not be received in time for them to reach the customer before the ship and cargo arrives at the port of discharge. The bank in question, noting the date on the bill and comparing this with the length of voyage, may fear that as the goods will arrive before the bill, some time may elapse before the consignee can clear at Customs and obtain delivery. Consequently, warehousing and dock charges may be accumulating and we have already seen that the ship-owner can exercise a lien on the goods for these expenses. Such bills are therefore described as 'stale' and can be extremely troublesome where short sea voyages are involved. Hence the indemnity procedure which is often resorted to as outlined above.

Groupage bills

Sometimes a forwarding agent will consolidate a number of consignments from different exporters on one bill of lading in order to simplify shipment, save charges and avoid minimum freight or obtain preferential rates. In such cases only one bill of lading is in existence and each individual exporter cannot, therefore, obtain a seperate bill of lading. 'Certificates of shipment' are issued, or sometimes the agent will have his own bills of lading printed which are known as 'shipping and forwarding agent's' bills or 'house' bills. It should be stressed that strictly speaking these documents are not sufficient to satisfy a CIF contract and are often expressly forbidden in letters of credit. If the exporter is in a position where he excepts to receive this lower order of document, then care must be taken to receive the approval and consent of the customer. Again, the progress in transportation methods and growing use of containers, together with increasing efficiency on the part of shipping agents consolidating consignments, are bringing about a greater degree of acceptance of shipping certificates and house bills.

Short form bills of lading

Basically, as the name implies, the short form of bill is an abbreviated type of document, smaller, and not containing the long list of detailed clauses that generally appear on bills of lading. In certain circumstances it may not, therefore, be considered a suitable form of evidence of contract of affreightment. Letters of credit and contracts of sale should always be checked carefully to see if there is any mention that short form bills will not be accepted so that the necessary type of bill of lading can be obtained from the shipping line. Based upon a United Nations Recommendations both the General Council of British Shipping (GCBS) and SITPRO have developed the use of what is known as the 'common short form bill of lading' and this has largely overcome the reluctance that has in the past been shown to the use of this type of document. Unlike the more standard 'long form' or previous 'short form' types, the common short form bill does not bear individual shipping line logos. These can be inserted by the exporter or freight forwarder and simplifies stockholding. It is now generally accepted that the bill retains the three essential characteristics of the more conventional bill of lading as mentioned on page 109.

Sea waybill

Because of the speeding up of transportation and therefore shorter voyage periods, use is now being made of this species of document *Figure 6.5 (a)*. It serves as a receipt for goods and evidence of contract of carriage but does not act as a document of title. Because of this the consignee does not usually need to possess this document in order to obtain the goods upon their arrival. The importer may well be able to be provided with a complete set of other documents such as invoices, certificates of origin, etc., thus being able to arrange clearance much sooner than if negotiable bills of lading were awaited.

It must be stressed that this whole question of transfer of title will hinge upon the attitude of the exporter towards security of payment. It will be seen in Chapter 10 that the new banking rules in ICC Brochure No. 400 have broadened their approach to the spectrum of transport documents acceptable against letters of credit. Similarly mention will also be made in this chapter of a recent Midland Bank/SITPRO Survey which examined the administration of letters of credit and dicrepancies encountered during their administration. Amongst the various reasons for rejection by banks of documents, one section devoted to bills of lading listed the undermentioned problems:

© GCBS 1979

*Applicable only when document used as a Through Sea Waybill

Particulars declared by Shipper

Shipper		**NON-NEGOTIABLE**	UK Customs Assigned No.	SWB No.
		SEA WAYBILL	Shipper's Reference	
			F/Agent's Reference	

Consignee

Name of Carrier

Notify Party and Address (leave blank if stated above)		
		The contract evidenced by this Waybill is subject to the exceptions, limitations, conditions and liberties (including those relating to pre-carriage and on-carriage) set out in the Carrier's Standard Conditions of Carriage applicable to the voyage covered by this Waybill and operative on its date of issue; if the carriage is one where had a Bill of Lading been issued the provisions of the Hague Rules contained in the International Convention for unification of certain rules relating to Bills of Lading dated Brussels 25th August, 1924, as amended by the Protocol signed at Brussels on the 23rd February, 1968 (the Hague Visby Rules) would have been compulsorily applicable under Article X, the said Standard Conditions contain or shall be deemed to contain a Clause giving effect to the Hague Visby Rules. Otherwise the said Standard Conditions contain or shall be deemed to contain a Clause giving effect to the provisions of the Hague Rules. In neither case shall the proviso to the first sentence of Article V of the Hague Rules or the Hague Visby Rules apply. The Carrier hereby agrees: (i) that to the extent of any inconsistency the said Clause shall prevail over the said Standard Conditions in respect of any period to which the Hague Rules or the Hague Visby Rules by their terms apply, and (ii) that for the purpose of the terms of this Contract of Carriage this Waybill falls within the definition of Article 1(b) of the Hague Rules and the Hague Visby Rules.
Pre-Carriage by*	Place of Receipt by Pre-Carrier*	The Shipper accepts the said Standard Conditions on his own behalf and on behalf of the Consignee and the owner of the goods and warrants that he has authority to do so. The Consignee by presenting this Waybill and/or requesting delivery of the goods further undertakes all liabilities of the Shipper
Vessel	Port of Loading	hereunder, such undertaking being additional and without prejudice to the Shipper's own liability. The benefit of the contract, evidenced by this Waybill shall thereby be transferred to the Consignee or other persons presenting this Waybill. Notwithstanding anything contained in the said Standard Conditions, the term Carrier in this Waybill
Port of Discharge	Place of Delivery by On-Carrier*	shall mean the Carrier named on the front thereof. A copy of the Carrier's said Standard Conditions applicable hereto may be inspected or will be supplied on request at the office of the Carrier or the Carrier's Principal Agents.

Marks and Nos; Container No.	Number and kind of packages; Description of Goods	Gross Weight	Measurement

Freight Details; Charges etc.	**RECEIVED FOR CARRIAGE** as above in apparent good order and condition, unless otherwise stated hereon, the goods described in the above particulars.

GCBS SWB 1979		Ocean Freight Payable at	Place and Date of Issue
			Signature for Carrier: Carrier's Principal Place of Business

711

Authorised and Licensed by the General Council of British Shipping © 1979   Printed & Produced by A. C. Shaw (Export) Sales Co., Ltd., 127 Cheapside, London EC2V 6DH

Figure 6.5(a) Non-negotiable sea waybill

Discrepancies in bills of lading	*% of total admin errors*
Absence of full set	1.3
Absence of 'on board' notation	0.7
B/ladings require endorsement	0.7
Claused/Dirty B/ladings	0.8
Goods consigned to wrong party	1.5
Port of shipment/discharges incorrect	1.0
Others	4.9
Sub-total	10.9

The above will give some idea of the importance of the exporter's awareness of the details of the various aspects of bills of lading as it can be seen that errors in this field can lead to 10.9% of all rejections of letters of credit owing to incorrect documentation.

Ship-owner's liability

The original Carriage of Goods by Sea Act 1924 basically limited the ship-owner's liability to £100.00 per package or unit. Provision could be made to increase this when arranging the contract of affreightment and of course a higher freight rate could be charged. A typical B/L clause referring to this aspect might be as follows:

> The extra freight rate payable on goods the value of which has been declared by the shipper to exceed £100.00 per package or unit, has been based and calculated upon the description and value furnished by the shipper. If such description or value has been mis-stated, the shipper, consignee, and/or owner of the goods shall if required by the carrier pay such freight as would have been charged by the carrier if the goods had been accurately described and valued, and a certificate signed by the carrier or his agents shall be conclusive evidence of the amount that would have been so charged.

The Act provided that the monetary units applying to the £100.00 figure were to be taken as gold value. This led to some confusion and in 1950 an agreement was concluded between merchants' organizations, ship-owners and underwriters who were members of the British Maritime Law Association that the liability should be limited to £200.00 sterling lawful money of the United Kingdom, assuming, of course, that no other agreements existed between ship-owner and shipper. This is sometimes known as the 'Gold Clause'.

In 1968 there took place a reform of the rules relating to bills of lading by means of the Hague-Visby Rules. The amendments to the original Hague Rules proposed by the Brussels Protocol were enacted in the United Kingdom by the Carriage of Goods by Sea Act 1971. Included in this Act was the provision for the ship-owner's liability to be increased to £401 approximately per package or unit. This figure was related to the gold franc so that in the course of time changes in various currency equivalents could be encountered.

Shipping note

The standard shipping note developed by SITPRO replaces many different kinds of existing shipping notes by a standard form, for use when delivering export cargo to the receiving Authority at any British port, containerbase or other freight terminal. Stocks are available either in gummed sets for completion by ballpoint pen or typewriter, or loose for use in spirit duplicating, 'xerographic' or offset litho machines. The forms may also be produced on to blank Baron self-copy paper by means of 'xerographic' or other plain copiers, using a film overlay – in this case, the second, third, fourth and fifth sheets of the set should be coloured or marked pink, yellow, blue and green respectively.

The distribution of the standard six-part set is normally as follows:

1 – retained by docks or terminal
1 – returned by ocean carrier as a
    'received for shipment' return
1 – HM Customs
1 – Truck driver as his receipt
1 – Ocean carrier as 'shipped on board' return
1 – retained by shipper as administrative copy

Figure 6.3 shows a standard form which should always be completed carefully. Attention is drawn to some of the box numbers as follows:

Box 2   A reminder that there may be a facility available at the port or terminal for arranging appointments for the delivery lorry.

Box 3　Very important, as here we would expect to see references to such items as the ECI number or reference to pre-entry, etc; in other words, linking the shipment with the particular customs procedures involved (see Chapter 4).

Box 7　For some destinations the process of booking shipping space may involve registration and the obtaining of a number. If this is the case it is most important that it should be quoted as goods may be shut out if arriving without details of the registration.

Box 8　A reminder of the distinction of employing a shipping line in the conventional sense of the use of a CTO (Combined Transport Operator). In the latter case the procedures and shipping documents involved will possibly cover a journey by multimodal transport units.

Box 17　Possibility of special stowage requirements on deck refrigeration, away from boilers, etc. This should to some extent be differentiated from dangerous or hazardous cargo which will need a special form of shipping note, the DGN (Dangerous Goods Note).

The note must be lodged *either* with the vehicle at the receiving point or at the receiving authority's designated office *before* arrival of the goods, according to local port practice. Only goods for shipment to one port of discharge on one sailing and sometimes relating to only one bill of lading, may be grouped on one shipping note.

Port practices

It will have been seen in the Distribution chapter that there are various patterns and structures of ports and container depots both in the UK and overseas. There will always to some extent be the possibility of variations in practice and procedures. The development of such documents as the SITPRO standard shipping note and DGN, etc., have brought about a greater degree of standardization internationally in port/shipping operations.

Containers

A brief consideration of the above will show that the mechanics of the container process will influence considerably the question of the nature of the bill of lading encountered in container shipments. Emphasis will be placed by container operators on the concept of a 'through delivered' service in order to extract the maximum benefits from container operations. Therefore, the exporter will encounter more frequently:

(a) groupage bills of lading
(b) through bills of lading, and
(c) 'received for shipment' bills of lading.

Operators often consolidate several exporters' cargoes into one container which will be shipped under a main bill of lading. The individual shippers will receive either *certificates of shipment* or *house bills of lading*. Container operators are more likely to arrange to collect shippers' cargoes in order to enable them to control the whole process. They will therefore handle the 'pre-carriage' and often final inland delivery to overseas customers. This will frequently enable the exporter to receive 'all-in' freight quotations which will be a tremendous boon to him and enable 'franco' prices to be quoted with more accuracy and precision than in previous cases when often an exporter would have to build up his costing on the basis of several prices covering inland transport, dock charges, handling, loading and unloading, ocean freight and charges involved in the overseas country. The more orthodox type of shipment would have often meant that some four or five separate organizations might have been involved in a shipment, with all the associated difficulty of obtaining from each one a particular cost quotation.

As to the bill of lading itself, the exporter will have to consider the nature of the receipt to be obtained from a container operator and the type of negotiability of the bill of lading with its resultant title of ownership and acceptability by the banking system when documentary bills or credits are involved and where the bill may perhaps, on occasions, be presented as security for an advance or for discounting of bills of exchange.

As in many cases containers will be loaded at exporter's premises or at an ICD, the operator will provide the equivalent of a 'received for shipment' bill of lading. This is understandable because, at this stage, an actual 'shipped on board' bill is just not a possibility.

When presented as security for an advance, such documents will be evaluated with due regard to all the relevant circumstances in the same way as any document presented as collateral.

The banks emphasize that the use of containers implies that some goods inevitably will be carried 'on deck' and that suitable and adequate insurance must be arranged.

The Uniform Customs and Practice for Doc Credits ICC

Brochure No. 400 has introduced fresh articles which provide much wider scope for the utilization and acceptance of these more 'anticipatory documents' as they are obviously now in very wide usage.

The question of the liability of the shipowner in terms of value per package or unit has already been discussed on page 120, and consequently the definition of such units when shipping by container can be important. If for example the liability figure of £401.00 was applied to a whole container load as a 'unit' there would be some concern both for exporters and insurance regarding the level of recourse against a shipowner.

The amendments to the Hague Rules have as their main objectives the readjustment of liability limitation in order to counteract monetary depreciation since 1924 and also the adaptation of the rules to suit the new transportation techniques such as containerization and other methods of unitization of cargo. A container clause has been developed to cover consolidated goods when containers, pallets or similar articles are used. The number of packages or units enumerated in a bill of lading as packed in the container will form the basis for calculation of liability. For example, if a bill of lading indicated 2000 cartons of whisky loading into Container No. 2356, then the carton would be the basic unit for liability. There is also provision for a weight limitation of liability to cover general merchandise which cannot be expressed clearly in units or cases.

It is felt in many quarters that the importance attributed to the level of liability on the part of the ship-owner is somewhat exaggerated as, in any case, freight rates are adjusted to cover such liabilities and that in practice there often results a certain amount of double insurance.

Container insurance

The other important aspect is, of course, the application of insurance to container consignment. Much has been written about this and there are a number of different viewpoints as to how insurance cover and the resultant policies and premiums are affected. Experiments with combined insurance certificates and bills of lading have so far not succeeded because the adoption of such cover might mean that companies with advantageous premiums owing to their sheer size and business might find themselves faced with higher insurance costs which might result from container companies issuing their own insurance cover. Nevertheless, there is very little doubt that further developments will solve this type of problem and that such combined documents will eventually be developed.

There are a number of special factors which will influence the outlook of insurance companies with regard to container risk cover. For example, it represents a 'concentration of risk' and it is possible that certain types of damage such as sea or rainwater might take place and not be detected at all throughout the voyage whereas such damage might be easily noticed in an orthodox consignment of a number of separate wooden cases. Such damage, in a container, might slowly and steadily affect the entire contents of a container. Insurance companies also point out that a container is like a miniature hold of a vessel and needs specialized personnel to handle packing, loading and stowage. This may not always be possible, for example when, as in some instances, exporters load containers themselves.

There is also the vital question of on deck stowage. It is calculated that the payload of a container ship consists of approximately 40 per cent of deck stowage. In many cases, where computerized documentation is being employed, it is not possible for the container operator to indicate on bills of lading that particular containers are either below or above deck. This might well mean that insurance premiums have to be averaged out to cover the possibility of on deck risk exposure. Close attention is being paid to these problems by the container committee of the International Union of Marine Insurance (IUMI).

The other international body deeply concerned is the Comité Maritime International (CMI) and the aim of the April 1969 Convention (known as 'the Tokyo Rules') was to lay down a framework for the provision of a suitable combined transport document giving a satisfactory document of title which will enable each combined transport operator to carry out his work efficiently and at the same time provide suitable receipts and title for the exporter.

The need for inter-modal transportation backed by a suitable CTO (Combined Transport) document has led to the formulation of a set of provisions and rules for the satisfactory operation of such a document. These rules have found expression in Brochure 298 of the International Chamber of Commerce entitled *Uniform Rules for a Combined Transport Document*. Such a document should be a great step forward for CTOs (Combined Transport Operators) who provide start-to-finish delivery services.

Air freight

We can envisage much of the mechanics of shipping as being applicable to air freight except that obviously the overall tempo is much faster. The Carriage of Goods by Air Acts, 1932, 1961 and

1962, based upon the Warsaw Convention Rules, provide the background legal framework establishing the relationship of the trader to air carrier. The Acts set out basic definitions, regulate the documents relating to air carriage, and establish the liability of the carrier.

Most exporters will employ forwarding agents and the latter's activity in the sphere of consolidating cargoes to obtain better freight rates is of great importance due to the need to minimize the comparatively high freight costs of air transport. In the field of aircraft charter there is a growing number of brokers on the Baltic Exchange who specialize in this work and they collectively form the Airbrokers' Association. Because of the speed of transportation, air forwarding agents will often offer many services including, in many cases, delivery of goods to the ultimate consignee on a COD basis.

Air freight rates

The exporter can keep in touch with the various scheduled airline flights to all parts of the world by referring to such publications as *Cargo by Air*, a supplement to *Lloyd's Loading List*. This can of course, be supplemented in greater detail by the schedules and other information issued by the airlines themselves. The various permutations of air freight rates can be a little more complex than sea freight and can be summed up briefly in the following categories:

Method of Calculation: airline rates are based on the kilo. Volume does not normally become a factor until it exceeds the $6\,m^3/K1000$ ratio (6 cubic metres to the tonne). Thus, $6000\,m^3$ can be described as a chargeable kilo or volumetric unit on which the freight rate will be based if they exceed the weight kilograms of a consignment.

This shipper of airfreight will encounter several different types of freight classification, such as:

(1) General Cargo (GC)
(2) Specific Commodity Rates (SCR)
(3) Unitized Load Device (ULD)
(4) Container rates
(5) Classified rates
(6) Freight All Kinds (FAK)

'Classified rates' represent a percentage discount or surcharge based upon a general cargo rate and apply normally to specialized and high cost items such as furs, precious metals and live animals, etc.

'Freight all kinds' represent a more simplified structure where freight is charged at a set rate per kilo irrespective of the commodity. This was originally based upon the assumption that a shipper could offer a guaranteed volume of cargo during a twelve-month period. Many FAK rates are now, however, available without this contractual stipulation.

Mention has been made of COD deliveries and these are avialable for most European destinations. The charge for such consignments is usually 1 per cent of the COD amount, excluding freight. COD is not usually accepted where consignments involve on-carriage by other airlines. Similarly, it cannnot be used on UK domestic routes, and perishable cargo, livestock and newspapers are excluded. 'Charges forward' represent the charging to the consignee at the point of destination the cartage, export fees, freight and insurance premiums.

An exporter would normally commence the air transaction by the completion of 'shipper's letter of instruction', which corresponds basically with a shipping and forwarding agent's instruction form used for sea freight. This would call for information pertaining to:

(a) Method of despatch to airport and the party responsible for making arrangements
(b) Instructions to prepare or obtain *air waybill*
(c) Consignee's full address
(d) Notify party – if applicable
(e) No. of packages, type of packing
(f) Nature, quantity of goods and markings and numbers
(g) Weight and measurement details
(h) Value for Customs and value for carriage
(i) Instructions regarding insurance
(j) Details of charges to be paid by shipper
(k) Details of charges to be paid by consignee
(l) COD details, if applicable
(m) Details of any documents attached, i.e. export specifications or shipping bills for Customs entry, consular invoices or certificates of origin
(n) Instructions in case of non-delivery, i.e. hold and notify shipper or abandon

Shipper's Name and Address | Shipper's Account Number

Not negotiable

Air Waybill

Issued by

Copies 1, 2 and 3 of this Air Waybill are originals and have the same validity

Consignee's Name and Address | **Consignee's Account Number**

It is agreed that the goods described herein are accepted in apparent good order and condition (except as noted) for carriage SUBJECT TO THE CONDITIONS OF CONTRACT ON THE REVERSE HEREOF. THE SHIPPER'S ATTENTION IS DRAWN TO THE NOTICE CONCERNING CARRIER'S LIMITATION OF LIABILITY. Shipper may increase such limitation of liability by declaring a higher value for carriage and paying a supplemental charge if required.

Issuing Carrier's Agent Name and City

Accounting Information

Agent's IATA-Code | Account No.

Airport of Departure (Addr. of first Carrier) and requested Routing

to	By first Carrier (Routing and Destination)	to	by	to	by	Currency	Chgs Code	WT/VAL PPD	WT/VAL COLL	Other PPD	Other COLL	Declared Value for Carriage	Declared Value for Customs

Airport of Destination | Flight/Date | For Carrier Use only | Flight/Date | Amount of Insurance

INSURANCE – If carrier offers insurance and such insurance is requested in accordance with conditions on reverse hereof indicate amount to be insured in figures in box marked Amount of Insurance.

Handling Information

No. of Pieces RCP	Gross Weight	kg lb	Rate Class / Commodity Item No.	Chargeable Weight	Rate / Charge	Total	Nature and Quantity of Goods (incl. Dimensions or Volume)

Prepaid | Weight Charge | **Collect** | Other Charges

Valuation Charge

Tax

Total other Charges Due Agent

Shipper certifies that the particulars on the face hereof are correct and that insofar as any part of the consignment contains dangerous goods such part is properly described by name and is in proper condition for carriage by air according to the applicable Dangerous Goods Regulations.

Total other Charges Due Carrier

Signature of Shipper or his Agent

Total prepaid | Total collect

Currency Conversion Rates | **cc charges in Dest. Currency**

Executed on (Date) at (Place) Signature of Issuing Carrier or its Agent

For Carriers Use only at Destination | **Charges at Destination** | **Total collect Charges**

TATE FREIGHT FORMS 0908 313656 3/86

Original 3 - (For Shipper)

Figure 6.5(b) Air waybill

Preparing the air waybill

The next stage after this is for the air waybill (see *Figure 6.5 (b)*) to be prepared. This document is approximately the equivalent to the sea freight bill of lading in as much that it functions as a receipt and evidences a contract of carriage. However, the air waybill is not a negotiable title to goods in the same way as is a sea bill of lading although, of course, it is widely used as a valuable receipt and evidence of despatch and can at times be utilized within the framework of letters of credit, etc. When the sets of waybills issued by the various airlines are studied, *three originals* can be distinguished. These, however, do not function as a set of bills of lading would to a sea transaction. They would cover the following stages:

Original No. 1 for issuing carrier
Original No. 2 for consignee
Original No. 3 for shipper

Under normal conditions, the exporter would receive Copy No. 3; Copy No. 1 would be retained by the airline and Copy No. 2 would automatically go forward to the consignee to enable the goods to be collected at the destination point. The passing of ownership by a transfer of documents against payment can in consequence follow a different pattern compared with that relating to sea deliveries. Sometimes an exporter might consign the goods and address the air waybill to an oversea bank or agent who can then, in turn, arrange to hand over the goods to the importer when appropriate payment is made. On other occasions, a COD method might be possible.

Apart from the above three copies, airlines issue a number of extra sheets for purposes such as the following:

Delivery receipt
Airport of destination
Third carrier (if applicable)
Second carrier (if applicable)
First carrier (if applicable)

Normally IATA recommend a set of nine air waybills although most carriers seem to provide ten or twelve which provide extras for local inward clearance and payment of charges, etc.

The details inserted in the air waybill would consist of all the routine description of cargo, etc., and are largely an extension of the particulars mentioned in the letter of instruction. In addition, the following points would be of particular importance to an exporter.

Declared value for carriage

Within the framework of the General Conditions of Carriage, the liability of the carrier is normally restricted to approximately £11.80 per kilo or to the value which might be declared by the exporter on the air waybill. In the event of a higher figure being inserted, a valuation charge would be made by the air carrier. The insertion of the letters 'NVD' (No Value Declared) in this particular section would indicate that the normal carrier liability would prevail and no valuation charge would be incurred. The latter case is most likely to be encountered in practice as shippers will normally cover through their own insurance operations. There can sometimes be problems when shipping very high value cargoes and an insurance premium may be based on the assumption that a shipper is in fact inserting value declarations thus increasing the carrier's liability cover.

As in the cases of sea shipment where groupage/consolidation services are utilized, the agents arranging despatch may issue House Air Waybills (HAWB) in place of the normal airline Master Air Waybill (MAWB).

Rate class

There would usually be encountered various code numbers applying to certain aspects such as the particular freight rate being applied, e.g. SC, GC, FAK, etc.

Restricted articles

The IATA lays down certain regulations for articles of a dangerous or hazardous nature and there exists a Restricted Cargo List which defines the commodity, gives it Class Code Group classification and prescribes packing and suitable labelling. The exporter must indicate on the air waybill the relevant particulars as per the list and provide the following certificate:

'I hereby certify that the contents of this consignment are fully and accurately described above by proper shipping name and are classified, packed marked, labelled and in proper condition for carriage by air according to the current Edition of the IATA Restricted Articles Regulations and all applicable carrier and governmental regulations. I acknowledge that I may be liable for damages resulting from any mis-statement or omission and I further agree that any air carrier involved in the shipment of this consignment may rely upon this certification.'

Such a certificate is on a printed form not unlike the shipping note but with a bold red diagonally-striped border.

Rail systems

The exporter to Europe is served by a constantly-growing rail system. This provides a variety of services enabling him to send his goods to Europe. In many cases, through deliveries can be made. The through railway wagon is an excellent method of transport although expansion has been limited to a certain extent by a shortage of wagons capable of operating on the Continent. It is thought that through services carry some 4 per cent in volume and 7 per cent in value of merchandise exports to Europe. British Rail have accumulated a vast amount of experience in handling procedures and documentation and offer some of the simplest methods available by the use of various *consignment notes*.

Normally, a shipper is likely to utilize the railways either simply to convey his goods to the docks for subsequent shipment by vessels not operated by BR, or, via one of the systems of railferries, to convey the goods to a Continental port or even, at times, to carry the consignment right through to a customer's address.

For sending the goods to the docks for subsequent shipment outside the railway system, it is likely that a BR number consignment note would be used. This is a very simple form and requires only basic details of cargo, dock to which goods are to go and name of carrying vessel, together with wagon number and specification of consignment. The relationship of the railways to the particular dock in question should always be checked by an exporter as this may affect the manner in which charges are made.

If the goods are being consigned to a Continental port, then for most goods a form of 'Declaration and Consignment Note' should be completed for destinations entailing carriage by water and the passing through Customs. Such consignments could be forwarded from the Continental port to the final destination, of course, but for this last segment of the journey the terms and conditions of the particular country in question would apply. Some salient details required by the consignment note would be as follows:

(1) Type of service, for example for the Continent:
    Mail service (express parcels)
    Grande vitesse (fast goods)
    Petite vitesse (ordinary goods service).

(2) Any document attached, i.e. Customs Entry, 'T' forms, invoices and certificates of origin or export licences, etc., and instructions regarding the issue of bills of lading.
(3) Full specification of goods, including accurate trade description and units of quantity.
(4) Whether there is any question of duty relief or goods under bond, etc.
(5) FOB value
(6) Origin of merchandise.
(7) Payment of charges – if BR do not require payment, are charges for sender or consignee?
(8) Type of risk cover.

For deliveries right through to a Continental destination, one of the best methods is the use of a CIM (Convention Internationale de Marchandises). This form is known as a 'consignment Note/Lettre de voiture' or 'Frachtbrief'. Goods so carried are subject to the provisions of the International Convention concerning the Carriage of Goods by Rail 1961. The details of the consignment note are very much as per that covered above.

Sheet 1   Consignment note (to be handed to the consignee when the goods are delivered)
Sheet 2   Invoice (for accountancy purposes and where all charges are shown; retained by the destination railway authority)
Sheet 3   Arrival note (goes forward to, and is retained by destination station)
Sheet 4   Duplicate of consignment note (given to sender after consignment has been accepted)
Sheet 5   Duplicate invoice (retained by forwarding station)

The movement of railway wagons is covered by the TIF (Transports Internationaux par Chemin de Fer) Convention which prescribes a TIF International Customs Declaration to facilitate the crossing of frontiers for goods carried by rail. When shipping to the Continent under a CIM consignment note, it is necessary to utilise a TIF BR Form. Two copies of this declaration are normally required for every Continental country involved in the consignment journey.

TIR road transport

One of the problems facing road transport was of course the complications, in relation to Customs examination and possible duty payments, facing a haulier when a lorry was involved in crossing several frontiers. There were also the problems involved with the actual vehicle itself which was sometimes regarded as actually being exported and then re-imported with all the associated complications and paperwork. To cope with these emerging problems there has emerged the TIR (Transports Internationaux Routiers) Convention. This is an international convention established by the Economic Commission for Europe, to which the United Kingdom is a party. Other countries in which the convention operates include:

Austria; Belgium; Bulgaria; Czechoslovakia; Denmark; Federal Republic of Germany; Finland; France; Greece; Hungary; Italy; Liechtenstein; Luxembourg; Netherlands; Norway; Poland; Portugal; Republic of Ireland; Romania; Spain; Sweden; Switzerland; Turkey; United States of America and Yugoslavia.

In essence, the purpose of the Convention is to make it possible for goods packed in Customs-sealed road vehicles or containers to travel across one or more national frontiers with the minimum of Customs formalities. This avoids the examination of goods at each frontier post and means that the carrier does not have either to pay duty or give security for these payments. The operation of this procedure hinges upon three main requirements:

(1) That prior approval has been received for road vehicles or containers which have to fulfil certain requirements laid down by the Convention.
(2) That a TIR carnet is used as the basic documentation.
(3) That this carnet is issued by an approved association and that adequate control of this document is undertaken.

Prior approval of vehicles or containers

The approving authority in the UK is, of course, the Department of Transport and application has to be made to the appropriate licensing authority for examination. Such approval will depend upon a number of factors, for example:

(a) That Customs seals can be easily and effectively used.
(b) That goods cannot be removed from, or introduced into, the sealed part of the vehicle without obvious damage or breaking of seals.
(c) That there does not exist any possibility of concealed areas where goods may be hidden.

After inspection and approval, the carrier will receive a GV 60 or certificate of approval which is usually valid for two years.

There is also the 'certificate of type approval' which is given to a manufacturer covering a particular design which enables him to affix a metal plate to the vehicle approving the design. Plates measuring 250 mm × 400 mm showing in white the letters 'TIR' on a blue background must be fitted to the front and rear of the vehicle in question. Three photographs of the vehicle – front, rear and one side – should be carried to assist the Customs authorities in their control. Great care must be taken by the carrier that all vehicles are maintained up to the TIR standard and that no damage or modification takes place that might adversely affect this compliance.

TIR carnet issued by approved association

Application may then be made to some approved guaranteeing association such as the RHA (Road Haulage Association Ltd) for admission to the scheme and for the necessary carnet. Two types of carnets are available, namely a six-volet (voucher) or a 14-volet type. A pair of vouchers is necessary for the country of departure, the country of destination and each country traversed. The main component parts of the carnet consist of:

(a) Guaranteeing association (the RHA) and the international organization to which it is affiliated, in this case the IRU (Union Internationale des Transports Routiers)
(b) Declaration and undertaking by the carrier to abide by all the necessary regulations and requirements
(c) Goods manifest
(d) Details of carnet, e.g. offices of departure; vehicle certificate number and date
(e) Stipulated itinerary; seals and identification marks
(f) Detachable vouchers

Also will be shown the validity period (two months from date of issue).

The carnet obtained from the RHA will include a loose-leaf form which can be used as a schedule of the movements and whereabouts of a carnet. This form has the following headings for completion:

Carnet No.	Volet
Expiry date	Date issued
Sent to	Destination
Trailer/vehicle No.	Job No.
Returned from	Date returned

Plus a space for any other explanatory notes

Great care has to be taken with the handling and use of the TIR Carnet as loss of this document or infringements can result in suspension from the scheme or the need for an exporter to stand indemnity for any violation of Customs authority which might result from the loss.

A check should be made to see if there are any other accompanying documents which, although not always obligatory, may be necessary in some countries and often assist in obtaining a trouble-free passage. For example, in France a 'Carnet de Passage' is used and this can be obtained either from the French Ministry of Transport or rather more easily through the Automobile Association in the UK. The Carnet de Passage is in essence a Customs document applying to the vehicle and not the load. Similarly, any goods vehicle travelling into, from or through the Federal Republic of Germany, and carrying goods in connection with the operator's own trade or business, should carry a document (which can be obtained, for example, from the TRTA (Traders Road Transport Association Ltd.)) giving detailed information regarding the vehicle, points of unloading or loading, names of companies being visited, etc.

Damage to the vehicle due to accidents or any other emergency must be reported to Customs or Police who may be called upon to fill in a declaration on carnet. Otherwise, the carrier will be liable for duty, etc. payments which may become due as a result of seals or canvas being broken or torn, of if the TIR regulations are in any other way infringed.

The carnet itself is printed in French but additional pages may be inserted giving a translation in the language of the country of issue. Translation may also be required by countries en route.

Standardized international road consignment note

The IRU (International Road Transport Union) have developed a consignment note satisfying the requirements of the CMR (Convention de Marchandises par Route). This can be obtained from the RHA and is normally issued in English, French and German with some other translation being available. It acts as a waybill and covers all road transport up to £3000 per ton weight of goods. On board ship it gives the road carrier recourse (under certain conditions) to the shipping company.

There are four main parts to a CMR consignment note set, namely:

(1) for consignor
(2) for consignee

(3) for carrier
(4) copy

In addition, there are some six other copies which may be used for such purposes as internal accounting and record keeping. Altogether there are some 31 items for completion covering such data as names of consignor/consignee, specification of goods, metric volume, by whom charges are payable, currency special requirements, etc. Items 1–12 inclusive are completed by consignor. Consignee's signature for receipt is obtained on carrier's copy.

Postal services

For many exporters the use of parcel post for their exports can be of considerable advantage, as a very efficient system of overseas parcel post exists covering a wide variety of markets. Essentially, it should be borne in mind that goods sent by parcel post are liable to Customs examination at point of desination or any appropriate payment of duty, etc. Reference should be made to the current *Post Office Guide* to obtain all the applicable regulations such as the maximum weight (at present 10 kg), types of items that cannot be sent, for example hazardous or dangerous goods etc. Reference should also be made as to the particular destination in order to ascertain what appropriate documentation is required.

It is likely that the following types of documentation will be encountered:

(1) An adhesive form to be affixed to the parcel.
(2) An alternative tie-on version of the above for small parcels or where it is not practicable to use an adhesive form.
(3) A non-adhesive form of which one or more copies may be required.

Reference should be made to the regulations governing the particular market, in order to see which specific category is involved. For certain letter-post dutiable items a 'green label' system is operated.

The value and nett contents should be shown on the above documents, together with all other relevant information which will facilitate customs clearance. Equally, any certificates of origin should accompany the parcel, if necessary, and this should be stated on the customs declaration under the list of contents. To some countries there exist services such as 'Franc de Droits' (Free of Charges) whereby delivery may be made to a customer free of

Customs and other charges. This system is indicated by the initials 'FDD'. Such parcels as a rule must be posted at a head or branch office and the sender must pay a deposit on account and undertake to remit any balance on demand.

It has been the task of this chapter to examine some of the main categories of transport documentation and procedure in addition to the more orthodox bill of lading/title of ownership transactions. It is in this former category that the greatest changes are likely to occur, particularly in relation to container and road transport. The task will be for UK commercial practice to adjust the transfer of ownership and payment methods to suit the new form of through delivered/combined transport operator type of consignment. A very encouraging factor is that great strides have been made by the various international institutions and organisations, coupled with real progress towards standardization of documents and procedure, particularly in road and rail transport, and showing great potentialities when applied to European trade.

It will be seen in Chapter 7 that the enlarged EEC has made considerable impact upon transport documentation. The Full Community Transit System, using the appropriate 'T' form for example, can in certain cases supplant TIR operations. For postal despatches to EEC countries of *non*-free-circulation goods, a yellow label should be affixed. Postal consignment of qualifying goods under EEC/FTA agreements not exceeding certain low values call for the use of form EUR2.

7 International trading areas: documents and procedures

The growth and development of the European Economic Community (EEC) has naturally had considerable impact upon international trade and has brought about a series of re-alignments of relationships between many countries. Taking the UK for example, not only is there the dimension of operating between the Community but also the second dimension of that Community's relationship between other trading groups and individual countries.

The Community at present consists of the following full member countries:

Belgium	Holland
Denmark	Italy
Eire	Luxembourg
France	Portugal
Germany (Fed Rep)	Spain
Greece	United Kingdom

Turkey is an Associate Member.

Some of the more important administrative developments of the EEC can be categorized under the following headings:

(1) *Transport,* through a pattern of forms and procedures which are necessary to accompany our goods both within and sometimes outside the EEC.
(2) A whole series of *regulations and requirements* which face the exporter depending upon the nature of his product and markets.
(3) The series of *trade agreements* concluded between the EEC and other countries and trading groups resulting in preferential and free trade agreements.

This type of analysis should lead us on to examining the EEC framework in which exporters and importers will be interested, in order to see how it will impinge upon the activities of their particular companies.

Most companies are concerned to a greater or lesser extent
either directly or indirectly with the following:

(1) The Common Customs Tariff (CCT), also referred to as the
    Common External Tariff (CET).
(2) Moves towards certain areas of political and social
    harmonization, e.g. labour policy, transport policy, etc.
(3) Inward Processing Relief and Common Agricultural Policy
    (CAP) with levy and subsidy systems.
(4) The adoption of EEC rules of competition which will have a
    bearing on marketing and distribution policy and structure.
(5) A relationship between EEC/UK and other trading groups
    and areas such as the old EFTA system, Commonwealth
    preference and GSP (General System of Preference) areas,
    and a number of specially-negotiated relationships with
    other countries such as, for example, the Mediterranean
    area.
(6) A pattern of T-form documentation covering the status and
    transit of a consignment and the possible use of a variety of
    movement certificates and certificates of origin.

It will be seen, therefore, that the above six headings
considerably influence the activities within a company's export
department. The export sales function now has to keep abreast
with tariff matters and their impact upon cost and pricing strategy.
The many complex and individual arrangements between 'third
countries' need to be studied, together with new definitions of
origin criteria. The shipping and transport specialists need to
familiarise themselves with new documents and Customs procedures, etc. As always, the company will be in many cases
employing outside specialists, such as forwarding agents and other
transport operators, who will undoubtedly bear a large part of the
responsibility for the T-form operations.

Background of the EEC

It is not proposed to go deeply into the origins, history and
institutions of the Common Market since much has already been
written and published on this subject. To give only one example,
there is the excellent Barclays Bank publication on the enlarged
Common Market which provides a 'bird's eye' picture of the
growth and structure of the EEC, together with a statistical
survey. It should be borne in mind that basically there are three
communities, namely the EEC, the lesser-known ECSC (European Coal and Steel Community) and Euratom (European Atomic

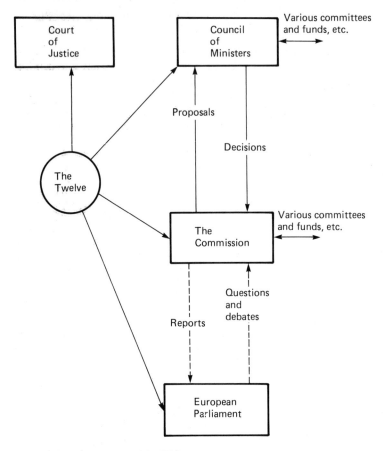

Figure 7.1 Basic structure of the EEC

Energy Community). *Figure 7.1* shows the relationship between the institutions of the EEC.

The basic 'core' of EEC operations and legislation is of course the Treaty of Rome which instituted the EEC on 25 March 1957. A good text is available from HMSO published as Command Paper 4864. The Treaty consists of a series of Articles which are concerned with broad objectives and intentions and it is to these that the exporter can turn as an initial point of contact. For example, Articles 1, 2 and 3 provide a clear and concise description of what the original six members of the Community hoped to achieve. Articles 38-47 deal with agricultural policy and Articles 85-94 deal with Rules of Competition which could have very far-reaching implications for some companies.

The Treaty goes on to make provision for the Secondary Legislation of the European Community to take place through the Council and the Commission by means of regulations, directives and recommendations. For example, when we are considering T forms we will see that Article 41 of Council Regulations 542/69 permits the use of a two-page type of T2 form.

Exporters should turn to HMSO for publications covering instruments in force appropriate to various aspects, e.g. budgetary policy, agriculture, technical standards and transport, etc.

Tariffs

When the original EEC achieved Customs union, a common external tariff was adopted against goods from outside the Community. This tariff is known as the Common Customs Tariff (CCT). The main four-figure headings in the CCT are similar to those in the United Kingdom tariff, since both are based on the CCCN, but each contains its own sub-headings dictated by special needs.

Constant efforts are made to modify and adjust the tariff headings of products to achieve a growing degree of international accord. It is anticipated that the current tariff trade code numbers will be replaced by the new extended numerical pattern of the Harmonized System provisionally due to come into operation during 1988. It should be borne in mind that correct usage and employment of the tariff numbers is essential both from the point of view of exporters and importers to ensure both accurate classification of trade figures and appropriate assessment of duty or tax rates if applicable.

A specialized feature is the use of tariff sub-headings which base a rate of duty on 'end-use headings' rather than the 'essential character' of the product itself. For example, we might think of maize as a product but its use in brewing is the end-use application.

The EEC also operate 'tariff quotas', which for special reasons permit a member to import a certain amount of a product annually at a lower duty rate than normally.

EEC Customs procedures

T forms and the Community transit system

Of all the administrative aspects of the EEC, perhaps of most importance to the practical exporter are the documentary and procedural requirements of the Community. This means a working knowledge of the Community Transit (CT) system and the variety of T forms and the other documents that may be required both to accompany a consignment of goods from one member country to another or perhaps to cover goods moving outside the EEC area.

UK exporters have, of course, been familiar for many years with the concept of exporting goods to an area which gives some form of preferential treatment with regard to duty, etc., such as EFTA and Commonwealth preference areas. In order to qualify for this preferential treatment, it has been customary to provide some form of documentary proof of origin and entitlement.

In parallel with this has been the development of some form of documentation to cover the appropriate mode of transportation. This ranges from the traditional type of bill of lading to the TIR carnet system developed to cover the transit of consignments over international frontiers without individual customs clearance and payment of duty.

We can therefore see that the EEC T form system can in various ways cope with the concept of the *status* of the goods in question *plus*, in certain circumstances, the *transit* of the consignment. The resulting Community Transit (CT) system is intended to combine these two functions of 'evidence of entitlement' and 'international transit' system. Depending upon the exporter's choice, he may be considering a system which will cover only evidence of entitlement (status) or a combined system (status/transit). By entitlement, we are of course alluding in the EEC sense to providing the appropriate paperwork to ensure that the goods are treated as community goods and should therefore be free of any duty between member states.

The CT procedures are governed by regulations and decisions of the European Communities contained within the main provisions of Council Regulations 542/69. The use of CT procedures does not in any way affect the need to comply with any relevant UK import or export prohibitions or restrictions.

Types of document

We must now consider the different types of document available for use under the CT system. Each has a particular significance and is for use in particular circumstances. It should be borne in mind that certain CT documents may themselves constitute a declaration as to the nature of the goods in question and therefore the incorrect use of forms may render the signatory liable to penalties.

Basically, the trader will encounter a range of T forms to cover movements of goods *within* the Community itself. The range will cover:

T1   Non-Community goods, transit purposes only
T2   Community goods plus transit
T2L   Community goods status only
T   A special control copy

When considering the above form types it will be necessary to refer to appropriate HM Customs Notices for information. The key notice would be No. 751 which sets out the detailed background of qualification for Community treatment and the operation of the various forms. It is necessary to be quite clear about the terminology employed:

Status: Whether the goods qualify for a nil duty position within the community which will mean that they must be goods originating wholly in the community, or: Any imported items from outside the EEC have paid all appropriate (if any) import duties.

Free circulation: If the above requirements have been met, then they can be expected to enter the community country in question free of duty.

Transit: Basically the nature of the possible movement of goods over a number of frontiers or customs posts within the EEC area.

Depending, therefore, upon the degree to which goods satisfy or otherwise the above criteria, various *types* of T form will be utilized.

It should always be borne in mind that member countries *may* apply other forms of prohibition to imports from fellow member countries in order to protect public security, morality or national treasures, etc. In the same way, import licensing may be applied to prevent a deflection of trade.

In the light of the above let us now examine the use of the various forms, T1, T2, T2L, and T, as used by the original six member countries and *still* used by them in the enlarged community.

Form T1

This automatically indicates that the consignment it covers is *not* in free circulation in the EEC member states. It is, therefore, a signal to the Customs authorities in the countries of transit and destination that the goods are not entitled to free entry or to intra-community rates of duty under EEC arrangements.

Bearing in mind that the *absence* of a suitable T form also indicates that the goods in question do not qualify for preferential EEC treatment, what is the purpose of a T1? The answer is that in this case the T1 is being used as a 'transit' document only; in other words to provide a unified documentary system that enables the goods to move over a number of EEC frontiers without Customs clearance, even if at the arrival at the final destination appropriate EEC duty is levied. Thus we have an example of a document being used purely as a transit document; in fact, to use the official terminology, it implies 'negative status'.

Form T2

This is a combined 'status' and 'transit' document. The five-page form (*Figure 7.2*) is a unified documentary system which enables a consignment to be monitored across a number of frontiers. It also implies 'free circulation'.
Note: A dual-purpose T form can be numbered either T1 or T2.

Form T2L

The L suffix indicates that this is a two-page status document only and is used when consignments cross just one internal frontier. It is obviously suited to air-freight despatches or shipment from port to port. The purpose of this form is simply to certify 'free circulation'.

Form T

This is special control form and is likely, for example, to be used for goods eligible for a Common Agricultural Policy (CAP) refund, production subsidies or goods subject to some form of prohibition or restriction on exportation from the Community. The T form may be used as an additional fifth control copy when used with a four-page T2 or by itself if some other transit procedure such as TIR or rail is being used.

Examples

A German exporter air-freighting goods from Frankfurt to Paris could use a T2L *form*. A German exporter putting goods on a lorry and sending them from Cologne across France to Brussels

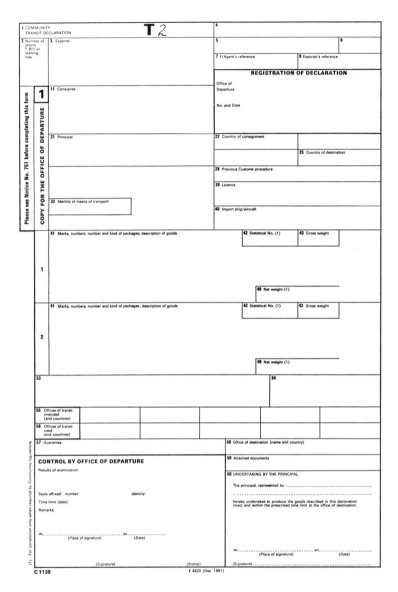

Figure 7.2 T2 form

would employ a *five-page* T2. This is assuming in both cases that the goods in question are in free circulation. It will be seen, therefore, that the T2 form in some respects is similar to the TIR carnet system. An exporter using a T2 system must, however, ensure that his vehicle complies with any particular legislation and also that there is no question of conflict between EEC or bilateral transport quota systems that might be in force.

These T forms have to be made available to the Customs, duly completed by the exporter (or his agent) and presented to an approved office of departure for certification by Customs.

Where the T-form system is being used as a transit operation (T2 five-copy set), a form of guarantee will have to be provided on behalf of the exporter. Also, as the consignment passes across frontiers, a transit advice note (Form C1128) should be deposited at each point. When the copies of the T forms are delivered to the destination office, a receipt (C1129) should preferably be obtained showing that the T forms were in fact presented. A guarantee is not required for goods dispatched by approved airlines.

When goods go by rail, a simplified system can be utilized: the T forms are not actually used and the railway authority becomes the 'principal'; there is no need for duty deposits or guarantees. For consignments sent by post, a yellow label (C1130) is used if the goods are not of the appropriate 'free circulation' status.

It should be noticed that, although Switzerland and Austria are not EEC members, they do accept the appropriate Community Transit T forms covering the transit of consignments across their territory. Naturally this refers only to the 'transit' aspect of the documentation. This extension is covered by HM Customs Notice No. 750B.

It should be borne in mind that the Community is a living and therefore developing organism and consequently administrative and documentary changes can be expected from time to time. Much work is at present being done. The Internal Market Council approved in 1984 two regulations which should lead to modification of intra-Community documentary practices and procedures.

A detailed breakdown of the procedures will, in due course, emerge from a series of implementing regulations to be drawn up by a committee of the Commission's Customs Union Service. In general, however, it appears that the aim will be eventually to introduce a Single Administrative Document (SAD) to cover Community export, transit and import operations. It is envisaged that the SAD will comprise a seven-part set using sensitized paper which captures simultaneously all the export information common to the transit and import functions.

Together with a standardization of coding information and using the SAD full procedure, this should lead to a single document and it is claimed that in the Community as a whole it could lead to the disappearance of over seventy individual Customs forms.

The procedure which is in an advanced stage of development is envisaged at present as 'coming on stream' in 1988.

EEC special agreements

The aspects of documentation and procedure so far considered apply, in the main, to purely EEC operations within the Community. However, it must be appreciated that the enlarged Community has woven around itself a vast complex network of trade and association arrangements. The UK export manager must therefore be in a position to check the particular market in which he is selling to see if there is any special agreement that might affect the duty on his products and, therefore, his price policy. Should there be any special arrangements in force,some special documentary procedures will invariably be necessary. As already mentioned, the arrangements are numerous and complicated; reference can be made to the many HM Customs notices that cover the various agreements, but broadly speaking we can distinguish the following categories:

(a) *Association Agreements*, such as with Turkey dating from 1963 and envisaging eventual full membership.
(b) *Preferential Trade Agreements (PTAs)* concluded, or in process of being concluded, between the EEC and certain Mediterranean countries (e.g. Egypt, Cyprus) and Africa, Caribbean and Pacific (ACP) countries (e.g. the Bahamas, Nigeria and Tonga).
(c) *Free Trade Agreements (FTAs)* cover trade between the EEC and all individual members of EFTA (those that did not join the Community). The agreements will allow free trade in the great majority of industrial products covered by Tariff Chapters 25 to 99.
(d) *Generalized System of Preference (GSP)* covers certain developing countries belonging to the UNCTAD Group of

77, and allows many goods from these countries into the EEC either duty free or at reduced rates.

The above relationships, resulting from preferential and free trade agreements, have to be based on some fairly precise rules of origin in order to enable products to qualify for favourable treatment and at the same time to avoid 'deflection of trade' – that is to say, where products might simply be shipped via a third country to obtain a tariff concession to which they might not be entitled. Basically, running like a thread through most of the trade agreements, the following criteria can be detected:

(1) Whether or not the products in question do actually originate, or are wholly produced, in the country in question (EEC Regulation 802/68 sets out the definitions of originating products);
(2) The concept of 'sufficient transformation', which is based on change of tariff heading, i.e. a finished product from a number of imported items has a different tariff heading compared with the imported items;
(3) The satisfying of some value-added percentage or qualifying process.

The following example of sufficient transformation can be found in HM customs Notice 828 dealing with the EEC/EFTA free trade agreements:

'Rubber waste (heading 40.04) is imported into the EEC (e.g. the UK) from the USA and processed into reclaimed rubber (heading 40.05). The imported material undergoes a change in tariff heading in the EEC and becomes an originating product for the purpose of claiming FTA treatment in an EFTA country'.

In order to check the application of the above criteria, the exporter must check the HM Customs chapter heading of his commodity or product. An example, taken from HM Customs Notice No. 828, is shown as follows:

Chapter 79 Zinc and articles thereof
Manufacture which causes all non-originating materials used to change tariff heading, provided the value of all non-originating materials used does not exceed 50 per cent of ex works price.

Finished product	Qualifying process
79.01 Unwrought zinc; zinc waste and scrap.	Manufacture which causes all non-originating materials used to change tariff heading.

Naturally, these rules of origin are very complex and must be studied in detail in the case of individual products and materials. Also, as increasingly the flow of components, raw materials and manufacturing processes transcends individual frontiers, complicated cumulative processes can be encountered. An importer of components may seek from his supplier some form of manufacturer's declaration to enable decisions to be made regarding percentage origins, etc.

From the 1 April 1983 an experimental alternative set of rules have been in operation determining the origin of products exported to EFTA countries applicable to Chapter Headings 84 – 92. Originating status for such goods will be determined by a maximum non-community/EFTA percentage content varying according to the product but generally between 25 and 40 per cent. These rules are considered as being optional to those mentioned above.

It should be borne in mind that exported goods that have benefited from drawback or temporary duty-free admission will not normally be able to qualify for preferential treatment.

Documentation

Consideration should now be given to the category of documentation that is necessary to support individual exporters and importers to claim benefits of nil duty or some preferential treatment under the umbrella of the above-mentioned structure of various EEC preferential arrangements. The basic document is the 'movement certificate'. This certificate has to be completed, verified by the Customs authorities of the exporting countries and a copy made available to the exporter's customer so that the latter can claim whatever tariff benefits may exist under a particular agreement. An example of such a certificate is the EUR 1 (Customs reference C1299 – see *Figure 7.3*), which is used for trade between EEC countries and ex-EFTA (FTA) areas. The EUR 1 form is also

DUPLICATE
APPLICATION FOR MOVEMENT CERTIFICATE

1. Exporter (Name, full address, country)

EUR1 No. N 768232

2. Application for a certificate to be used in preferential trade between
THE EUROPEAN ECONOMIC COMMUNITY
and
....
(Insert appropriate countries or groups of countries or territories)

3. Consignee (Name, full address, country) (Optional)

4. Country, group of countries or territory in which the products are considered as originating
EEC

5. Country, group of countries or territory of destination

6. Transport details (Optional)

7. Remarks

(1) If goods are not packed indicate number of articles or state "in bulk" as appropriate.

8. Item number: marks & numbers	Number and kind of packages (1): description of goods	9. Gross weight (kg) or other measure (litres, cu. m., etc.)	10. Invoices (Optional)

Duplicate Application Form for retention by Chamber of Commerce (if not required, detach before presentation to (Customs).

C 1299 5 Printed in the UK for HMSO
Dd 8857711 3/85 500M FCS/0107

Figure 7.3 EUR 1 form

being used in trade with a variety of countries embraced by the preferential trade areas mentioned on page 147. In the case of all present movement certificates, simpler forms such as the EUR 2 are used for low-value consignments and in some cases for postal despatches. The EUR 1 movement certificate consists of four pages (plus a duplicate sheet for countersignature by Chamber of Commerce if required). The top copy (page 1) is presented to HM Customs for certification and endorsement. It is this copy that must eventually be transmitted by the exporter to his customer. Page 4 represents the exporter's declaration, and it is here that he will specify how his goods qualify for the particular benefit in question, e.g. wholly produced, sufficient transformation, or satisfying some process or added-value critreion. The tariff heading number should be given. In certain circumstances, the exporter can make special arrangements with HM Customs to have his movement certificates pre-authenticated to avoid delays.

Quite apart from the T form and movement certificates, there will remain instances when a UK exporter will need to supply his customer with a Chamber of Commerce type of certificate of origin, which may be needed for a variety of reasons by overseas authorities both in and out of the Community. The EEC format for the three-part set has been adopted and in the case of British products, the term 'European Communities – United Kingdom' must be used. Otherwise, its completion and handling with the local issuing Chamber of Commerce follow very much the lines of the old type of certificate.

8 International invoices and certificates of origin

Some of the most important categories of international trade documentation are represented by various types of invoices and certificates of origin. These documents in themselves are often called upon to satisfy a whole range of international trade agreements and import and export Customs authority regulations.

Invoices

To any form of trader, the basic commercial invoice is a document of fundamental importance since it fulfils the following functions:

(1) It is a supplier's bill for goods and services.
(2) It is a detailed list showing unit prices, totals, weights and other specifications, and certain other elements of the total price such as packing and delivery charges.
(3) It provides a check list for the customer and generally enables a particular consignment to be identified against a specific order.
(4) On occasions it may be a key document inasmuch as it will be used as evidence of value in, say, an insurance claim. Equally, to a bank, it may prove to be an essential part of the shipping documents which it may be holding as security.
(5) Although the invoice, as such, may not be a contract of sale, it can in certain instances act as evidence of the contract.

Invoices for duty payment purposes

So far, the above data is of general application to all invoices, whether employed in normal domestic trading or in international business transactions. It is when we consider *export invoices* that we realize the very wide variety of the types that may be encountered, and also the different requirements that they might be called upon to fulfil. In the first place, the overseas buyer will invariably need his supplier's invoice to present to his Customs authority. This will, in fact, be a key document because the value and description shown on the invoice may provide the basis for any duty or tax assessment and indeed, the description of the goods on the invoice may play a part in their identifications as to whether they are allowed to be imported or not, i.e. subject to any import licensing. At all times, therefore, the invoice must be made out clearly to enable correct assessment to be made and to enable the importer to obtain speedy Customs clearance and take delivery of his goods. One of the key pieces of information that the exporter will require, therefore, is the basis upon which the particular overseas market in question assesses import duty. Duty may be assessed in a number of ways:

(1) *Ad valorem* – according to the value of the goods.
(2) *Specific duty* – based perhaps on gross weight of article or upon the particular unit itself, such as per case or per bundle.
(3) The application of the above may in turn depend upon whether any particular international trade agreements or preferential systems are involved. These might be exemplified by various GATT agreements EEC/FTA, Latin American Free Trade Agreements (LAFTA) and Generalized System of Preferences (GSP) etc. Clearly today there is a wide and constantly changing pattern and network of international trade agreements. Consequently, the Customs authorities of the importer's country are bound to need to scrutinize amongst other items, the invoice to decide:
What is the nature of the product?
The value
Whether subject to a rate of duty or entitled to receive some preferential treatment because it has emanated from a specific country or group of exporting countries.

It will be seen that the above provides one of the major keys to the problem of what type of invoice an exporter should use and how it should be completed. It would be impossible to attempt an identification and examination of every type of invoice that might be encountered because these are so numerous. Nevertheless, it is hoped that the following comments will enable a practitioner to make an analysis of a given market and to decide upon which principles his invoicing should be based.

First of all, when the question of *ad valorem* duty is considered, it is most important to find out the actual value on which duty is to be assessed; for example, is the *ad valorem* percentage to be levied on the FOB or CIF price? It is probably true to say that in most cases the CIF contract price is chosen as the basis of duty assessment. However, it must be borne in mind that certain variations may be encountered in different markets. If for example, *ad valorem* rates are operating, there may sometimes be questions of royalty, agent's discounts or other component parts of the price structure. Similarly, cost of packing or computation of freight might play a part in determining the ultimate dutiable figure. In the case of *specific* duties the number of units, gross or nett weight might all influence duty assessment.

It will be seen, therefore, that considerable thought must be given to the layout and completion of an export invoice. A simplified example is shown in *Figure 8.1.*

Of course, much more information than that shown would often be needed but essentially this example shows some of the basic elements of the export invoice structure. For Finland, an FTA country, a special EUR form would be needed as will be seen later.

Internationally-speaking there has been a steady move towards a degree of harmonization in the methods of valuation for Customs purposes based upon the Brussels Convention on the Valuation of Goods for Customs Purposes, known as the 'Brussels Definition of Value'. Emerging from the 'Tokyo Round' of the GATT Multilateral Trade Negotiations has been a new package of agreements on valuation. This agreement was accepted by the EEC and a number of the other more important countries; it is expected to be progressively adopted by most other countries. The new valuation code was accepted by the UK and other Community countries in 1980.

Whereas the Brussels definition of valuation adopted the 'notational' system whereby the criterion is the price the goods would fetch on a sale in specified open market conditions, the later GATT agreement employs a 'positive' system employing a range of specified methods of valuation. The broad classifications of this system are:

Transactive Value
Transaction Value of identical goods
Value derived from selling price of goods in importing country
Computed Value based upon build-up cost

It will be borne in mind that the relationship between buyer and seller may play a part in the choice of valuation method. Sales between associated companies may mean that the actual transactive value, as evidenced by the contract sales invoice, is not

Bought of:
   Southern Exporters Ltd.,
   Winchester, Hants, England

9th August 19.................
                                              EX 7051
Customer: Invoice No.   ....

OY Bemberg AB
PO Box 101   Customer's
Helsinki 10   Order No.   ......571...........
Finland

Invoice of ONE CASE CONTAINING ONE HEAVY-DUTY
COMPRESSOR
Shipped per mv 'BALTIC MERCHANT' from London to
Helsinki

Marks:	Description of Goods	£ p	£ p
B.A.B.	ONE WOODEN CASE		2000.00
571	CONTAINING ONE MK		
HELSINKI	11-B COMPRESSOR		
	380V INDUSTRIAL		
Specification:	Charges:		
1.5 × 1.5 ×	Case including packing	25.00	
1.5m	Carriage to docks	14.00	39.00
cu.m. =			
3.375			
Gross wt: 100 kilos	FOB London	39.00	2039.00
Nett wt: 90 kilos			
	Freight, incl B/L,	50.00	
	etc., charges		
	Marine insurance, incl	15.00	
	policy stamp, etc.		65.00
	CIF Helsinki	65.00	2104.00
With appropriate		*Finnmarks 16 832 00	
EUR Form			

Figure 8.1 Example of an export invoice

applicable; there may be the need for the Customs authorities to take into account a comparison of other prices. Similarly, the computation of the price may have reference to any tools, designs or other factors supplied but not included in the actual invoice price.

A vital point to remember is that goods always have some value in the eyes of the importing Customs authorities even if they are supplied genuinely free of charge. In such cases it is always wise to indicate on the invoice a value for customs purposes even if no charge is being made to the overseas importer.

Different types of export invoice

So far, the commercial invoice has been considered and emphasis placed upon the information it should contain, with particular stress on duty assessment. It is necessary now to look at all the possible categories of invoice encountered in exporting. These can be considered under the following headings:

(1) *Commercial invoice by itself.*
(2) *Commercial invoices plus some form of declaration* which the exporter himself is responsible for typing and signing.
(3) *Commercial invoice plus declaration* as above but requiring some form of independent verification by, say, a Chamber of Commerce or the appropriate embassy.
(4) *Consular invoice*, in some sense a parallel document as it is needed as well as the commercial invoice.
(5) *A specific invoice form* which is required by some countries. In a case such as this the exporter has to obtain the requisite invoice form which is laid down by the appropriate authorities.

The reasons behind the various types of invoice set out above can be seen to stem from:

(a) The possible need for the invoice actually to contain a signed declaration by the exporter that the invoice is showing the correct price structure and other data.
(b) The need at times for some independent verification to ensure that the prices actually shown on the invoices are *bona fide*, that no attempt is being made to show inaccurate prices to avoid Customs duty.
(c) Sometimes an invoice is designed to show a comparison between the domestic selling price and the export price. This may very often be conditioned by a country's desire to

avoid any form of dumping activities by exporters, or where it wishes to foster and protect infant industries.

Bearing in mind the above classification of the various invoice types and some of the main reasons behind them, some examples can now be considered.

Commercial invoices with declaration

France requires two copies showing the terms of sale, e.g. FOB, CIF, etc., and invoices should bear the following declaration:

'Nous certifions que les marchandises faisant l'objet de cette fourniture sont de fabrication ... (country of origin), et que la valeur sur mentionnée est juste et conforme à nos écritures.'

This could be translated as 'We hereby certify that the goods to which this invoice relates are of ... origin, and that the value stated is correct and in accordance with our account books.'

Normally, at least two copies of the commercial invoice would be needed and details shown should include packing and packaging details and, of course, utilize the metric system.

Sweden, on the other hand, does not actually call for a declaration as such, on the invoice, but apart from the normal data it requests the inclusion of the CCCN and the provision for Customs of three copies. Facsimile signatures are accepted.

The signatory would normally be a director, secretary or partner.

When completing declarations such as this, the exporter should be careful to note whether facsimile signatures can be used. In some cases this is so but some other countries prohibit facsimiles and require that signatures be original. This point can be of some importance when simplified systems of documentation are being produced by reprographic or computerized systems, or if carbon copies are being utilized.

An example of an *independently verified declaration* would be the case of Iran which requires that a commercial invoice should show the following types of declaration:

'We hereby certify this invoice to be true and correct and in accordance with our books, also that the goods are of ....origin.'

'We hereby certify that the prices stated in this invoice are the current export market prices for the merchandise described therein and we accept full responsibility for any inaccuracies or error therein.'

Normally, such invoices will need counter-signing by a Chamber of Commerce and perhaps, in certain cases, legalization by the Iranian Embassy.

Care may have to be taken on invoices with regard to geographical place names etc. With Iran no mention should ever be made of the 'Arabian Gulf' but rather 'Persian Gulf'. Obviously, to certain other countries the reverse could be true.

Consular invoices

This type of invoice is distinctly different, it being a particular set of forms which have to be purchased from and used in conjunction with the appropriate embassies or consulates. Their use has diminished dramatically over the years and they represent nowadays a rather specialized requirement. Two examples are given below in order to gain some idea of the type of detail encountered. The charges quoted are naturally always subject to change.

Honduras

'Five copies, to be completed in Spanish, obtainable at London Consulate at £6.00 per set of five: must show values in US dollars and 8% of total FOB value at the foot of the invoice to facilitate calculation of charge in Honduras; must not be included in CIF value.

To be presented to the Consulate: Legalization fee £12.50. Letter of correction £12.50.

Immediate legalization may be obtained for additional fee of £12.50.

Consular invoices not required for shipments of a CIF value less than US dollars 25 or for air freight shipments irrespective of value.'

Paraguay

'Four copies required for each consignment, to be in Spanish, obtainable at the London Consulate at £24.00 per set of four. Consular legalization fee is 5% of the FOB value of the original invoice payable in Paraguay at port of destination. A Consular invoice is now advisable for consignments under US dollars 100 especially for direct shipments.'

Specific invoice forms

As has been mentioned, these are usually encountered when some special form of duty preferential system is in operation, or when there is a need to scrutinise very carefully the relationship of the export price to the exporter's current domestic value. Examples of such forms would be the Customs invoice called for by Canada. This form was introduced 1 January 1985, aligned to the UN/ECE (United Nations/European Commissions on Economy) and takes into account the GATT valuation system referred to earlier in this Chapter.

Similarly, many countries may require this specific type of form which can be purchased from commercial stationers and used by the exporter. Or, in a large number of cases, it may possible for the shipper to employ his own basic commercial invoice but to ensure that all the required data is incorporated to satisfy the particular country's Customs requirements.

Much progress has been made over recent years towards this growing international standard of invoicing but care must always be taken to ensure whether ordinary commercial invoices plus specialized data can be used, and if it can, is any prior approval of the invoice format required?

Many of the above-mentioned types of specific invoice incorporate declarations of the origin of the goods and indeed are often referred to collectively as 'Certificates of Value and Origin' (CVO). It is here that SITPRO systems can be of immense benefit since they have developed a wide variety of 'overlay' systems. By this means, specialized invoices can be produced *within* the framework of the exporter's own documentary systems as the overlays can contain the specific text and data required by individual countries.

Set out below is a list of the main categories of information that may be required in these types of invoices.

(a) Importer (name and address)
(b) Purchaser – if other than importer (name and address)
(c) Vendor (name and address)
(d) Exporter – if other than vendor (name and address)
(e) Consignee (name and address)
(f) Description of the imported goods, including marks and numbers, number and kind of packages and characteristics
(g) Quantity
(h) Total weight (net and gross)
(i) Unit selling price
(j) Current domestic value or open market value in exporting country at factory/warehouse/port of shipment and details of any export subsidies or similar benefits received in the exporting country

(k) Conditions of sale and terms of payment (i.e. sale, consignment shipment, leased goods, etc. Whether prices are FOB, CIF, duty paid, etc. Details of discounts and other special arrangements)

(l) Currency of settlement

(m) Place of direct shipment to overseas market

(n) Date of direct shipment to overseas market

(o) Transportation charges, expenses and insurance to the place of direct shipment

(p) Transportation charges and expenses from the place of direct shipment

(q) Insurance costs from the place of direct shipment

(r) Amount for packing costs incurred by the buyer.

There is a growing tendency also for many international invoices to require the insertion of the appropriate trade classification of the merchandise. The most widely used is of course the CCCN. Some thought may have been given to this aspect; there can at times be differences in interpretation of the particular classification heading which could lead to incorrect duty assessment because, it will be remembered, the CCCN is not merely a statistical number but also indicates the possibility of a direct linkage to a given rate of duty. Consequently, there may be the need for some liaison between exporter and importer concerning the correct application of the tariff heading.

Of all areas where it is essential to have accurate reference material, the invoicing sphere is perhaps the most outstanding as requirements change so quickly and are of such vital importance. The following are three major works of reference which, apart from providing much valuable information in many spheres, are of particular value in checking the invoicing requirements of an importing country: Croner's *Reference Book for Exporters*; Tate's *Documentation Guide* and National Westminster Bank's *Monthly Export Bulletins*; *Consular Requirements* – a supplement to *Lloyd's Loading List*.

Such works of reference enable a constant watch to be kept on a country's documentary requirements and for an accurate profile to be maintained.

Certificates of origin

As has been seen above some export invoices may in fact require some indication of the actual origin of the goods being shipped. The concept is an important one and it must be confessed that there can often be many uncertainties. There is much virtue in the exporter having a firm grasp as to the particular reasons lying behind the need for a country to insist upon certificates of origin or at least some form of declaration from the exporter when goods are being imported into an overseas market.

First of all let us consider the particular formats in which questions of origin can materialize, namely:

(1) A sample statement on the export invoice prepared by the exporter, remember the example given earlier for France.
(2) Some official form such as the standard type available from Chambers of Commerce. (see *Figure 8.2*)
(3) A geographically-specialized standard form such as the Arab British Chamber of Commerce (ABCC).
(4) One of the specific type of Certificates of Value and Origin (CVO) referred to above.
(5) Although perhaps not strictly comparable, forms such as T2L, T2 and EUR.2 which in their own specialized way have a bearing upon origin.

Another point which may have to be borne in mind is also the possible distinction between 'originated in ....' and 'manufactured in ....'.

There is really no basic international definition as such pertaining to origin, although the gradual process of harmonization is constantly taking place. Certainly between trading groups such as EEC, FTA, LAFTA and GATT agreement; of necessity there must be a large degree of coalescence of basic understanding and systematization of rules of origin, but as has been said, much depends on the reason behind the need for this information.

Some main reasons are:

(1) In order to qualify for some form of preferential treatment regarding the levying of duty.
(2) To administer the application of a quota agreement.
(3) Backing up a political sanction.
(4) To link the purchasing of goods to some form of financial assistance.
(5) Statistical purposes.

The degree of importance and precision of the rules will therefore depend to some extent upon the relevance of the above-mentioned reasons.

For the purposes of tariff preference the most widely encountered basic rules can be illustrated by those formulated by a series of EEC directives which can extend origin from either 100%

1 Consignor	No. PQ 100251	ORIGINAL
2 Consignee	**EUROPEAN COMMUNITY** ——— **CERTIFICATE OF ORIGIN**	
	3 Country of Origin	
4 Transport details (Optional)	5 Remarks	
6 Item number; marks, numbers, number and kind of packages; description of goods		7 Quantity
8 THE UNDERSIGNED AUTHORITY CERTIFIES THAT THE GOODS DESCRIBED ABOVE ORIGINATE IN THE COUNTRY SHOWN IN BOX 3 **SOUTH BUCKS. & EAST BERKS. CHAMBER OF COMMERCE & INDUSTRY** Place and date of issue; name, signature and stamp of competent authority		
19	South Bucks. & East Berks. Chamber of Commerce & Industry	

DTI/XP/1302

Figure 8.2 Chamber of Commerce certificate of origin

origin in the country concerned, or for goods processed or utilizing components and materials from other outside countries, can nevertheless certify that the last, substantial economically-justified process has in fact been carried out in that exporter's country. In some cases the criteria may be based upon a simple percentage, e.g. 50% or 75%, etc.

On the other hand, if it is a question of political boycott or economic sanctions then the definition of origin may be much more exacting and relate to materials or components that, although substantially processed in the exporting country, may nevertheless be excluded since they contain items obtained from a country which itself is on a 'black-list'.

In the case of, say, developing countries which are recipients of financial aid, loans or lines of credit, it is becoming customary in some cases to link that aid to purchases from the donor country and thus bring about the need to identify origin.

Therefore, this segment of documentation usually linking up with the invoice, will in most cases play an important role in the importer's clearance of goods and any mistakes could lead to quite severe penalties or sanctions, and in any case delays or problems with the buyer's authorities.

9 Methods of payment

The payment risks

No export transaction can be said to be successful until payment has been received for the goods delivered overseas, and the proceeds have been safely credited to the exporter's account. Many of the problems of payment, such as length of credit period, checking the financial stability of a customer, or debt recovery, are similar to those that any businessman would face in the home market of the United Kingdom. In exporting, however, we are bound to be faced with a number of extra risks, the main elements being associated with the following:

(1) Distance; even if not geographically distant, the market is nevertheless across a frontier.
(2) Different legal systems provide varying frameworks within which the exporter must decide his payments policy.
(3) Currency differentials – fluctuating rates of exchange.
(4) Greater difficulty involved in the recovery of goods.
(5) As export markets tend to become more competitive, there is greater demand by customers for longer credit periods and discounts, etc.
(6) As most exporters usually find themselves dealing with a number of different countries, so there must be more risk of their sales contracts being upset by political disturbances or sudden unexpected foreign legislation.

Bearing in mind the above considerations, it would seem that the broad background of export finance which it is our task to consider can be examined under three main headings, namely:

(1) The mechanics of arranging for and receiving payment.
(2) Foreign exchange and its relation to the sales quotation, and the receipt of the proceeds.
(3) The institutional aspect – the operations of the banking mechanism – factoring and credit support facilities.

(2) and (3) will be considered separately in the next chapter.

Bound up with the mechanics of payment will, of course, be the process of invoicing, but this is rather a specialized aspect and is dealt with separately in Chapter 8. Also, the export practitioner will have to be very flexible in his outlook, as there are many different ways in which companies handle their exports payment. In many, the accounts departments look after drawing of bills of exchange and preparing invoices, whereas in other organizations shipping and payment functions are linked directly together, within the framework of a self-contained export department.

There is little doubt that many potential exporters are dissuaded by payment problems. Time and time again companies relate difficulties they have experienced in getting their money, and often a first venture into the export field results in either a number of bad debts, or payment being made over so protracted a period that all the profit has disappeared. Again, failure to allow for variations in rates of exchange or banking charges results in a severe shock when the money is finally credited to the exporter's account.

Many of these problems are due to a complete lack of appreciation of the technology of overseas payment and a failure to adopt a systematic approach and a well defined export price and payments policy. In many cases, companies complain that long credit periods are required by their overseas customers and that to grant them would completely 'kill' the business because of the cost involved. Often this type of problem can be solved by the skilful use of bills of exchange and co-operation with bankers or one of the many excellent export houses that exist in this country. Certainly there is no lack of basic information on this subject. The banking system in particular produces excellent booklets giving advice on methods of payment and showing how they themselves can assist. It would appear that the main need is for a really integrated approach. This approach should start right from the quotation stage when the price and conditions are being formulated for presentation to the potential overseas buyer.

A vital point to bear in mind is that it is not merely a question of a passive response to a customer's enquiry, such as deciding whether or not we can concur with their wishes. For example, a customer's enquiry or order may stipulate payment 'thirty days after acceptance of the goods' on an open account basis. In this case, the export manager must judge whether this is possible or not and respond accordingly. But many enquiries from overseas do not in themselves mention any payment terms and therefore the reaction to this aspect, and what payment terms are put forward, is going to have an important bearing on a company's competitive position. This will call for a dynamic and creative response. Thus the payment terms and conditions will function as vital marketing tools in their own right.

Formulation of a payments policy

A check list covering the salient features of a payment policy could be as follows:

(1) Financial position of country of import.
(2) Any exchange restrictions in importing country.
(3) Any restrictions applying to methods of payment in importing country.
(4) The credit standing and financial status of the buyer.
(5) Type of product involved in the transaction, e.g. consumer products, consumer durable goods, capital equipment or perishable goods.
(6) The amount of money involved in the transaction.
(7) The particular customs of the trade in question.
(8) Competitive conditions.

It is not suggested for a moment that the above represents the exact order of priority but, broadly speaking, this should represent the various stages to be checked when deciding payment policy. Items (1), (2) and (3) listed above are largely outside the control of the exporter, but his success or otherwise in export transactions will depend to a great extent upon his knowledge and assessment of all the relevant factors. Whatever the financial standing of the overseas customer may be, and however glowing the credit status report is, the financial and political position of the importer's country will be a controlling factor. The buyer may have the funds and be only too anxious to meet his commitments, but should his country experience economic, political or exchange difficulties, it may be forced to impose restrictions on payment abroad. This could lead to delay in settlement or even complete loss. Therefore, it is essential that consideration be given in the first place to the financial, economic and political standing of the importer's country, before deciding on the credit terms and methods of payment that are to be extended. Obviously, the larger the sum of money and the longer the period of credit involved, the more vital becomes the factor of country and exchange risk.

Credit status enquiries

Having analysed the position of the importing country, the exporter's policy will then be determined by his knowledge of the customer's financial and credit status. To this end he may enlist the help of

   (a) his bank,
   (b) overseas agent,
   (c) a fellow manufacturer – trade references,
   (d) a professional institution specializing in the credit status,
   (e) organizations concerned with the exporter's business, such as the Export Credits Guarantee Department.

Banks offer help to an exporter by using their extensive overseas intelligence networks in order to check the financial standing of prospective buyers. Most banks possess a vast amount of information about the standing of traders and agents in all parts of the world and, in addition, can always make further enquiries through their numerous overseas correspondents. Reports by telex and cable can generally be obtained at very short notice and banks can be assisted in their efforts by the provision of the name of the bank where the overseas importer keeps his account, if this information is in the possession of the exporter. The bank should always be given a clear idea of the extent of the actual monetary value and length of credit involved. A potential customer may be perfectly sound for business up to, say, £10 000 every three months, but should an exporter begin to speed up the tempo of his business with this particular account, his customer may be tempted to commit himself beyond his financial resources. If the course of business extends over a long period of time, it is advisable to renew the enquiries periodically, at least once every twelve months.

If a good agency system has been built up by the exporter in his various overseas markets, this too, should be a source of information about customers. An agent can supplement banking information by knowing how the prospective customer is paying his bills, his stock levels, the quality of his products and services and how his business is being affected by the prevailing economic climate. As in all agency relationships, a great degree of care is necessary when selecting agents and acting on their advice. It is imperative in the field of financial status enquiries that the exporter has the utmost confidence in his agent. It might be very tempting for an unscrupulous agent, thinking only of his commission, to introduce a wide circle of customers, some perhaps of doubtful financial stability. On the other hand, with a del credere type of agent, it is an integral part of his duties to ensure that business is done only with financially sound and reliable companies.

A very good source of information, and one which is not always exploited, is the mutual exchange of information between fellow manufacturers and exporters. Often this can be done without either party revealing any secrets or betraying any confidences. Sometimes it is possible to obtain more intimate details which can be of help in framing credit policies. For example, an exporter might learn that a particular importer is very sound and highly respected in the trade, but simply has a bad habit of invariably taking a long time to settle debts, even though he does eventually discharge his obligations. This might help in making decisions as to whether to offer cash discount incentives or to employ documentary bill systems.

The UK is also very well served by professional institutions which specialize in credit reporting services. This is usually done on a subscription basis and provides such information as company history, management, operations, reputations, affiliations, financial structure, payments record and credit opinions. Most of these organizations also offer a specialized consultancy service particularly suitable for unusually large initial orders or contracts or where heavy capital commitments are likely to be incurred. For rapid, on the spot decisions, which are so necessary for the present day export manager, there are a number of registers and directories produced by such organizations which give a lot of background information on a wide range of companies throughout the world.

Such organizations as the Export Credits Guarantee Department incorporate credit status checks as an integral part of their insurance facilities.

The skilful use of the above-mentioned services is becoming an essential part of modern management technique and the investigation of customer financial standing is as important to corporate strategy as the forecasting of production and sales schedules.

Having therefore considered the importing country and the status of the overseas customer, the exporter will begin to investigate the alternative methods of payment open to him and relate them to specific transactions in order to achieve a balance between on the one hand making the offer attractive and competitive to the customer and on the other, minimizing the risk and ensuring the maximum profit return obtainable.

Methods and mechanics of payment

There are six basic methods of obtaining payment for export orders and in order of preference for the *exporter* they are

(1) Cash with order,
(2) Documentary letter of credit,
(3) Documentary bills,
(4) Open account,
(5) Payment against goods shipped on consignment, and
(6) Compensation or barter trading (see Chapter 10).

From the trader's point of view, the ideal method of payment would be by cash, either on confirmation of order or when the goods are ready for shipment. This state of affairs is only likely in a seller's market as it is naturally very unpopular in the eyes of importers. Nevertheless, in cases where specialized products are being made to suit an individual customer, it may be essential to ask for at least part of the purchase price with the order. This would apply particularly in instances where the exporter may be locking up considerable capital in the preparation of the goods. In practice, compromises are often sought. As an example, a scientific instrument manufacturer, with an order to equip a whole medical laboratory in France, might arrange to receive one-third of the purchase price with the order when the contract is signed, one-third when the consignment is ready for shipment and the balance when the apparatus has arrived, been installed and is operating satisfactorily. Many variations of this theme will be found in different trades. The other extreme is presented by the methods of *payment against consignment* or *open account* and these are the most favourable methods from the point of view of the importer.

Goods shipped on consignment enable the exporter to place his stocks in the importing country (usually through an agent) without actually giving up the title of ownership. For certain categories of goods, particularly fast-moving consumer and consumer durable products, the maintenance of stocks will be essential. Normally, the exporter will not receive any payment until sales are made in the overseas country and the goods may always be sent back to him without liability on the part of the importer/agent. Stocks therefore might represent a considerable amount of capital locked up in the overseas market and exposed to all the normal commercial, plus political and climatic risks. Consignment operations are best based on a well-established and trusted agency system.

Open account

The open account system is now rapidly becoming the main method of settlement in today's international trading practice. The mechanism is simple. The exporter despatches his goods, sends the appropriate documents of title, e.g. bills of lading, together with his invoice, and then has to wait for payment. The goods thus pass into the customer's possession before payment is made and the exporter has only the protection of the particular contract of sale. Should anything go wrong it is always difficult and expensive to enforce this by methods of litigation. There is no special procedure or documentation, however, and therefore the open account system has the advantage of simplicity; terms and methods of settlement need attention. Very often some form of discount incentive is offered for prompt payment and might be phrased as follows:

2½ per cent discount for payment within seven days,
or terms nett monthly account.

Sales on this basis are usually settled by periodic remittances against statements.

Transmission of funds

It is important that the method of transmission of the proceeds be allowed for, and to a large extent this applies to the operation of *all* methods of payment. Funds might be transferred in the following ways.

(1) TT (telegraphic transfer) – this is a speedy method of settlement as the importer's bankers will send to their correspondent in the exporter's country a coded message ordering that the seller's account should be credited accordingly.
(2) AMT or MT – in this case funds would be transferred either by Air Mail Transfer or ordinary Mail Transfer.
(3) SWIFT messages: A computer network at present utilized by about 800 European, North American and Hong Kong banks. The initials stand for The Society for Worldwide Interbank Financial Telecommunication.
(4) Cheque – the importer, depending upon the exchange control regulations of his country, may be able to discharge the debt by simply sending a cheque to the exporter who would pay this into his bank.

(5) Banker's Draft – this is really a cheque drawn by one banker on another.

It is really important that these methods of transmission of funds should be considered because the cost of each method will, of course, vary. The quicker methods of transmission will obviously cost more, but at the same time they will have a bearing on the time period during which the exporter is out of funds. It could make a big difference as to whether the proceeds of an export transaction are received in a day or so by cable or perhaps take up to three or four weeks to arrive by ordinary mail.

In times of high interest rates this might amount to a considerable out-of-pocket expense for the exporter.

This 'float time' therefore will have an impact upon the cash flow aspects of an exporter's business and needs to be carefully monitored. The starting point of such control might utilize the following type of calculation:

$$\text{Breakeven point} = \frac{\text{TT cost} - \text{MT cost} \times 36\,500}{\% \text{ interest rate} \times \text{days saved}}$$

(SITPRO Check List for International Money Transfers)

Circumstances suitable for 'open account methods':

(1) If the exporter knows his overseas customer very well and has had previous commercial dealings.
(2) Inter-company relationships.
(3) The importing country is politically stable and financially sound.
(4) Where one is selling in competitive, sophisticated and demanding markets such as department stores in France and Germany, where one has to compete in terms of price and methods of payment as well as quality and delivery.

So far then we have considered two extremes, namely 'cash with order' on the one hand, and 'open account' and 'consignment' on the other. We have seen how they affect both importer and exporter, the relative risk on either side and the fact that none of them needs any complicated documentary procedure. Between these two extremes many export consignments are paid for by 'documentary bills' or 'documentary letters of credit'. Banking experts calculate that about 30 per cent of the export business of the UK is still conducted by these methods of payment. The essential characteristic of these documentary systems is that the exporter in one way or another makes the handing over of the appropriate documents of title of ownership (such as bills of lading, air waybills, etc.) dependant upon payment by the

importer. With this characteristic is usually coupled the employment of bills of exchange and the close liaison of the exporter and
importer with the banking mechanism.

Documentary bills

In outline, the exporter despatches his goods, assembles the
appropriate documents (in most cases consisting of bills of lading,
invoices and insurance certificate – a typical set of documents for a
CIF contract); he then arranges to draw a bill of exchange on the
importer and this 'documentary bundle' is then transmitted
through his own bank (known as the 'remitting bank') and
presented to the customer through a bank overseas in the buyer's
country (known as the 'collecting Bank') on either a D/P
(Documents against Payment) or a D/A (Documents against
Acceptance) basis. In the former case, the customer will usually
receive the documents and therefore title to the goods, when he
pays to the overseas correspondent bank the appropriate sum of
money. With documents against acceptance he will receive the
documents of title when he 'accepts' the bill of exchange, namely
signs his name and date across the face of the bill undertaking to
pay the sum involved at some specific time in the future. For
example, a 90-day bill duly accepted would mean that it would
mature (become payable) 90 days from the date of acceptance.

The basic mechanism of the documentary bill is illustrated in
Figure 9.1 but before we consider the processes and procedure
more closely, it would be useful to study further the bill of
exchange.

Although mainly the term 'bill of exchange' is employed in the
text it should be appreciated that in commercial practice the term
'draft' is often encountered.

The bill of exchange

This document has a very long history and was widely used in
international commerce in the Middle Ages. It is defined in the
Bills of Exchange Act 1882 as

> '... an unconditional order in writing, addressed by one person
> to another, signed by the person giving it, requiring the person
> to whom it is addressed to pay on demand or at a fixed or
> determinable future time a sum certain in money to or to the
> order of a specified person, or to bearer.'

This must be closely adhered to in order to ensure that a fully
negotiable instrument is produced and, indeed, the wide use of
bills of exchange (or drafts as they are also called) stems from their
negotiability which enables them to be passed from hand to hand.

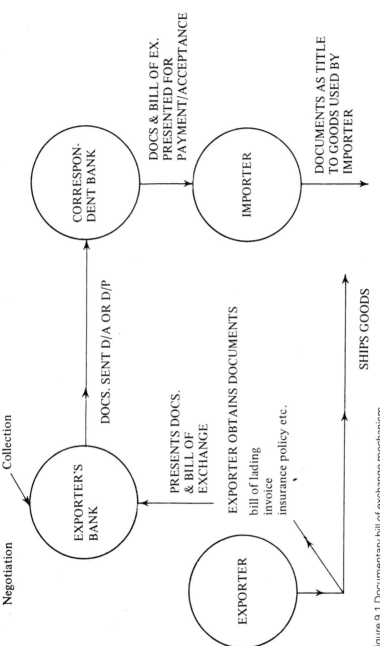

173

Negotiation

Collection

CORRESPON-
DENT BANK

IMPORTER

DOCS & BILL OF EX.
PRESENTED FOR
PAYMENT/ACCEPTANCE

DOCUMENTS AS TITLE
TO GOODS USED BY
IMPORTER

DOCS. SENT D/A OR D/P

EXPORTER'S
BANK

PRESENTS DOCS.
& BILL OF
EXCHANGE

EXPORTER OBTAINS DOCUMENTS

bill of lading
invoice
insurance policy etc.

SHIPS GOODS

EXPORTER

Figure 9.1 Documentary bill of exchange mechanism

At this stage it must be borne in mind that this type of bill can be used in other fields of trade but here we are concerned principally with the bill of exchange linked to the handing over of shipping documents, in other words a 'documentary bill'. Bills can be employed without being so linked and are then known as 'clean bills', but care must be taken not to confuse these with clean bills of lading.

There are three parties to a bill of exchange, namely the drawer, drawee and payee. Applying this to a typical export transaction we have

Exporter (drawer) draws bill on drawee (importer), usually instructing that the sum of money should be paid into exporter's account (payee).

In most cases the drawer is also the payee but this need not necessarily be so; it might be that instructions are given for the proceeds to be placed to the account of a third party.

The terms 'documents against payment' and 'documents against acceptance' have already been mentioned and these provisions would decide whether the bills were 'sight' or 'period' or 'time bills'.

The 'tenor' of the bill is the period of time involved. This can be clarified by looking at the following specimen:

No. 1246

LONDON, 5th September, 19.... For £2500
At ..... Sight ...... pay this ..... SOLE BILL of Exchange
.... to the Order

of .... OURSELVES ....
    TWO THOUSAND FIVE HUNDRED POUNDS

Value Received ....   for and on behalf of
    A. B. PEINTURE   Silcometer Instruments
                         Ltd
To ....
    LILLE, FRANCE
                            ....
....   Secretary/Accountant

In the above case, the drawer and payee is, of course, Silcometer Instruments Ltd.; the drawee is A.B. Peinture. The sum of money which is shown in both figures and words is £2500.

The specimen indicates that the 'tenor' of the bill is 'at sight'. If the bill had been a time bill (sometimes referred to as 'usance bills') for a period of, say, 60 days, then the wording could have been 'At sixty days after sight'. In the absence of any other arrangements, the 60 days would 'run' from the date of acceptance or 'sighting'. Note that the wording is 'Pay this sole bill' which means that in this case only one copy of a draft is actually being drawn. It might well be that two copies are, in fact, needed and in this event, one copy would have the wording 'Pay this *first bill* of exchange, second of same date and tenor unpaid'. The second copy would read 'Pay this *second bill* of exchange, first of same date and tenor unpaid'. Note that each copy is by itself negotiable but once one has been paid or accepted, then the other one is void. In practice this operates in much the same manner as sets of bills of lading.

The wording 'value received' suffices to indicate the aspect of 'consideration' which is necessary for a contract between the exporter and his customer. Sometimes a note can be put on the face of the bill which identifies more specifically the nature of the transaction, e.g. 'Shipment of 20 compressors per the ss *Arabella*'. The bill is normally signed by the parties empowered by the individual company to sign cheques, i.e. secretary, accountant, or director and should be endorsed by the drawer on the back of the draft itself.

When completing bills, the following additional points should be noted:

(1) Bills may be printed by companies rather like their cheques, or pads of forms can be obtained from commercial stationers. The number shown on the specimen, 1246, would be an identification number which would be entered on a counterfoil for retention. If necessary, a bill can be typed on a plain piece of paper.
(2) United Kingdom bills no longer need stamp duty at home but an exporter should not overlook the possibility of some form of revenue stamp charge being incurred in some overseas countries.

In the above example of the 60-day draft it was seen that the bill would mature in 60 days after the date upon which the drawee made formal acceptance. In practice, however, there could be other options. For example, a bill could be drawn payable at 60 days from date of bill of lading or some other reference point such as date of ship's report. This approach can, of course, inject a greater degree of flexibility, but when employing such maturity periods, the legal definition of 'at a fixed or determinable future date' must not be overlooked. Any unacceptable vagueness in the wording could weaken the legal character of the bill of exchange.

Looking back on our definition, therefore, we find: 'requiring the person to whom it is addressed to pay on demand (*sight*) or at a fixed or determinable future time (*time*).'

Negotiating and discounting bills of exchange

An important by-product of the use of bills of exchange in export transactions is the possibility of utilizing them with the object of obtaining advances of money. This is usually carried out by the widely used process of 'negotiation' and also in some cases the 'discounting' of bills. Care must be exercised in the use of the term negotiation because obviously it is a widely-used term in a general commercial sense, i.e. negotiating a contract or negotiating a set of documents, etc. In the sphere of negotiating bills of exchange we normally mean that when, say, sending drafts and documents on either a D/P or D/A basis through the bank, arrangements are made whereby the bank in question actually pays the exporter immediately. Subsequently, when the bills have been appropriately honoured, the bank will debit the exporter with the cost of interest, etc., involved in the time taken for them to obtain reimbursement and the time they initially credited the exporter. Naturally, there will be a relationship between the prevailing rates of interest and other charges and the exporter's cash flow needs.

The second, perhaps more formal term 'discounting', implies that a term bill, duly accepted, is discounted by a bank or other financial house. This means that the exporter will receive the value of the bill *less* a discount rate. The bank will hold the bill and then present it to the drawee (acceptor) for due payment. It is probably true to say that formal discounting tends to be more applicable to larger value transactions involving larger companies and not so widely encountered as negotiation operations.

Discounting is very often linked with the term 'acceptance credits' whereby a bank agrees to have the bill drawn upon it for acceptance. For this they charge an acceptance commission which can vary between about 1/8–3 per cent per annum. The accepted bill can then be discounted in the financial market through banks or specialized discount houses who will of course charge a discount rate. Such bills will generally be referred to as 'bank bills' and may of course attract rather more favourable rates (from the point of view of the exporter) as compared with 'trade bills' drawn and accepted by commercial companies. With the latter, of course, there will not be any acceptance commission.

Discount rates are usually based on a straight per annum basis and this is calculated on a 365-day period for sterling bills and 360 for foreign currency drafts.

A typical basic formula therefore used by exporter when viewing discounting financially, might be as follows:

£50 000 sterling draft at 90 days
prevailing per annum discount rate 14.50%
Acceptance Commission 1.2% per annum
Therefore:

$$£50\,000 \times \frac{14.50}{100} \times \frac{90}{365}$$

= amount of discount	= £1787.67
= acceptance commission	= £ 150.00
	£1937.67
Amount received by exporter	£48 062.33

The above may serve just to give a very approximate idea of the magnitude of the discounting process. Of course many fluctuating factors will affect the rate itself depending upon prevailing cost of money market rates, parties involved and underlying creditworthiness of the drawer and acceptor, etc. Another important factor for consideration is the question of 'recourse'. A bill discounted 'with recourse' means that should the holder of the bill find that on maturity it is dishonoured (i.e. not paid by the drawee) then recourse may be had to the drawer (i.e. exporter) for reimbursement of the money. 'Without recourse' would mean that the discounter would accept the credit risk in the event of non-payment by the drawee. The Bill of Exchange Act allows for such bills to be drawn *sans recours*. Naturally, bills with such clauses have less attraction for a discounter and have limited use in normal bill discounting.

When considering such instruments as bills of exchange it should be borne in mind that promissory notes may also be encounted and are provided for by the Bill of Exchange Act. In essence, instead of the exporter drawing a bill for acceptance he may ask for the importer to issue his promissory note making a legal promise to pay a sum of money in a prescribed period of time.

Nowadays, in international trade there is considerable use of 'forfaiting' which is a rather specialized international type of financing against bills and notes. This will be referred to in Chapter 10 against the wider background of finance and credit institutions.

Banks, when making advances of money or negotiating bills may sometimes require a degree of security over, say, shipping documents. This may lead to the exporter providing the bank with a 'letter of hypothecation'. This, in a sense, provides the bank with a degree of rights against the documents and goods in the event of non-payment. Reference is usually made to 'general letters of hypothecation' lodged by the exporter to cover the whole of the export business being transacted over a prescribed period of time, or a 'specific letter' which will apply to one particular transaction.

Of course, no form of bill can give the exporter absolute security. His customer can go bankrupt before the bill is presented or matures. We have seen that if it is discounted, he is normally liable to ultimate recourse by the bank. Nevertheless, a customer who has accepted a bill of exchange and wishes to keep a good reputation will have a much more difficult job in delaying payment compared with, say, an invoice and statement on open account terms. It is said that a trader dishonours a bill 'at his peril'.

Before considering the final procedural stage of the documentary bill, namely presenting the documents to the bank and the completion of the appropriate bill lodgement form let us sum up the type of situations suitable for D/P and D/A payment.

Situations suitable for documents against payment are

(1) Exporter may not be wholly satisfied with the financial status of his customer and therefore retains control of his goods by keeping the documents (in the banking channel) until payment is received.
(2) It does at least provide the importer with the opportunity of obtaining the documents (and title to the goods) at the time he makes payment. In fact it is almost like a COD transaction.
(3) Markets where it may be relatively easy to dispose of goods may exist in the overseas country.
(4) The sight draft, together with shipping documents, will often enable an advance to be obtained from the bank.

Situations suitable for documents against acceptance are

(1) Competitive selling conditions; customer wants to obtain, use or dispose of goods before he pays.
(2) A compromise for the exporter. He has parted with the goods before actual payment has been made but he does

hold an accepted bill which he may discount and obtain money quickly, albeit at a discount rate.

(3) The exporter can always reserve the right to unload the cost of credit on to the customer by putting an interest clause on the bill, which means, in effect, that although the importer will be getting credit for the period of 30, 60, 90 days, etc., he will have to add an interest rate to the principal sum shown on the bill when it arrives at maturity.

Charges incurred on bills of exchange

These charges include

(a) Possible overseas stamp duties.
(b) Negotiation charges by bank in UK.
(c) Collection charges by correspondent bank overseas.
(d) Cost of transmitting proceeds, cable, air-mail, etc.
(e) Interest charges between time when money is paid in to bank overseas and time it is received in UK.
(f) Sometimes question of exchange rate conversion.

A typical structure of a banking charge might be as follows:

Documentary Bills for Collection/Negotiation
0.25% (0.25 per £100). Min £8, max £50.
For negotiations, interest to cover the period until the bank receives reimbursements from its correspondents will also be charged.

Again, these figures are intended only to provide some quantitative idea of potential costs and could vary between banks and customers.

Wherever possible, the various charges and interest rate, etc., should be made quite clear when conditions of sale are being arranged. Nothing is more conductive to bad customer relationship than for there to be misunderstanding on this point. Equally, it is important, when calculating the selling price and profit margin, that these types of charges be included in the computation. There has grown up a practice of inserting various types of clause on the bill of exchange which clarify the position as to the party bearing responsibility for the particular charges involved.

Examples are

(a) 'Payable at the current rate of exchange for sight drafts on New York'.

(b) 'Payable at banker's selling rate for telegraphic transfers on London'.
(c) 'Payable with stamps and all charges for collection'.
(d) 'Payable with interest at … per cent per annum from date hereof until the appropriate date of arrival of remittance in London'.
(e) 'Payable with exchange and stamps as per endorsement'.

It will be seen that the above provide a number of permutations to cover the various charges, and some, such as (d), actually specify the mode of transmission of proceeds. Some clauses are traditionally used in certain countries, e.g. (d) which is often called the 'Eastern Clause'. Clause (e) is used where bills are going forward for negotiation mainly to Australia or South Africa, and in these cases the negotiating bank will insert an exchange figure endorsement on the bill so that the importer has to pay sufficient of his own currency to cover the various charges incurred, including possibly an interest element as well.

The point must be emphasized that clauses should not be used unless both the exporter and importer understand them completely and are in agreement. Equally, they should only be used when it is appropriate for the specific country or customary for a particular trade. Banks should be consulted as to the suitability of a clause and, as will be seen, there are plenty of facilities for clarifying these instructions when the lodgement form is completed and handed to the bank with the documents.

Collection order or bank lodgement form

A form is obtained from the bank and although it may vary from one bank to another, it will require basically the same treatment. The layout for a typical bank collection order is shown in *Figure 9.2*. This form is completed (generally in duplicate) and handed to the bank, together with the bill of exchange duly drawn and accompanied by the appropriate documents (usually bills of lading, invoice, insurance policy and perhaps other peripheral documents such as certificates of origin). A glance at the form will show that in the light of our above analysis we should know what instruction to issue, i.e. D/A or D/P charges, the mode of transmitting the documents and how the proceeds should be remitted. These are just a few points which deserve mention. Most important is the instruction regarding 'protesting'. If a customer refuses to accept or pay a draft correctly drawn and in conformity with the agreed contract, then this bill is technically dishonoured. Should litigation be resorted to, then it would be necessary for the bill to be 'noted' by a public notary in the overseas country and then officially 'protested', which is a legal process. This whole question is a delicate one and needs very careful handling as the processes can vary considerably from country to country. It is also quite easy to cause a perfectly sound customer considerable annoyance by protesting a bill. A typical cause of trouble is the synchronization of presenting bills with the actual arrival of a carrying vessel. Suppose a consignment of 300 cases of Carbon Black has been shipped to a customer in Italy who is going to use this in the process of manufacturing rubber. The terms of payment may have been agreed at 120 days to enable him to obtain the raw material and complete his manufacturing process. What may happen, is that the documents pass through the banking system and are presented to the importer immediately for acceptance. It may well be that because of unexpected delay the ship is not due to arrive for some time, and perhaps it might be up to 14 days before the Italian importer could hope to obtain delivery. As the 120 days would usually begin to operate from acceptance date, it would, in effect, cut down the period in which the importer would have the goods before payment is due. For voyages to more distant markets the effect would be even more noticeable. This can be taken care of by instructing the bank to re-present on arrival of ship and therefore no protesting at this stage is required. In any case, most exporters would instruct a bank to notify them if the draft has not been honoured, giving the reason and asking for fresh instructions before there was any question of protestation.

With regard to charges, it will be noticed that there is an opportunity to waive them if they are refused by the drawee. When small sums are involved, and where perhaps the question has not been clarified in the order, this is often a commonsense way of avoiding troublesome correspondence and a disgruntled customer.

For some time, the banks in a large number of countries have been interpreting documentary collection procedures in accordance with 'Uniform Rules for Collections' laid down by Brochure 322 of the International Chamber of Commerce. The rules state together (under the heading of 23 Articles) basic definitions, methods of presentation and payment, acceptance, protesting and charges, liabilities and responsibilities. They will form an ideal reference point between the exporter, the remitting and collecting banks and the overseas importer. To give an idea of the depth and approach of the rules, the following are some specimen Articles.

FOREIGN BILL AND/OR DOCUMENTS FOR COLLECTION

1976/77

Drawer/Exporter	Drawer's/Exporter's Reference(s) (to be quoted by Bank in all correspondence)
Consignee	Drawee (if not Consignee)
To (Bank)	For Bank use only

FORWARD DOCUMENTS ENUMERATED BELOW BY AIRMAIL. FOLLOW SPECIAL INSTRUCTIONS AND THOSE MARKED X

Bill of Exchange	Comm'l. Invoice	Cert'd./Cons. Inv.	Cert. of Origin	Ins'ce Pol./Cert.	Bill of Lading	Parcel Post Rec'pt.	Air Waybill
Combined Transport Doc.	Other Documents and whereabouts of any missing Original Bill of Lading						

	ACCEPTANCE	PAYMENT			Protest	Do Not Protest
RELEASE DOCUMENTS ON			If unaccepted ⟶			
If documents are not taken up on arrival of goods	Warehouse Goods	DoNotWarehouse	and advise reason by		Cable	Airmail
	Insure Against Fire	Do Not Insure	If unpaid ⟶		Protest	Do Not Protest
Collect ALL Charges			and advise reason by		Cable	Airmail
Collect Correspondent's Charges ONLY			Advise acceptance and due date by		Cable	Airmail
Return Accepted Bill by Airmail			Remit Proceeds by		Cable	Airmail
In case of need refer to					For Guidance	Accept their Instructions

SPECIAL INSTRUCTIONS:

1. Represent on arrival of goods if not honoured on first presentation.

Date of Bill of Exchange	Bill of Exchange Value/Amount of Collection
Tenor of Bill of Exchange	
Bill of Exchange Claused:—	Please collect the above mentioned Bill and/or Documents subject to the Uniform Rules for the Collection of Commercial Paper, ICC Brochure No. I/We agree that you shall not be liable for any loss, damage, or delay however caused which is not directly due to the negligence of your own officers or servants.
	Date and Signature

BANDA ALIGNED EXPORT DOCUMENTATION PACKAGE FORM No. 124

4122E OZALID (U.K) LTD

Figure 9.2 Documentary bill collection order: above—general purpose; facing page—specific bank issue

1 Copy to be retained by the Bank

To National Westminster Bank PLC ↻

| | Customer reference |
| | Bank reference |

Branch _____   Date _____

Please **Collect** the following clean or documentary Foreign Bill of Exchange payable abroad, subject to the conditions on page 4.

Bill of Exchange Details

Date Bill due (if fixed maturity date) | 0 5 8 | | | | | | | eg 030578 = 3rd May 1978

Drawer's Name | X 5 8 5 | | |

Drawee's Name and Town | X 5 8 2 | 1 |

| X 5 8 2 | 2 |

Bill is already accepted | 0 7 5 | | 1 = Yes

Document Details

Document delivery instructions | X 0 6 9 | | 1 = Against payment   2 = Against acceptance   3 = In accordance with special instructions below.

	Statement	Freightnote	Cons Inv	Cert of Origin	Insce Cert/ Policy	Negotiable Bills of Lading	
Number of major documents	5 9 2	S	F	C	R	I	B	Only appropriate boxes must be completed.

Number of Invoices | 4 7 8 |

| 1 | 2 | 3 | 4 | Boxes 1 and 2 = No to make up Bill amount
Boxes 3 and 4 = No of copies per invoice (incl original)   Number forwarded   of   Number Issued   When used complete all boxes

		No	Description
Number of Other Documents	5 9 3	1	
	5 9 3	2	
	5 9 3	3	
	5 9 3	4	

Insurance arranged by | 0 5 4 | | 0 = No insurance   1 = Drawer   2 = Drawee

Charges Instructions

Drawees Responsibility | 0 6 1 | | NWB charges   Agents charges   1 = Yes   0 = No   When used complete all boxes. Drawer is assumed responsible for all charges if left blank.

Drawer's Responsibility | 0 6 2 | |

Charges to Drawee may be waived if refused | 0 6 3 | | 1 = No   0 = Yes

Case of Need

Name and full address of Representative abroad who may be contacted in case of need | 5 8 6 | 1 |

| 5 8 6 | 2 |

| 5 8 6 | 3 |

Case of need's powers | 0 6 6 | | 1 = Unconditional   0 = Advisory

Special Instructions to Collecting Bank Abroad

Bill is to be returned after acceptance | 0 6 7 | | 1 = Yes

Protest instructions | 0 7 0 | | | Box 1 = on non-acceptance   Box 2 = on non payment   When used complete both boxes   1 = Yes   0 = No

Payment/Acceptance may be delayed until arrival of goods | 0 5 5 | | 1 = Yes   0 = No

Cable required | 0 6 8 | | Leave blank if cable not required
1 = Cable proceeds/dishonour-charges to drawee.   4 = Cable proceeds-charges to drawee
2 = Cable proceeds/dishonour-charges to drawer.   5 = Cable proceeds-charges to drawer
3 = Cable dishonour-charges to drawer

Other instructions

Reference should be made to General Instructions on page 4 | 5 9 5 | 1 |

If insufficient space enter:- 'see letter attached' and include letter as an item in 'Number of | 5 9 5 | 2 |

| 5 9 5 | 3 |

Article 7

Documents are to be presented to the drawee in the form in which they are received, except that remitting and collecting banks are authorized to affix any necessary stamps, at the expense of the principal unless otherwise instructed, and to make any necessary endorsements or place any rubber stamps or other identifying marks or symbol, customary to or required for the collection operation.

Article 9

In the case of documents payable at sight, the presenting bank must make presentation for payment without delay.

In the case of documents payable at a tenor other than sight the presenting bank must, where acceptance is called for, make presentation for acceptance without delay, and, where payment is called for, make presentation for payment not later than the appropriate maturity date.

Article 17

The collection order should give specific instructions regarding protest (or other legal process), in the event of non-acceptance or non-payment. In the absence of such specific instructions, the banks concerned with the collection have no obligation to have the documents protested (or subject to other legal process) for non-payment or non-acceptance.

Any charges and/or expenses incurred by banks in connection with such protest or other legal process will be for the account of the principal.

It will be seen from the above specimen Articles that a careful relation of these to the bank's instructions form will bring the whole processing of documentary bills into a very clear perspective. Note how Article 9 makes clear the importance of synchronizing the presentation with the availability of the goods, as we have already discussed with our example of the Italian importer.

When considering the collection order instruction form it is important to remember that in some cases for various reasons, the exporter may instruct the bank to send forward documents but without actually drawing a bill of exchange. This may be quite common when, perhaps, dealing with a well-known regular customer. Both parties might be quite content to rely upon payment against the invoice and handing over of the documents without the formality of the bill of exchange. This is sometimes referred to as 'Cash Against Documents' (CAD). Care must always be taken to distinguish this from 'Open Account Terms'.

Looked at from another angle, bills could be drawn and sent through the bank *without* any shipping documents, namely a 'clean collection'. The *documentary* collection is of course the synchronization of the handing over of documents only against a prescribed mode of payment or acceptance of drafts.

Documentary commercial letters of credit

As has been seen, next to cash-with-order the most favourable method of payment for the exporter is a form of Letter of Credit (L/C). With many qualifications, which will be considered, the letter of credit places a sum of money in the United Kingdom to be made available upon presentation of the required documents. Compared with the documentary bills already discussed, it will be seen that the L/C provides for payment to be made in the *exporter's* country and also that the *importer* is himself responsible for undertaking all the necessary initiative and procedure in establishing the credit (although this would often be done in close consultation with the exporter).

The parties to an average L/C transaction will be: (1) the importer (opener), (2) the bank in the importer's country (issuing bank), (3) the bank in the exporter's country (advising correspondent bank), and (4) the exporter (beneficiary).

The loose term 'credit' can at times be a little confusing, and should not be confused with private letters of credit provided by banks for persons travelling abroad. In banking terms, a commercial documentary letter of credit has been defined as:

'.... a promise given by a banker to accept or honour bills of exchange if drawn on him or, if drawn on the buyer or the issuing or paying bank by the seller, to negotiate them, security for the payment or acceptance of the obligation to pay reposing in the pledge of the documents of title to the goods exported, in the special property thus obtained'.

The above definition reveals a factor of fundamental importance to major areas of export documentation, namely the use of the documents as title to the goods. It is this which makes the manner in which bills of lading are made negotiable so vital, i.e. to order and endorsement.

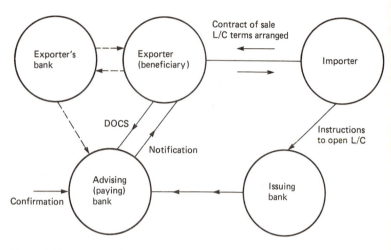

Figure 9.3 Letter of credit diagram

The security offered by letters of credit has to be earned because, as we shall see, this method must by the very nature of the relationship between importer/banks/exporter demand a great degree of precision of procedure, with particular reference to the type and description of the shipping documents required.

Figure 9.3 can be used to trace the main mechanism of the L/C process which goes through the following stages:

(1) Importer completes a bank form which contains full instructions on how the L/C should be constructed. See *Figure 9.3.*

(2) Importer's bank transmits the L/C to its correspondent bank in the exporter's country.

(3) Correspondent bank notifies exporter, sends him the detailed L/C containing all the requirements and showing the value of the credit and length of time for which it is valid.

(4) Exporter then proceeds with shipment and careful collection of all the required documents, ensuring that they conform one hundred per cent with the L/C.

(5) When documents are complete, exporter presents them (usually together with a draft) to correspondent/advising bank who checks them for conformity and then pays according to the terms of credit.

(6) Note that in the diagram, the exporter's bank is also shown. This is because many exporters pass the documents through their own bank for checking and presentation. There is no absolute necessity for this, but it can often be more convenient for the exporter to have his own bank's assistance and guidance.

A point of some significance is the fact that the overseas customer has to complete his instruction form for his bank and it is important to remember that the professional exporter will, wherever possible, ensure that when the details of the transaction are being formulated, he will give every assistance to his customer by advising him of any details which streamline the credit requirements. In practice, many orders get off to a bad start by insufficient co-operation on this point and, as soon as a L/C arrives, the exporter finds it contains requirements which are impossible for him to fulfil and immediately correspondence, delay and expense can result. A simple example is that of part shipments being permitted. Broadly speaking, and all other things being equal, an opening bank would tend to favour a L/C for a complete shipment but if there is a possibility that the exporter may have to ship more than one consignment, then advance information on this point to the customer might lead him to state in the letter of credit under 'partial shipments/not permitted/ permitted', deleting 'not permitted'.

So far, the credit has been referred to in general terms but it is important that the practitioner is able to identify the main types that are encountered in trade, and to distinguish between their relative advantages and disadvantages. Letters of credit can be classified as follows.

Types of letters of credit

(a) Revocable credit

As the name suggests, this type can be cancelled or modified by the customer (the opener of the credit) without prior approval of the exporter. Obviously this leaves much to be desired since, although the credit is opened and notified by the bank, by the time the goods have been shipped and the documents presented, the customer may have changed his mind and cancelled the credit. The exporter, who has shipped the goods, is therefore left with the documents on his hands. This type of credit is really only a mere mechanism for providing payment and guidance to the exporter as to the form the documentation should take.

(b) Irrevocable credit

This is far more common to letters of credit and constitutes a legally binding agreement between beneficiary/issuing bank and importer to the effect that (amongst other things) the credit cannot be revoked or modified without prior agreement of the beneficiary. Here the exporter has the degree of security that is more classically associated with credits.

There remains one important aspect which has a bearing upon the above two types of credit, namely that of 'confirmation'. We have seen that an irrevocable letter of credit establishes a bond between the issuing bank and the exporter, but this bond will not extend to the notifying or paying bank in the UK unless the credit is confirmed. If the credit is unconfirmed, we would expect to see clauses on the L/C, such as

> 'We have no authority from our clients either to confirm this credit or to guarantee the acceptance/payment of drafts drawn thereagainst. The credit is therefore subject to cancellation without notice and the above particulars are for your guidance only.'

or

> 'We have not been requested by the above named (issuing) bank to confirm this instrument, and consequently this advice conveys no engagement on our part.'

It is important that there should be no misunderstanding on this point. If the letter of credit is not confirmed, then the UK bank which has notified the exporter is not itself a party to the credit but is acting merely as an agent, authenticating the origin of the credit instructions, but not automatically obliged to negotiate drafts drawn. Supposing some political or economic crisis should arise which prevents, at the last moment, the issuing bank (in the importer's country) from transferring currency to the UK advising bank; then if the L/C was unconfirmed, the advising bank would not necessarily be obliged to pay against the credit when the exporter presents the documents.

Confirmation of a L/C by the advising bank is, then, normally desirable and we would look for a clause such as

> 'The above credit carries our confirmations and we hereby agree with the drawers, endorsers and holders in due course of drafts drawn under this credit that such drafts will be duly honoured on presentation provided that all the terms and conditions of the credit have been complied with.'

Therefore, provided that the exporter meets all the conditions of the credit, and produces the necessary documents within the period of validity, the advising bank will ensure that the money is there to honour the draft without recourse to the drawer. The exporter will then always hope to receive wherever possible an 'Irrevocable Confirmed Letter of Credit Without Recourse' and this would represent, as far as is ever humanly possible, one hundred per cent certainty of obtaining payment. The validity of the confirmation must, however, always be considered. The mere description on a letter of credit to the effect that it is confirmed may not always be sufficient if the bank does not possess the correct status. If there is any doubt, a London Bank should be consulted and sometimes asked to add its confirmation.

Naturally, the varying degrees of security of letters of credit will mean a scale of charges which vary accordingly. Some specimen charges are:

For confirming a credit (inclusive of the fee for advising) 0.10% (£0.10 per £100), Minimum £25, each three months or part thereof, charged for full period of validity at time of confirmation.

Amendment Fees £12.50 per amendment.

Although prima facia charges are for the account of the opener, that is of course the customer, the exporter must be prepared for sometimes having these charges or at least a part of them debited to himself. It is a point therefore that must be considered both in relationship to pricing and costing and customer relationship.

The above are only intended to give some idea of magnitude as far as possible charges are concerned, and detailed reference should be made to individual banks where charges will often vary.

It is important to remember at this juncture the aspects considered against D/P and D/A bills of exchange have certain factors in common with letters of credit, namely drafts drawn against credits can also be at sight or term and may be paid, accepted, negotiated or discounted. Clearly the major difference is that in credit operations various banks are more directly implicated in the various financial undertakings. The degree of involvement as has been seen will vary with such aspects of irrevocability and confirmation.

In the general course of export trade, a number of different variations on the letter of credit theme may be found, all designed to fit in with special types of transaction and trading pattern. The following represent the main categories likely to be encountered.

Transferable credit

Can be transferred by the beneficiary to another party. Often used by brokers or merchants where they can assign part of the credit to the primary supplier. Where the credit is split, it would be known as a 'transferable and divisible credit'. These credits are not often encountered in the UK but can be found frequently on the Continent.

Revolving credit

One which is automatically renewed as amount of credit used by drawing of bills. Very useful in a case where a buyer places a contract for regular, say monthly, shipments. If he normally buys £5000 monthly, then the revolving credit would be opened for £5000 and, as the draft is drawn and honoured, another £5000 would automatically become available.

Countervailing or back-to-back credit

Used in triangular or entrepôt trade. For example, a UK merchant may receive an order from Sweden for some heavy machinery which he is buying from Germany. The Swedish customer opens a L/C in London in favour of the merchant. If the German supplier requires cash against documents, to avoid being out of funds the merchant may arrange with his bank to use the existing L/C as a security for the opening of a credit in Germany in favour of the supplier. The bank is able to keep control of the operation, maintaining shipping documents throughout as security and charging the merchant accordingly when final settlement has been made.

Anticipatory or packing credits

In this case the credits permit payment (usually partial) against documents obtained early in the shipping process; for example, warehouse receipts, dock receipts, wharfinger's receipts. Final payment is generally made when the bill of lading is produced. Used a lot in raw materials, commodity and livestock transactions. In the wool trade there is usually a clause in the credits known as the 'red clause' which enables such advances to be made to the beneficiary.

Stand-by credits

This type of credit now finds mention in UCP (1983) (see below) which described it as often used in lieu of a performance guarantee. As such it may transpire that the underlying guarantee is linked to the performance being symbolized by the provision of some documentation and procedure. It usually functions in rather the opposite way to other credits, inasmuch that the applicant will be the seller arranging a standby credit with a bank to underpin his obligation to carry out a contractual performance.

Deferred credits

There has been growing use of deferred payments being made a condition of a credit without the drawing of a time draft. Instead of a period of time being, say, geared directly to a bill maturity date, i.e. 90 days from sight, it could be 90 days from receipt and installation of goods and issued of an acceptance certificate by the buyer. There are many variations possible.

Mention has been made several times of the high degree of precision which is necessary when attempting to fulfil the requirements of a letter of credit. Because the documents represent the goods called for by the opener of the credit, the bank has no alternative but to reject any documents which do not conform precisely to the credit. This is known as the doctrine of 'strict compliance'. We have seen that for documentary bills, the ICC has formulated a series of internationally-accepted rules. Similarly, for letters of credit, we have brochure No. 400, the *Uniform Customs & Practice for Documentary Credits*. In a series of 55 Articles it defines terminology and sets out the rules and procedure to be adopted by banks which conform to these rules. In practice, this represents the main international trading countries. Usually there will be a note somewhere on the credit to the effect that 'I/We agree that, except so far as is otherwise expressly stated, this Credit will be subject to the Uniform Customs and Practice for Documentary Credits (1983 Revision) International Chamber of Commerce Brochure No. 400.'

This brochure should be studied in detail by the practitioner since, quite apart from the formulation of procedure and terminology, it is a mine of information about letters of credit and the usual type of documentation used against such credits. Let us take a look at six specimen Articles.

Application to Open a Documentary Credit
(To be completed in triplicate, Typescript or Block Capitals, The
Applicants attention is drawn to the notes overleaf. If necessary,
further guidance may be obtained from your Account holding Branch.
Where applicable boxes should be marked by an 'x'.)

Original
(for despatch by
Branch to
Overseas Branch/IBC)

Leave this space blank

To be completed by Branch (NWB29)

Tel No
and ext

To: National Westminster Bank PLC ↻

1   Please open an ☐ **Irrevocable** ☐ **Revocable Credit**
    by ☐ Airmail ☐ Tele-transmission.
    If tele-transmission, send ☐ Brief Details ☐ Full details.
    (If contact cannot be made, despatch will be effected by Cable unless otherwise instructed in Section 23)

2   For Bank use only

3   Applicants full name and address _____

    _____ Account Number _____

4   In favour of (Full name and address) _____

    _____

5   Currency and amount (Figures and words) _____

    _____

6   Available either by (A) Drafts at ☐ sight ☐ _____ days sight ☐ _____ days from date of _____

                          Or (B) By Deferred Payment (without drafts)   ☐ _____ days from _____

7   Expiry date _____ In (Country) _____

8   Documents must be presented within _____ days from On Board Date of the Marine Bill of Lading or from the
    date of 'Taking in Charge' as indicated upon any other Transport Document but in any event not later than the expiry date of the
    Credit. (If left blank 21 days will be applied)

    Documents Required

9   ☒ _____ Signed Invoices

    Either number 10 or number 11 must be completed

10 ☐   Insurance ☐ Certificate ☐ Policy in negotiable form dated not later than the On Board Date of a Marine Bill
    of Lading or the date of 'Taking in Charge' as indicated upon any other Transport Document covering the
    ☐   CIF or ☐ CIP value plus _____ % and the following risks: 'War, Strikes, Riots and Civil Commotions'

    ☐   Institute Cargo Clauses 'A'   (All Risks)   **These alternatives will be accepted**
    ☐   Institute Cargo Clauses 'B'   (WA)   **unless otherwise instructed**
    ☐   Institute Cargo Clauses 'C'   (FPA)

    Any other risks required:

11 ☐   Insurance will be cared for by the undersigned and I/we undertake to keep the Merchandise adequately covered by Policies
    of Marine, War, Fire and other usual risks in approved companies and to lodge with you or produce upon demand the policies if
    called upon to do so and in the event of failure to do so you may insure the Merchandise at the expense of the undersigned.

12 ☐   Full set (if issued in more than one original) Clean 'On Board' Marine Bills of Lading issued to order and Blank Endorsed
    marked ☐ Freight Paid ☐ Freight Collect ☐ Notify (Full name and address)

13 Full set (if issued in more than one original):   Signed by the Carrier or signed on behalf
    ☐   Combined Transport Bill of Lading issued   of the named Carrier by his Agent marked
        to order and Blank Endorsed   ☐   Freight Paid
    ☐   Railway Consignment Note
    ☐   Roadway Bill   ☐   Freight Collect ☐ Notify
    ☐   Other Document of Movement _____   (Full name and address)

    Evidencing goods consigned to (Full name and address)

Figure 9.4 Application form to open a letter of credit

Article 5

Instructions for the issuance of credits, the credits themselves, instructions for any amendments thereto and the amendments themselves must be complete and precise. (*Figure 9.4* illustrates a typical Credit Opening Instruction form.) In order to guard against confusion and misunderstanding, banks should discourage any attempt to include excessive detail in the credit or in any amendment thereto.

Article 11

  (a) All credits must clearly indicate whether they are available by sight payment, by deferred payment, by acceptance or by negotiation.
  (b) All credits must nominate the bank (nominated bank) which is authorized to pay (paying bank), or to accept drafts (accepting bank), or to negotiate (negotiating bank), unless the credit allows negotiation by any bank (negotiating bank).
  (c) Unless the nominated bank is the issuing bank or the confirming bank, its nomination by the issuing bank does not constitute any undertaking by the nominated bank to pay, to accept, or to negotiate.
  (d) By nominating a bank other than itself, or by allowing for negotiation by any bank, or by authorizing or requesting a bank to add its confirmation, the issuing bank authorizes such bank to pay, accept or negotiate, as the case may be, against documents which appear on their face to be in accordance with the terms and conditions of the credit, and undertakes to reimburse such bank in accordance with the provisions of these articles.

Article 34

  (a) A clean transport document is one which bears no superimposed clause or notation which expressly declares a defective condition of the goods and/or the packaging.

Article 37

  (a) Unless otherwise stipulated in the credit, the insurance document must be expressed in the same currency as the credit.

Article 41

(c) The description of the goods in the commercial invoice must correspond with the description in the credit. In all other documents, the goods may be described in general terms not inconsistent with the description of the goods in the credit.

Article 47

(a) In addition to stipulating an expiry date for presentation of documents, every credit which calls for a transport document(s) should also stipulate a specified period of time after the date of issuance of the transport document(s) during which presentation of documents for payment, acceptance or negotiation must be made. If no such period of time is stipulated, banks will refuse documents presented to them later than 21 days after the date of issuance of the transport document(s). In every case, however, documents must be presented not later than the expiry date of the credit.

These examples will indicate the precision and detail required but reference should be made to the full brochure when administering credits. This should also be supplemented with Brochure 411 which gives a detailed interpretation of the Articles and compares them with the previous 1974 rules which were superseded in October 1984.

A check list for letters or credit

(1) Type of letter of credit – irrevocable, confirmed, etc.
(2) Period of validity – expiry date.
(3) Are there any other limiting time factors? Does bill of lading have to be dated before a certain time? Is there any expiry date of import licences or currency permits?
(4) Are description of goods, names, etc., correct?
(5) Check total value of credit. It is enough? What currency? Are there any tolerances?
(6) What documents are called for, such as bills of lading, air waybills, certificates of shipment, etc? Are clean shipped-on-board bills required? Should they be made out 'to Order'? Is part shipment or transhipment allowed?
(7) If insurance is involved, is a policy or certificate called for? What value should be covered for insurance purposes?

Where should claims be made payable and in what currency? And, of course, what risk cover is required?

(8) Are there any special peripheral documents called for such as quality certificates or inspection notes? Check to see if inspection by an outside authority is specified.

(9) Check port of departure and port of destination.

(10) Ensure that the advising bank's instructions as to the manner in which the draft should be drawn and presented are carefully noted and adhered to.

(11) Pay particular attention to any specialized documents, such as consular invoices and certificates of origin, that may be required. Remember that many of these will have to be obtained from outside sources such as consulates and chambers of commerce. The cost and time involved in obtaining them must be borne in mind. Check most carefully to see if there are any obligations as to the dating of these documents. For example, it may sometimes be the case that a certificate of origin must be dated prior to the date of a despatch document such as bill of lading or air waybill.

(12) Finally, remember that a letter of credit should be checked immediately it is received. Any discrepancies or confusing items can often be easily rectified by contacting the customer via the bank. This is often easy if done in the early stages but becomes expensive and annoying to the customer if left to the last moment.

It will be seen from the above that, when the letter of credit is being analysed, reference to the *Uniform Customs and Practice* brochure (where applicable) will enable many points to be clarified.

Dealing with discrepancies

Naturally, the experienced exporter will expect transactions to proceed smoothly and for his draft and documents to be negotiated without difficulty. There will, however, always be the possibility that some problem or discrepancy will arise and it is necessary, therefore, for the various techniques of overcoming these problems to be studied.

The following sequence should be followed, wherever possible, when the exporter finds himself with documents which contain some irregularity or discrepancy which has resulted in the bank refusing to meet his draft.

(1) First of all, the discrepancy should be rectified by the exporter himself, if at all possible.
(2) On many occasions it might be preferable to cable the customer requesting an alteration in the terms of credit to enable the paying bank to meet the draft.
(3) The exporter may use a form of indemnity countersigned by his own bank against which he may receive payment.
(4) Payment is made under reserve.
(5) The documents are sent forward for collection.

Some examples of the conditions which might give rise to the above courses of action are as follows:

(1) When presenting the documents, a mistake might have been made on the exporter's commercial invoice. It is usually a simple task for a fresh invoice to be prepared and re-presented.
(2) A bill of lading may have been 'claused' when the credit calls for 'clean shipped on board' bills. In this case, the exporter cannot himself rectify the position and, if time permits, he might be able to cable the customer asking for the claused bill to be made acceptable under the credit.
(3) Very often there is not time to take the necessary steps to rectify discrepancies and the possibility of using a letter of indemnity has to be considered. This document, signed by the exporter and countersigned by the exporter's bank, would be submitted to the paying bank with the documents. The draft could then be paid but, of course, when the documents arrive for the overseas importer, he would be free to reject them if the discrepancy in question ran counter to his wishes and he perhaps regarded it as of fundamental importance. In such a case as this, the paying bank could then return to the exporter and ask for reimbursement under the terms of the indemnity.

In many cases the use of a letter of indemnity can act as a very useful form of 'lubrication' and help considerably in certain types of discrepancies. It might be the only possibility in a case where a 'stale' bill of lading is involved. After all, the customer will still normally want the goods, but the indemnity might well protect the importer's interest should heavy warehousing or other expenses be incurred due to the delay.

It should, however, be realized that in practice the raising of a letter of indemnity must to some extent weaken the 'without recourse' concept which is, as we have seen, of paramount importance to the exporter in letter of credit transactions.

(4) 'Payment under Reserve' is basically the same approach as the letter of indemnity but in this case there is no formal document and the payment is made under a verbal agreement and represents a high degree of trust between exporter and banker.

(5) Should the case arise where a set of documents contain numerous serious discrepancies, then it may be impossible to employ any of the above techniques. In this event, the bank will not pay against the exporter's draft but simply send the documents forward to the issuing bank overseas who will present them to the importer, who will then have the choice of either accepting or rejecting them and paying or not paying. This in effect has reduced the original letter of credit to the status of documents against payment.

It must again be emphasized that banks, when handling and paying against letters of credit, are really bound within very precise limits to observe the doctrine of strict compliance and therefore the requirements called for by the letter of credit must be precisely observed. Again, let us also remember that we can in many instances render assistance to our customer by advising him when he is on the point of completing his instructions to his bank calling for the establishment of the documentary letter of credit.

A most important publication, *Letter of Credit Management and Control,* published by SITPRO (January 1985) as a result of a joint survey with Midland Bank, gives some very interesting data on the degree of problems and expense incurred by UK exporters when operating against credits. It estimates that the annual cost to exporters as a result of discrepancies, delays and cost of guarantees, etc., amounts to a total of about £50 million. Some example figures are given of a comparison with a previous SITPRO survey in 1981.

	MIDLAND BANK 1983–84	4 BANKS 1981
Total sets prepared for survey	1215	3261
Total sets unpaid on first presentation	595	1778
Failure Rate	49.0%	54.5%
Documents late*		
Credit expired	9.5%	7.3%
Late shipment	4.6%	4.4%
Late presentation	11.9%	7.9%

*These are just some of the reasons for rejection.

It can be seen that in three years there has been an improvement in efficiency but obviously much more remains to be done.

10 Aspects of foreign exchange and credit institutions

In the previous chapter we examined the various mechanisms of payment encountered in international trade. They were examined from the viewpoint of security, competitiveness and cash-flow considerations. This, however, was really only half the story and the exporter needs to be familiar with other elements of the overall financial background to overseas payments. Essentially, these fall under two broad headings, namely: the possibility of foreign exchange units entering the picture; plus the need to appreciate some of the financial, credit insurance institutions and other sources of finance that may be available. In some high-level and sophisticated transactions there may even be the question of barter deals.

A working knowledge of various schemes of credit insurance and availability of lines of credit and inter-government financing may, in many cases, make all the difference to penetrate export markets. Perhaps no other field in exporting has seen such a rapid development as the financial operations devised and operated by banks, governments, state trading organizations, factors and varieties of merchants banks, etc.

Let us first of all consider some of the salient features encountered with the possible involvement with foreign exchanges.

The mechanism of foreign exchange

A feature of foreign trade is that in many cases the question of foreign currency and exchange rates will arise at some time during the transaction. It may of course transpire that the exporter will transact orders expressed in his own currency, i.e. dollars, francs or sterling, and of course some currencies do not take upon themelves international roles. Consequently, from say a UK exporter's point of view, the sterling unit will often be employed. In other cases, however, the overseas importer will pay an equivalent sum in his own currency unit, e.g. dollars, to pay his debt to a UK exporter who normally will receive his payment in the UK in sterling.

The first practical questions which face an exporter when dealing with such a situation are as follows:

(1) How will he express his quotation? In sterling or in the currency of his overseas buyer?
(2) Is an exchange variation possible and, if so, how much risk is there of losing money owing to this variation?
(3) What steps can he take to remove the risk?

It should be borne in mind at this early stage that in many countries various forms of exchange control may operate and needless to say these will have a profound effect upon the currency options open to both exporters and importers.

Before considering the above in detail, let us look briefly at the mechanism of exchange rates. In a sense, a foreign exchange transaction, resulting from trade between countries, is a system which operates by inter-bank settlements. Let us assume a UK exporter has sold goods to a customer in Paris. That customer, in order to pay the exporter, will arrange to have his franc account at his own bank debited to the value of the invoice for the goods. The UK exporter will expect in due course to have his sterling account credited by the corresponding amount. By one method or another, therefore, the francs debited to the importer's account have to be transmuted into sterling credited to the exporter.

Usually this will, of course, be arranged between, in this case, the French and United Kingdom banks and this could be done in two ways.

(1) The French bank could literally use the importer's francs to buy the necessary amount of sterling to meet the needs of the UK exporter, or
(2) the French bank could credit the account of the United Kingdom bank in francs, which would mean that in effect the UK is holding francs in Paris.

In the latter case the UK bank would credit the sterling account of the exporter and would itself hold francs in Paris. Thus, we might represent the position graphically, as in *Figure 10.1*.

Now suppose that at a later stage a French exporter secures an order from a buyer in the United Kingdom. In this case, the UK importer's sterling account will be debited and the French exporter's account in francs will be credited. What could well happen is that the UK banking system could utilize francs from the

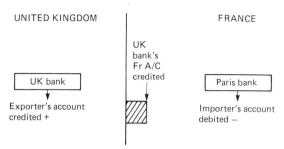

Figure 10.1 International banking mechanism

account it was holding in the French bank. Should the UK banks hold no francs in this way, then they would have either to buy francs in the foreign exchange market, or the French bank could elect to hold a sterling balance to its credit in, say, London. In other words, in the case of a French export the procedure would have been reversed.

Naturally, inter-banking operations nowadays are much more complicated due to the existence of the Euro Market which in essence means that foreign currencies will often move out of their own countries to be borrowed and utilized in overseas financial systems. Such movements, against varying interest rates in the money market, will naturally exert a marked influence on exchange rates.

Nevertheless, the simple example outlined above is sufficient to show that, in order to support international trade, the banking system will find itself either buying or selling foreign currency or at times holding foreign currency balances in other countries. When one enlarges upon this and thinks of the volume of trade throughout a large number of different countries, all involving the exchange of many different units of currency, it will be seen that the net effect of these transactions will have an impact upon the demand for, or supply of, a particular currency unit.

If one regards a unit of currency in the same way as any other commodity, then one could postulate that if the demand for, say, the French franc increased (perhaps because of a large outflow of exports from that country) then the overall effect would be that foreign banks would be buying larger quantities of francs, and the price of the franc in terms of the respective importing countries' currency would increase. It would be possible, therefore, to say at this stage that the exchange rate would be a result of the combined effects of supply and demand for a particular currency unit. Of course, apart from trade causing movements in exchange rates, the combined effect of overseas investment, short-term capital movements and the payment for invisible imports and exports, i.e. shipping, insurance and banking, would all play their parts in shaping rates.

Underlying all these movements, foreign exchange specialists also recognize the concept of the 'Purchasing Power Parity' theory. Briefly stated, this theory holds that the ratio of one currency to another will approximate to the relative purchasing powers of those two currencies in their respective countries. If, for example, £1 sterling in London will buy a parcel of goods costing, say, 12 French francs to buy in Paris, then the exchange rate would be in the neighbourhood of £1 = 12 Fr fr. There are, of course, certain objections to this concept. It is not always easy to compare purchasing habits of different countries and consequently comparable parcels of goods cannot always be obtained. Nevertheless, in the long run, the value of currency compared with those of other countries must of necessity determine the ultimate exchange rate. The various monetary policies practised by different countries, and the UK attempts to combat inflation, are all examples of the practical significance of this theory.

Although mention has been made above of the price of a currency (exchange rate) in terms of another currency, and this likened to any other commodity which can be allowed to respond to the mechanics of supply and demand, there are very great difficulties when applied to foreign exchange. The aim of monetary authorities is usually to stabilize exchange rates to allow for a smoooth flow of international payments and to avoid erratic fluctuations which can become a prey to speculation, thus playing havoc with internal economies. Only a very few countries are in a position to isolate themselves from the effect of international currency. The more involved in international trade a country is, the more exchange rates will affect its internal economy and vice versa. The UK is, of course, an example of a country which is heavily involved in the international currency market.

One of the classic mechanisms which in the past has been used and advocated as a stabilizing factor is the gold standard. Without going into the intricacies of the various types of gold standard, it can be summed up as a system which relates a particular series of currencies to a gold value. If a currency tends to fall in exchange rate compared with other currencies, there will come a point when gold will begin to flow out of that currency's country; conversely, it will flow in if the currency in question appreciates in relation to others. In both cases, the assumption is that the movement of gold will affect the monetary policy and operations of the particular country involved. A drain of gold, for example, should lead to a tight and dear monetary policy, restricting the economy and causing a fall in the price level. This should be followed by a discouragement of imports and a stimulation of exports. Logically this should lead to an improvement of the exchange rate in relation to its gold value and a subsequent flowing back of gold into the country which can then bring about an expansion in industrial activity.

The years between 1919 and 1925 had been a period of instability and fluctuation of exchange rates accompanied in some cases by severe inflation. In 1925 there was a return to the gold standard but in 1931 this collapsed due to certain basic distortions in exchange rates and accumulations of gold in the hands of some countries, notably the USA and France. After the abandonment of the gold standard, a number of countries still maintained their currency link with the UK, notably of course in the Commonwealth system. Despite this, however, the period up to 1939 was one of chronic instability with wide variations in exchange rates and great confusion in the field of international trade.

It is fully appreciated that some of the above and following comments are very largely purely historical. However, it is to some degree necessary to discuss the evolution of various types of international mechanism in order to appreciate and understand current operations and to follow future developments. Indeed, for some time the original six members of the EEC have operated the 'snake-in-the-tunnel' pegged system whereby they have kept their own currencies within a 2.5 per cent fluctuation band within a 4.5 per cent world 'tunnel'. The UK is not yet a party to the European Monetary System (EMS) but obviously, looking to the future, there may be some developments within the field of currency harmonization.

The International Monetary Fund

The end of the Second World War brought in its wake a determination by most of the leading nations to do all in their power to create a stable international economy. The International Monetary Fund was conceived at the famous Bretton Woods Conference in 1944 and established in 1946 with the following principal aims:

(1) To create an atmosphere conducive to international monetary co-operation.

(2) to expand international trade to the benefit of the economies of countries and the resulting full employment of labour and resources.

(3) to achieve this against a background of stability of exchange rates, and

(4) to encourage efficient facilities for settling international debts.

In essence, the IMF sought to achieve the above objectives by:

(a) Accumulating a pool of gold and foreign currency,

(b) the fixing of exchange rates, and

(c) the creation of institutions such as the International Bank for Reconstruction and Development.

The reserve pool of gold and currency

The necessary pool of exchange is obtained by the member countries who originally paid 25 per cent of their quota in gold and the balance in their own currency. A member country's ability to borrow from the fund is based upon the 'drawing Rights' that he obtains and represents a percentage of the quota originally contributed. A country could borrow up to 25 per cent of the value of the quota automatically but larger proportions than this would need the specific approval of the managers of the fund.

When requesting drawing rights from the pool, the country in question must be able to show that it is taking the necessary political and economic steps to improve its position in world trade.

The pool, then, acts as a stabilizer. If a particular country is experiencing a rather hard time and showing a deficit in its balance of payments, and consequently a diminution of foreign currency reserves, the ability to draw from the pool might give it just that breathing space necessary to improve its position. To work smoothly it is essential that countries do not experience persistent adverse trends since there must be a limit to the funds upon which they can draw at the expense of other countries who are satisfactorily maintaining their balance of payments. Equally, it is necessary that at some time the amounts drawn from the pool should be repaid.

Exchange rates

Initially the IMF determined the value of each member's currency in terms of gold and this, therefore, gave rise to a series of official rates of exchange known as the 'par' rate of exchange. There was a certain degree of flexibility built into the scheme obtained by allowing the rates to fluctuate up to 1 per cent above or below the par figure.

The UK, therefore, was bound to take all the necessary steps to maintain the exchange rate within these limits. This it did through the operation of the 'Exchange Equalisation Fund' which in effect meant that the Bank of England would at times *sell* sterling and at other times *buy* sterling in order to maintain the exchange rate. The UK and other IMF member countries were therefore obliged either to maintain their exchange rates within the limits or to seek authority to devalue, or in the case of a very stong currency, to revalue.

Since June 1972, however, most currencies have been free to float and respond to supply and demand, although in the UK, for example, the Bank of England will often intervene to support sterling when it is under pressure.

The inflationary effect of the downward-floating pound has been considerable. *Figure 10.2* shows the abrupt effect upon sterling, and *Table 10.1* shows the declining value of sterling in terms of a wide range of currencies over one-year and two-year periods.

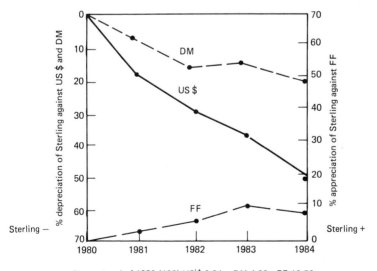

Rates at end of 1980 (100) US|$|2.34   DM 4.62   FF 10.70

Figure 10.2 Depreciation of sterling - 1980-1984

Table 10.1 The sterling effective exchange rate index during 1984 plotted against twenty different currencies (*1975 Average exchange rate* = *100*)

JAN.		FEB.		MAR.		APR.		MAY		JUNE	
3	82.8	1	81.8	1	82.9	2	79.8	1	79.8	1	79.5
4	82.0	2	82.0	2	82.4	3	79.7	2	80.0	4	79.5
5	81.9	3	82.0	5	82.1	4	79.9	3	80.1	5	79.3
6	81.7	6	82.1	6	81.6	5	80.0	4	80.5	6	79.7
9	81.7	7	81.7	7	81.4	6	79.8	8	80.0	7	79.7
10	81.8	8	81.5	8	81.1	9	80.1	9	80.0	8	79.6
11	81.7	9	81.7	9	80.8	10	80.2	10	80.1	11	79.6
12	81.8	10	81.4	12	81.0	11	80.1	11	80.0	12	79.5
13	82.1	13	81.6	13	80.9	12	80.1	14	80.1	13	79.5
16	82.2	14	81.8	14	81.1	13	79.9	15	79.9	14	79.5
17	82.3	15	81.8	15	80.8	16	79.8	16	80.0	15	79.5
18	82.0	16	82.1	16	80.9	17	79.8	17	80.5	18	79.5
19	82.3	17	82.5	19	80.8	18	79.7	18	80.4	19	79.6
20	81.8	20	82.3	20	80.6	19	79.9	21	80.5	20	79.4
23	82.0	21	82.7	21	80.5	24	79.9	22	80.0	21	79.4
24	81.6	22	82.4	22	80.3	25	79.9	23	79.5	22	79.4
25	81.8	23	82.7	23	80.4	26	79.8	24	79.5	25	79.2
26	82.0	24	82.6	26	80.3	27	79.7	25	79.4	26	79.0
27	81.9	27	82.7	27	80.3	30	79.7	29	79.6	27	78.8
30	81.9	28	83.4	28	80.5			30	79.5	28	78.8
31	81.8	29	83.1	29	80.4			31	79.6	29	79.1
				30	80.1						

JULY		AUG.		SEPT.		OCT.		NOV.		DEC.	
2	79.0	1	78.2	3	78.1	1	76.5	1	75.0	3	74.5
3	79.6	2	78.7	4	77.8	2	76.5	2	75.7	4	74.7
4	79.6	3	78.8	5	77.7	3	76.6	5	76.2	5	74.7
5	78.7	6	78.9	6	77.6	4	76.5	6	76.3	6	74.7
6	78.3	7	78.5	7	77.6	5	76.2	7	76.6	8	74.7
9	77.6	8	78.7	10	77.7	8	76.4	8	76.5	10	74.8
10	77.2	9	78.6	11	77.9	9	76.3	9	76.3	11	74.7
11	77.6	10	78.5	12	78.0	10	76.3	12	76.5	12	74.5
12	77.7	13	78.5	13	77.9	11	76.3	13	76.8	13	74.3
13	78.2	14	78.8	14	77.7	12	76.6	14	76.5	14	74.2
16	78.2	15	78.7	17	77.0	15	75.9	15	76.6	17	74.1
17	78.4	16	78.7	18	76.4	16	75.5	16	76.4	18	73.6
18	78.2	17	78.5	19	76.9	17	75.2	19	76.0	19	73.3
19	78.6	20	78.5	20	76.3	18	74.3	20	76.0	20	73.0
20	78.7	21	78.4	21	76.9	19	74.0	21	75.1	21	73.2
23	78.9	22	78.1	24	76.7	22	74.4	22	75.1	24	73.6
24	79.0	23	77.9	25	76.5	23	74.6	23	74.9	27	73.3
25	79.2	24	77.8	26	76.4	24	74.9	26	74.2	28	73.2
26	79.0	28	78.1	27	76.7	25	75.2	27	74.6	31	73.0
27	78.4	29	78.2	28	76.6	26	75.1	28	74.2		
30	78.5	30	78.2			29	74.9	29	74.3		
31	78.5	31	78.1			30	74.8	30	74.9		
						31	74.9				

The result of many of these currency movements is that the UK exporter has to consider very seriously the currency units in which the overseas sales contract is expressed. To the exporter the floating downwards of his currency will makes his goods cheaper in many overseas markets, or enable him to maintain his price but increase the profit margin. The particular price/currency policy adopted will of necessity have to be adapted to the type of commodity, the degree of competition and the volume of sales required. In any case, the exporter will have to be prepared for some of his own costs to rise owing to the corresponding increase which will take place in the price of imports.

How the quotation will be expressed

A trader may of course quote his overseas customer in sterling. In this case, the exchange variation risk is in effect passed to the customer because, when the time for settlement of the debt arrives, the customer will have to pay a sum of his own currency to produce sufficient sterling to meet the invoiced value. However, in a growing number of cases, UK exporters are being called upon to quote in the currency of their overseas buyers. This enables the prospective customer to ascertain the value of the transaction at a glance. In addition, they will know just what sum of money they will be called upon to pay when the time for settlement of the debt arrives. Generally speaking, therefore, a competent exporter will quote in foreign currency thereby being faced with a possibility of an exchange variation.

We will cite the case of a manufacturer who is going to sell £1000-worth of machine tools to a buyer in Paris.

Rate of exchange prevailing at time of transaction = 12.10 Fr–£1.

Therefore quotation for 12 100 Fr, payment within three months.

Now supposing, when the debt is settled in three months, the rate of exchange has moved to 12.20 Fr (i.e. the franc has weakened) then:

$$\frac{12100}{12.20} = 991.80$$

and the exporter has lost a little in the transaction. On the other hand, if the rate has moved to 12.05 (i.e. the franc has strengthened) then:

$$\frac{12100}{12.05} = 1004.15$$

In this case the exporter has gained.

Naturally, if large sums of money are involved in the transactions the gains and losses involved might be considerable and the exporter will have to consider what steps must be taken. These might be as follows:

(1) No action at all if the sums of money are small; experience shows that over the year there are gains and losses which tend to cancel themselves out.

(2) To incorporate an exchange clause in the contract such as 'the price quoted is based on an exchange rate of 12.10 Fr. = £1 and that any variation is for buyer's account'. This type of clause might be necessary, expecially in long-term contracts, but it does leave the customer in a state of uncertainty which in some areas of trade might not be acceptable.

(3) To cover the risk by using the forward exchange market.

Forward exchange cover

It must be remembered that when an exporter concludes an overseas contract there will usually be a period of time before he gets paid by his customer. If his business is being transacted in a foreign currency unit the floating up or down that might take place in exchange rates will to some extent have a bearing upon the amount of sterling he will obtain with the currency he receives when payment actually takes place. The act of covering forward exchange, therefore, is one of attempting to remove uncertainty and to know exactly what proceeds he will receive when the transaction is completed. Depending upon the nature and degree of forward movements it might also be possible to gain a little from the transaction. It should be borne in mind however, that the exporter himself rarely wishes to get involved in exchange speculations and is concerned mainly with stabilizing his trading position.

In the foreign exchange market there are two basic component parts: (1) the spot market, and (2) the forward market. Spot rates are those quoted for immediate sale or purchase of foreign currency. Forward rates are those which dealers or banks quote for (a) purchase of a foreign currency at some point in the future, or (b) sale of a foreign currency at some future date. Usually the popular periods of time are three, six and nine months forward. A simplified example might be represented as follows:

Spot Rate Dutch Guilder   4.48 = £1
1 month forward   2c premium
3 months forward   6c premium

The above are rather simplified figures but they are useful to illustrate the principles involved. It will be seen that the word 'premium' is used in this case. This means that the forward guilder is stronger in relation to the sterling equivalent and to arrive at the actual forward rate we must always *deduct* the premium figure. Therefore, in the above case the one month forward rate would be 4.48 less 2c = 4.46 and, for three months, 4.48 less 6c = 4.42. It will be seen in both cases that *less* guilders will be given in exchange for pounds.

Conversely, we might find that the forward market quotes for a currency at a *discount*.

Spot Rate Dutch Guilder   4.48 = £1
1 month forward   2c discount
3 months forward   6c discount

In this case, the forward guilder is weaker in relation to sterling and this time the figure is added to the spot rate. Thus, the result would be 4.48 plus 2c = 4.50, and 4.48 plus 6c = 4.61.

The exporter will then have to make his decision as to the forward sale of the foreign currency he expects to earn. This decision will be based upon his desire for certainty and the prevailing discount or premium which, in many respects, will in turn be based upon prevailing interest rates existing in the money market. It should also be remembered that, if the forward currency is strong, the exporter will stand to gain from the exchange rate. For example, if a spot rate is $1.30 = £1 and the forward rate $1.29, there will be a 0.01 advantage. Also, it should be borne in mind that a UK importer could be *buying* forward foreign currency to meet his overseas debts and an exporter will be *selling* forward the proceeds of his anticipated sale.

In practice, in the foreign exchange market, two rates are usually encountered, namely the buying and selling rates. For example:

French francs
12.10–12.15

The left-hand figure is the rate of which a bank or foreign exchange dealer will *sell* francs and the right-hand figure is the one at which he will *buy* francs.

We might in this case, therefore, envisage an importer arranging to buy French francs at the rate of 12.10 = £1 to meet his overseas debts and an exporter arranging to sell forward the francs he expects to earn from an overseas transaction at the rate of 12.15 = £1. The difference between the two is the profit margin of the dealer, and there will also be a commission charged.

The above franc rates can now be developed further and shown as follows:

Spot franc	12.10	–	12.15
Forward 1 month	2c	–	1c premium
1-month rate	12.08		12.14
Forward 3 months	4c		2c premium
3-month rate	12.04	–	12.12

Taking the above figures as an example, if an exporter has sold to a customer in Paris on the basis of three months credit, and had quoted in French francs, he could go to his bank or exchange dealer and arrange to sell the francs forward when they were received at a rate of 12.12 = £1.

The undermentioned represent a typical series of rates taken from a financial newspaper which indicates the premiums and discounts encountered in several series of exchange rates for different currencies:

Forward rates	*One month*	*Three months*
Austria	15–13 gr.pm.	40–37 gr.pm.
Belgium	30–24 c.pm.	79–70 c.pm.
Canada	0.52–0.46 c.pm.	1.31–1.23 c.pm.
Denmark	3¼–2 ore pm.	9⅛–7⅞ ore pm.
France	2½–1⅝ c.pm.	5¼–4 c.pm.
Germany (W)	2½–2¼ pfg.pm.	6⅞–6½ pfg.pm.
Holland	2¼–2 c.pm.	6⅜–6 c.pm.
Italy	par–3 lr.disc.	5–10 lr.disc.
Norway	¼ pm.–⅝ ore or.disc.	⅝–1¼ or.disc.
Sweden	3½–4⅜ or.disc.	11⅛–12 ore disc.
Switzerland	2¼–2 c.pm.	6–5⅝ c.pm.
United States	0.57–0.54 c.pm.	1.52–1.47 c.pm.

(Sterling–US dollar = 1.3087)

Depending upon the relationship between exporter and banker, it may sometimes be necessary for a deposit of money to be lodged with the bank when a forward contract is arranged. A typical set of conditions related to a forward exchange contract is set out as follows:

FORWARD EXCHANGE

Terms on which INTERNATIONAL BANK LIMITED enters into contracts with .... for the purchase or sale of foreign currency for forward delivery:

1 On the making of each contract the customer will deposit with the Bank by way of cover either cash or approved security equal to ....% of the sterling value of the currency calculated at contract price and maintain such cover until the completion of the contract.

2 At any time between the making of each contract and its completion the customer, if so requested by the Bank, will lodge and maintain with the Bank, in addition to the deposit referred to above, further cash or approved security sufficient to keep the Bank fully covered against depreciation (in the event of a sale by the Bank) or the appreciation (in the event of a purchase by the Bank) in the market value of the currency.

3 If the customer fails in any respect to fulfil the terms of his contract (including the provision above) the Bank is authorised (but not compelled) to close the contract without notice at the market price of the currency at the time of such default, notwithstanding that the maturity of the contract may not have been reached, and to debit or credit the customer with any resulting difference.

4 Any cover lodged with the Bank in accordance with the above provisions may be applied by the Bank in or towards satisfaction of any resulting difference.

To INTERNATIONAL BANK LIMITED .... Branch

I/We AGREE that the terms set out above shall be deemed to be incorporated in all contracts which from time to time I/We may conclude with you for the purchase or sale of foreign currency for forward delivery.

Date .... Signature ....

In cases where it might be uncertain as to the exact time of receipt of proceeds an 'option' contract could be utilized; for example, *3/4 months option* enabling the exporter to transact the exchange contract at any time between those two periods.

Credit institutions and sources of finance

Both exporters and importers need to be familiar with the various types of financial and credit institutions which will often play both a part in underpinning the credit risk and cash flow aspect or actually provide sources of funds available for international trade. These institutions both large and small will range from private and public sector and also increasingly international and multi-national organizations. They can be broadly categorized as follows:

International lending agencies

One such is the World Bank Group which consists of the International Bank for Reconstruction and Development (IBRD), International Development Association (IDA) and the International Finance Corporation (IFC). Within the broader international framework can be found a considerable number of more specialized agencies such as the European Development Fund (EDF), Inter-American Development Bank (IDB), the Arab Fund for Economic and Social Development (AFESD) and of course many United Nations Organizations such as the United Nations Industrial Development Organization (UNIDO). Naturally, most of these organizations will place considerable stress upon the infra-structures of developing countries.

Export houses

It has already been seen how confirming houses have traditionally acted on behalf of overseas buyers, and nowadays their services extend well into the financial field. Such confirming houses would provide finance to cover the gap between the goods leaving the factory and being purchased by the end user. Credit is provided for periods of 30 to 180 days and is available for all types of goods. Exports of capital goods can often be covered for periods of up to five years. The charges made usually take the form of a commission based on period of credit; average invoice value; volume of business; and the amount of other services provided. Also, interest is charged on an annual basis for the period of the credit granted. Usually, when acting on behalf of the buyer, all charges are borne by him, although he is credited with any cash discounts.

Factors

Another type of institution which enables the exporter sometimes to simplify his trading position is the factor.

In a sense, a factor is an organization which will buy from a trader his outstanding book debts. In practice, the exporter will send all his invoices at specified intervals and will receive a cheque for an agreed initial percentage of the total invoice value usually in the neighbourhood of 80 per cent. In fact, the invoices are assigned to the factor who mails them to the individual purchaser. As payments are made the balance of sums due are credited to the exporter. The cost of most factoring services depending on volume, and turnover lies between 1 and 2 per cent of sales figure. In addition, interest charges are made in the neighbourhood of 1½ to 2 per cent above basic bank lending rates. Factoring of this type originated very largely in the USA but its use is growing in the United Kingdom, where there has been considerable growth in the amount of exports operated via a factoring system.

Some of the major advantages stemming from the use of factors are that they

(1) remove the burden from senior management of credit control and debt collection,
(2) reduce funds tied up in outstanding debts, and
(3) simplify accounting and administrative work involved in sales ledger work.

Important in the field of factoring would be such companies as Alex Lawrie Factors Ltd., International Factors Ltd. and Arbuthnot Factors Ltd. These organizations have widespread international interests, and quite apart from the cash-flow advantage to the exporter is the wide range of services in the fields of collection of proceeds, credit control and foreign exchange which would be carried out on their behalf.

Banks

Moving away from the specific international institutions which operate over the wider field of overseas trade importers and exporters will be utilizing their own banking facilities. The United Kingdom exporter, for example, is fortunate inasmuch as he has at his disposal a wide range of experienced financial institutions which may at times help him in financing his exports. First of all there are the clearing banks such as Barclays, Midland, Lloyds and National Westminster. For many exporters, these are the banks which will provide short- or medium-term credit by means of loans and overdrafts, as well as a considerable amount of short-term credit financing by means of advances against bills or actually discounting these bills of exchange. As has been seen in an earlier chapter, they can provide considerable assistance and advice. They will also act as the main channel through which the various methods of payment, e.g. letters of credit and documentary bills, are transacted.

There is also the fraternity of merchant bankers who are playing an active part in financing exports on a long- and medium-term basis, particularly to the developing countries. They also undertake 'acceptance business', which means that they undertake to accept bills of exchange drawn on them by exporters, thus giving rise to 'bank bills'. These bills can then be discounted by merchant banks who specialize in the field of bill discounting. The bulk of the money used by these bill-brokers is obtained from the clearing banks on call and at short notice at fairly low rates of interest.

Some of the leading merchant banks are as follows:

Baring Brothers & Co. Ltd.	Brown Shipley & Co. Ltd.
Wm. Brandt's Sons & Co. Ltd.	Hambros Bank Ltd.
Kleinwort, Benson Ltd.	N. M. Rothschild & Sons Ltd.
Lazard Bros & Co. Ltd.	S. G. Warburg & Co. Ltd.

Credit insurance institutions

So far, the institutions considered have been those concerned with actually providing finance for the exporter, or smoothing his path by extending credit to his buyer, or enabling him to obtain his money more quickly as, for example, by factoring. In addition, however, different types of 'credit insurance' institutions whereby an exporter can obtain in the form of an insurance policy supporting cover against various risks that may be encountered internationally which might prevent or delay the payment for orders from overseas. These might be private or government organizations, or indeed, combinations of both, such bodies as COFACE in France, HERMES in Germany or Export Credits Guarantee Department (ECGD) in the UK. Appendix A gives a broad outline of some of the various international bodies encountered. In addition to giving actual credit risk cover, such organizations may extend various financial guarantees to buyer or seller, thus making lines of credit more easily available from banking or other financial institutions.

It may be instructive to consider in outline some of the facilities which the UK exporter may utilize with his own ECGD systems.

(1) *Commercial risks* – insolvency of the buyer or failure to pay, which is not due to the exporter's incorrect handling of the contract.
(2) *Buyer's refusal* to accept goods which have been consigned to him under the terms of the contract.
(3) *Political risks* – including import/export licensing restrictions, war, revolution and certain other risks.
(4) *Extra handling*, transport or insurance charges arising from interruption or diversion of the voyage.
(5) *Other causes* of loss occurring outside the UK and beyond the control of the exporter or buyer.

It is to be expected that the cover extended to an exporter will be based upon the assumption that he will at all times trade prudently and avoid any unnecessary risks. Therefore, ECGD will cover a *percentage* of loss to ensure that business is not entered into recklessly, without consideration of the financial consequences; it also ensures that the policy-holder has an interest in pursuing recoveries once a claim has been made. For example, against (1) above the percentage cover would normally be 90 per cent of the loss whereas with (2) the exporter would bear a first loss of 20 per cent of the full original price and ECGD 90 per cent of the balance. For many of the other types of risk ECGD would cover up to 95 per cent and there would be a distinction between the pre-credit risk where loss occurs *before* the despatch of the goods where 90 per cent cover could be expected.

Naturally, there will be many different needs to be catered for by ECGD such as those exporting, say, consumer goods on short-term credit periods on a fairly continuous basis compared to very large contracts for capital goods where payment terms may extend over a number of years. This leads to two main categories of policy, namely:

Comprehensive short-term guarantees

This is geared to the spread of the whole export business of a company, thus enabling a spread of risk and economic types of premiums. This type of cover probably accounts for about 75 per cent of ECGD cover.

Specific policies

Large contracts for capital goods or projects are not really suitable for the 'comprehensive' type of cover since there is no continuing pattern of trade. Instead, cover for each contract is arranged individually while the contract is under negotiation. Broadly speaking, such policies cover the same risks as the comprehensive policies and are most often on the *contracts* basis. There is cover in the event of the buyer's refusal to pay within six months of the date of accepted goods, and, where capital goods are sold to public buyers, the ECGD will cover the risk of default at any stage in the transaction.

Specific policy cover is normally for five years, although this can be extended if foreign competitors are backed by credit insurers or equivalent official bodies, usually by member organizations of the Berne Union, which comprises 26 full members and is concerned with the rational development of credit insurance in the international field. Union members agree to provide each other with full details of their methods of operation and to deal with each other in a frank and businesslike way, thus avoiding large-scale international competition in the field of credit cover.

When the exporter completes a proposal form applying for insurance, he sets out the following details:

(1) *Nature of business* – detailed description of goods and normal delivery period.
(2) *Existing contracts.*
(3) *Export turnover* showing exports for each market and total export turnover.
(4) *Bad debts* over three previous years.
(5) *Size of accounts.*
(6) *Declaration* that the applicant has not entered into any other contract of credit insurance or indemnity.

ECGD will then issue a quotation giving premium rates per £100.00 varying according to destination country and other factors. A discretionary limit (£5000 or more) will be shown, up to which the exporter can commit ECGD without specific reference. Once the cover is arranged, the exporter will list monthly the volume of business done in each market and from this declaration the premium is computed and invoiced accordingly.

Claims payment

For most types of cover claims are paid as follows:

(1) *For insolvency of the buyer:* immediately on proof of insolvency.
(2) *For protracted default on goods accepted:* six months after due date of payment.

Table 10.2 ECGD's coverage of United Kingdom exports (1949–50 to 1983–84)

Year	UK exports insured by ECGD* (£ million)	Total UK exports (£ million)	Proportion of UK exports insured by ECGD (per cent)
1949–50	218	1 901	11.5
1950–51	288	2 335	12.3
1951–52	400	2 866	13.9
1952–53	355	2 575	13.8
1953–54	344	2 733	12.6
1954–55	367	2 847	12.9
1955–56	388	3 067	12.7
1956–57	465	3 377	13.8
1957–58	482	3 445	14.0
1958–59	530	3 317	16.0
1959–60	660	3 595	18.3
1960–61	703	3 701	19.0
1961–62	805	3 835	21.0
1962–63	924	4 018	23.0
1963–64	1 081	4 315	25.1
1964–65	1 202	4 452	27.0
1965–66	1 355	5 051	26.8
1966–67	1 576	5 305	29.7
1967–68	1 784	5 389	33.1
1968–69	2 246	6 492	34.6
1969–70	2 487	7 589	32.8
1970–71	2 931	8 134	36.0
1971–72	3 439	9 467	36.3
1972–73	3 594	10 261	35.0
1973–74	4 313	13 210	33.0
1974–75	5 912	17 470	33.8
1975–76	7 479	21 021	35.6
1976–77	10 417	27 712	37.6
1977–78	11 405	34 251	33.3
1978–79	12 443	37 670	33.0
1979–80	14 134	46 477	30.5
1980–81	14 518	47 136	30.8
1981–82	14 537	45 339	32.1
1982–83	16 191	47 705	33.9
1983–84	15 408	52 139	29.6

*These figures exclude business declared under External Trade, Services, Constructional Works and Bank Guarantees, which does not represent direct exports from the United Kingdom. Advances made under economic assistance loans and refinancing are excluded.

(3) *For failure to take up goods:* one month after resale.
(4) *For sterling transfer delays:* four months after due date of payment or deposit of local currency.
(5) *For any other cause of loss:* four months after the date of the event causing loss.

ECGD does not cover risks which are readily insurable by commercial underwriters. Neither are exchange fluctuations or devaluation covered since, again, forward exchange operations are available to assist the exporter to cover this risk. Escalation clauses are now available in certain cases to help exporters in respect of rising costs when dealing with fixed-price contracts.

It should also be stressed that the Department as such does not advance money, but an ECGD policy can be the key to cheaper and easier export financing. There are three different types of direct guarantee to the exporter's bank which cover the whole field of export financing – from business done on open account, through bills or notes, from 30 days to ten years' credit or more. An ECGD guarantee to the exporter's bank covers 100 per cent of the money advanced to him and allows him to finance export credit given at a special rate. For medium-term business, generally speaking credit can be obtained at advantageous rates. ECGD are tending to 'phase out' bank guarantees.

Long-term credit for major projects or capital goods can be financed by special facilities known as 'financial guarantees', which in suitable cases allow a British Bank to make long-term loans for up to 12 years or more to the overseas buyer for the purchase of capital projects. These loans can usually be obtained at preferential interest rates and enable the buyer to pay the supplier in cash, while ECGD guarantees the repayment of the loans to the lender.

The use of ECGD can be gauged by the figures given in *Table 10.2.*

Other types of indemnity

In addition to the government-sponsored ECGD, there are commercial institutions, such as the Trade Indemnity Co. Ltd., which cover transactions both at home and abroad, although the cover afforded is principally concerned with insuring merchants or manufacturers against losses due to *insolvency* or *protracted default* and not against political risks, e.g. on losses arising from exchange transfer and import restrictions. 'Protracted default' is defined as failure to pay admitted debt for goods delivered on credit terms within 90 days of due date (excluding non-payment through political causes).

In some cases cover can be arranged to include work in progress and contractual loss on goods which cannot be delivered by reason of customer insolvency. It may also be possible to extend cover to insure credits opened or cash advanced.

The usual cover is around 75 to 85 per cent, the actual percentage of the risk varying with the quality of the business. The protection is valuable for exporters entering expanding markets.

There are two main policies, namely:

(a) *Specific account* – for one or more named customers.
(b) *Whole turnover* – which covers the whole of a trader's business.

With such a complex type of credit insurance, it is not possible to provide normal insurance tariff rates as there are big variations in individual proposals due to differences in product, type of market and customers.

Administration of such cover is relatively very simple. In the case of a whole-turnover policy, for example, the policy is issued on a perpetual basis from an agreed date and will cover deliveries made on or work done on or after a starting date. Earlier outstanding liability is not covered. At any time before the anniversary date in each year either party may give notice of termination to take effect at the next anniversary date. The assured is given a discretionary limit which must be justified by the current experience of the particular customer's account. Credit above the limit calls for the obtaining of consent and endorsement of the policy by the insurance company. There are some exclusions of cover such as dealings with government departments or nationalized industries, subsidiary or associated companies and deliveries to individuals (cover restricted to business concerns).

On the issue of a policy there is a payment of 25 per cent of the estimated annual premium. Every three months the premium is calculated and adjusted against this deposit and another 25 per cent is debited to the assured. In other words, the insurance company maintains a balance of three months premium in advance. Claims for insolvency do not have to wait until the estate of an insolvent customer is wound up but within 30 days of confirmation that the insured debt has been admitted to rank for dividend in the insolvent estate. In the case of protracted default, payment of claim is made within six months from date when default occurred.

It must be borne in mind that there will be many cross linking and co-operative operations between institutions. As has been mentioned lines of credit can be made available by banks to overseas importers. These credit lines might be backed by ECGD guarantees thus making possible quicker and cheaper forms of payment for the exporter. Below are some examples of such facilities recently available by NatWest group ECGD-backed lines of credit.

Colombia: £1.5 million with Banco de Bogota. Supply contracts to be entered into and approved for financing by 14 March 1986
Czechoslavakia: A third line of credit with Ceskoslovenska Obohodni Banka Prague for £5 million. Supply contracts to be entered into and approved for financing by 2 April 1986
Hong Kong: £3 million with Natwest Hong Kong Branch. Supply contracts to be entered into by 14 February 1986

The above types of lines of credit would be available to UK exporters and overseas importers to complete contracts by providing a source of attractive fixed rate finance (currently between 9.85 per cent and 12.15 per cent) normally for 85 per cent of the eligible value.

At another level the services of the Export Finance Co Ltd. (EXFINCO) could be utilized by companies selling on terms of up to 180 days which hold ECGD comprehensive short-term insurance cover. This could mean the exporter receiving 100 per cent of the credit insured value of the sales in sterling at the time of shipment. The balance, less any deductions resulting from credit notes or other adjustments, is paid on the average due date of the exporter's sales. Regular cash flow is thus fully assured. This facility is priced competitively and has the particular advantage that as the exporter's sales expand so does the facility without continual re-negotiation.

Another example of inter-bank mechanisms of financing exports is that of 'forfaiting'. This in essence is a specialized form of bill or promissory note discounting mentioned in the previous chapter. It provides an appropriate method of medium-term export finance without recourse and involves the purchase by banks of the trade debts. The mechanics of this method can be seen from the following example:

(1) The Hungarian International Bank was approached by a UK industrial goods manufacturer negotiating a contract for the supply of heavy industrial equipment to a state buyer in Turkey. The buyer desired repayment by four semi-annual instalments, i.e. over a two-year deferred payment term. Payments were to be guaranteed by Turkiye Is Bankasi.

(2) The relevant forfaiting rates were quoted to the UK company for financing deals in sterling, US dollars and Deutsch marks. The Turkish buyer opted for DM and the credit price and repayment values were calculated.

(3) The sales contract was negotiated upon the basis of four bills of exchange drawn by the UK exporter in advance of contractual performance. These were accepted by the Turkish importer and given an aval or guarantee by the above-named Turkish bank. The bills were then held by the Hungarian International Bank in the UK to be released to the exporter against presentation of the shipping documents in accordance with the contract.

(4) Once the bills were released against documentary presentation they were discounted by the Hungarian Bank at a committed discount rate and the exporter received cash payment for the full contract value on a *non-recourse* basis.

(5) The exporter, therefore, essentially deals on a cash contract basis whilst the buyer operates on deferred-payment terms. The costs involved are borne by the importer, apart from a commitment fee of 1 per mille per month charged on the value of the financing arrangment from time of commitment to when the bills are discounted. These costs could be taken into account at time of contract arrangment and included by the exporter in the contractual price.

Countertrade

Although somewhat specialized it would not be proper to conclude this chapter without a reference to countertrading or bartering. Essentially this represents a number of possible permutations whereby the sales of goods to an overseas market may be linked contractually to an obligation to buy goods or services from that country. A recent study suggest that no less than 83 countries have at times been involved in countertrade. *Figure 10.3* illustrates a straightforward Full Compensations Deal and a Triangular Compensation Operation.

The average exporter will need to rely heavily upon banks and specialized people such as commodity brokers, etc., to assist in matching up the disposal and sales of bartered goods in order to receive satisfactorily the resultant proceeds in cash terms. Barclays Bank PLC, from whom the information and diagram in *Figure 10.3* was helpfully provided, operate a special countertrade advisory unit.

TRIANGULAR COMPENSATION
(with Hard Currency Goods)

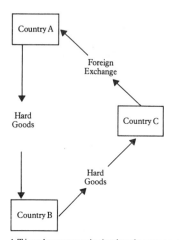

FULL COMPENSATION
(Value in Money)

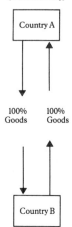

1. Triangular compensation involves the movement of goods between three countries.
2. This arrangement is appropriate when the hard goods offered in compensation by Country B are readily saleable, but not necessarily in Country A.
3. The goods are sold in Country C who then settle in foreign exchange with Country A.

1. One hundred per cent two-way transfer of goods, by means of a single contract.
2. The goods are valued in monetary units.
3. Settlement is often achieved by setting off the sale proceeds of the compensation goods against the amount due from the importer in Country B.
4. The compensation obligation may be transferred to a third party, against payment to that party of a subsidy, called a disagio.

Figure 10.3 Illustration of counter trading

It will be seen from this chapter, therefore, that exporters and importers need to keep constantly abreast of the fast-moving developments in this vital area of financial institutions, their operations and cross-linking systems. This will be necessary both to cushion the various types of credit risks that could arise with an export sale and to be able to identify various sources of finance and ways of improving cash flow. Obviously there is no one simple method since much will depend upon the nature of the product, type of market, length of credit period, etc. The skill required will be to identify appropriate sources suitable for a specific type of contract situation.

11 Cargo insurance

Insurance is a basic element both in our personal lives and in commerce. Privately, we insure our cars, our homes and possessions; in business, we insure our goods, our factories and transport. When we extend the practice of insurance to international commerce, it understandably takes upon itself a more complex pattern due to the wide variety of goods, countries and methods of transportation which are encountered in the exporting of goods and services. To the practising exporter, the class of insurance in which he is mainly interested is cargo insurance, particularly that falling under the headings of marine and air insurance policies. Marine insurance is not limited to transport by sea exclusively as it will in practice often cover any portion of a journey which is made over land. Similarly, insurance for exports by air is handled mainly through marine insurance brokers, and a specialized market at Lloyds deals with this type of cover. Air insurance still draws heavily upon the accumulated experience and principles of marine insurance. ⌐ ??!!!

No part of export is more interesting, or of greater antiquity, than marine insurance; plenty of evidence exists to show that forms of insurance for international trading were being practised in the Mediterranean before the Christian era. The very language and terminology used in insurance practice and documentation is rich and eloquent, still using Elizabethan and eighteenth century phrases and expressions. In 1601, an Elizabethan Act set up machinery to define insurance and marine insurance policies and to prescribe rules and regulations for their settlement. The definition itself is couched in beautiful language and expresses its meaning clearly, as is shown by the following extract:

'.... by means of which policies of assurance it cometh to pass that upon the loss or perishing of any ship there followeth not the undoing of any man, but the loss lighteth rather easily upon many than heavily upon few, and rather upon them that adventure not than those that do adventure, whereby all merchants, especially the younger sort, are allured to venture more willingly and more freely.'

Even today, it would be very difficult to describe the whole philosophy of marine insurance and its principles more clearly than this, as it sums up the whole basis of insurance, namely the spreading of the risk element amongst many. If a trader should lose his whole cargo without insurance cover, he might well be ruined. On the other hand, if a number of individuals undertake to cover a portion of the risk spread over many shipments and cargoes, then the risk becomes more acceptable. The term 'adventure' is still employed in insurance terminology to this day and refers to the actual consignment shipment covered. The last part of the quotation also shows how the tool of marine insurance can shield the trader from the hazards and losses, thus enabling him to enter international trade more willingly. A government department today would give its warmest approval to this Elizabethan incentive to exporters.

The experienced exporter, then, must be able to handle insurance as one of the many technical processes encountered in his profession in order to transact his business and make the necessary decisions. He must know how to apply the appropriate insurance elements to his transactions. This will mean having a working knowledge of the following:

(1) The extent of the exporter's liability for the insurance risk and the point at which risk passes from the seller to buyer. This will, of course, hinge upon the nature of the particular export contract, i.e. whether it is on an FOB, CIF or other basis.

(2) A background knowledge of the Marine Insurance Act of 1906 which originally encompassed the standard Lloyds policy which in turn has been developed into the more simplified Marine All Risks (MAR) policy incorporating various Institute of London Underwriters (ILU) clauses.

(3) The various parties and institutions involved in the marine insurance scene, for example, Lloyd's underwriters, insurance companies and brokers.

(4) The procedures involved in arranging insurance and the relevant documents employed such as policies, certificates and open cover.

(5) Payment of premium, calculations and procedures generally involved in the making and settlement of claims.

Even a brief expansion of these headings will show that a considerable amount of complex subject matter is involved in the entire process. It will be impossible for the average exporter to master completely such a specialized field and, indeed, there is no call for him to do so. He can utilize the skill and experience of his broker or insurance company who will advise him on the best type of cover and the cost of the premium. In practice, many shippers will instruct their forwarding agents to take complete responsibility for the insurance of their exports. Nevertheless, the professional exporter will feel that it is incumbent upon him to gain a knowledge of the basic principles of marine insurance so that he can relate them to the particular order he is handling and understand the background of the different types of risk and hazard, the appropriate type of cover available and how this will affect the premium to be paid. It will be necessary to achieve the correct balance between adequate cover for himself and his customer and yet at the same time to obtain as favourable a rate of premium as possible. Obviously, it would be a great mistake to ship goods which are not adequately covered against the types of hazard appropriate to the nature of the goods. Equally, it would be unsatisfactory to over-insure and pay high premiums covering types of risk which may not be particular relevant to the category of goods involved. Only a clear understanding of the various insurance risk clauses will enable the exporter to select the type of cover relevant to the transaction.

There must be sufficient understanding of the requirements specified by the customer. For example, an order may arrive calling for a specific type of cover which perhaps is not included in the exporter's normal policy. Action would have to be taken to make adjustments to the insurance cover and, if appropriate, to advise the customer of any extra premium payments which may be involved.

The two primary elements which will determine the exporter's course of action and condition his approach to insuring a transaction are:

(a) Terms of sale and type of contract.
(b) Insurable interest.

When we considered export sales clauses (Chapter 2), it was seen that cost and performance obligations arose between buyer and seller and that they would also impinge upon the transferring of the property in the goods and the risk transference. With an FOB contract, for example, the seller will need to arrange insurance cover and be responsible for its cost until the goods are actually loaded on board the designated vessel. We can say, therefore, that the risk passes to the buyer at that point and consequently he will have to arrange insurance. It should be stressed that, in the case of a pure FOB contract, the seller must advise the customer that the goods have reached this position, thus enabling the buyer to make all the necessary arrangements. After this point, the buyer will need to pay for them even if they are lost or arrive in a damaged condition.

With regard to the CIF contract, the duty of the seller is clear. He will have to arrange for appropriate insurance cover for sufficient value and to provide a correct form of insurance policy. The CFR contract will call for the buyer to arrange insurance from the same point as FOB but, as we shall see a little later, there can be complications because of a continuing interest, retained to some extent, by a seller.

Passing of risk in relation to passing of property

So far, then, the passing of risk has been considered. Export consignments are often complicated by the relationship of risk to the actual passing of the property. The FOB contract of a seller might, for instance, make provision for the passing of the property to take place upon satisfactory payment of a pro forma invoice. It may be, however, that property only passes after goods have been received and paid for. A CIF transaction would normally bring about the passing of the property by transferring shipping documents against some form of agreed payment such as documentary bill of exchange drawn at sight or on an acceptance basis.

In the case of a CIF contract, for example, the position is usually clear cut, as the property passing stage is synchronized with the handing over of the relevant documents such as bill of lading, invoice and insurance policy. Supposing that damage has occurred to the consignment, and that the customer, for one reason or another does not take up the documents; the effect of this is that the property does not pass to him as per contract. Now the risk, which technically passed to the buyer at port of departure, could revert to the seller who has retained a continuing interest in the transaction. This would not be very pleasing to the exporter but at least he would (1) possess the title to the goods in the form of the bill of lading, and (2) hold the appropriate insurance policy which would enable him to claim for the loss sustained. In short, we have identified the possibility of risk passing from, and reverting to, the seller.

The position under an FOB sale might be less clear cut and could expose the exporter to rather more risk. Again, we start from the point of risk passing to the buyer, but in this case, assuming damage to the consignment takes place as before, the buyer refuses to take up the goods, perhaps claiming that the advice of shipment indicated that the goods were not as specified in the contract. In this instance then, the risk might revert to the seller, but this time the seller might not be covered by any insurance and might not, therefore, be in a position either to obtain payment for the goods or to claim for the loss under an insurance policy.

A similar position would arise if the contract was a CFR one, with the added complication that the exporter's interest had been extended by the existence of a contract of affreightment between him and the shipowner. In this case, of course, he would have been responsible for booking shipping space and obtaining the bill of lading. Naturally the above concepts have to be applied in varying degrees to the whole range of quotation sales clauses from ex works up to franco domicile, but it is felt that the FOB, C & F and CIF clauses are the most widely used and involve the greatest possibility or risk reversion problems.

The essential factor is that the exporter must satisfy himself as to precisely when property passes and how his risk interest in the transaction is related to insurance cover. For FOB and CFR transactions, it is possible to allow for problems of this nature by both parties agreeing that the buyer's insurance policy could be used to cover the seller's interests if necessary. This would necessitate having the consent of the buyer's insurance company. Often this is a simple process, particularly when the insurer has offices in both the countries concerned. This type of arrangement is quite common in business transacted through the various types of export houses such as merchants and confirming organizations.

Another insurance practice is the use of special 'contingency insurance'. An exporter might elect to cover that portion of his business which he transacts on an FOB or CFR by the insertion of a contingency clause in his normal insurance policy. This means that in the event of risk reversion, the insurance can be attached retrospectively to the beginning of the journey, and loss or damage by insured perils is recoverable. A premium would be necessary for this component part of the cover, of course, but it represents a very sound form of operation for an exporter who deals with his overseas business on the basis of several different sales clauses.

The points covered so far can be summed up as follows:

(1) Nature of sales clause, FOB, CFR, CIF, etc.,
(2) where risk passes,
(3) passing of property,
(4) possibility of risk reversion, and
(5) methods of overcoming risk:
    (a) extension of buyer's policy to cover seller's interest,
    (b) arrangement by insuring company with branch office to hold exporter covered, and
    (c) contingency arrangements through exporter's own policy.

The law relating to the passing of property and risk is very complex and varies considerably from country to country. This point should be clarified wherever possible in the conditions of sale and embodied in the contract.

Marine Insurance Act of 1906

The legal framework for marine insurance is provided by the Marine Insurance Act of 1906, which represents the codification of law relating to this subject. Amongst other things the Act defines

Marine insurance,
insurable interest,
insurable value,
disclosure and representation,
the evidencing of the contract of insurance by the policy,
the voyage,
premium,
types of loss.

For example, it makes quite clear that 'a contract of marine insurance may, by its express terms, or by usage of trade, be extended so as to protect the assured against losses on inland waters or on any land risk which may be incidental to any sea voyage.'

Insurable interest

'Subject to the provisions of this Act, every person has an insurable interest who is interested in a marine adventure.
'In particular a person is interested in a marine adventure where he stands in any legal or equitable relation to the adventure or to

any insurable property at risk therein, in consequence of which he may benefit by the safety or due arrival of insurable property, or may be prejudiced by its loss, or by damage thereto, or by the detention thereof, or may incur liability in respect thereof.'

Note that with regard to insurable interest, the marine insurance policy covers not so much the actual goods but a relationship to those goods.

Disclosure and representation

'A contract of marine insurance is a contract based upon the utmost good faith, and, if the utmost good faith be not observed by either party, the contract may be avoided by the other party.' This principle is frequently referred to in Latin as '*uberrimae fidei*'.

The policy also makes it clear that the assured (exporter) must disclose to the insurer every relevant material circumstance which is known to the assured. It is therefore of utmost importance that all facts, such as those relating to packing of goods and nature of voyage, etc., are set out clearly when insurance is being arranged.

Insurable value

'In insurance on goods or merchandise, the insurable value is the prime cost of the property insured, plus the expenses of and incidental to shipping and the charges of insurance upon the whole.'

It is customary to insure for an agreed value which is in the neighbourhood of 10 to 15 per cent above the CIF value in order to cover incidental losses and out-of-pocket expenses should a loss occur. This is on the assumption that no other specific instructions have been received from the buyer. On occasions, the insured value might well be much higher than the CIF plus the 10 to 15 per cent figure. This is because there may be possibilities of duty payments being made and then loss or damage being sustained on long inland journeys after the discharge of the goods and clearance at the destination port.

A typical calculation might be as follows:

Consignment to Germany with FOB value of £1000 FOB London-insurance premium rate @ £0.30% plus War Risk of £0.05%.

FOB	£1000.00
Freight	57.50
Dock dues	10.00
Port rates	1.00
Customs Entry	3.75
Bills of lading	3.75
Attendance	7.50
	£1083.50·
Estimate insurance @ £1200 @ £0.35%	4.20
	£1087.70
Plus 10%	108.77
	£1196.47

Round up to £1200, the insurance premium is included in the value.

It has been seen earlier that the original basic policy covered by the Marine Insurance Act 1906 was the Lloyds Policy. This policy made provision for a number of different clauses covering particular degrees of risk to be inserted in the basic policy in order to tailor the cover to meet the varying needs of shippers. There were also basic rules for the construction and interpretation of these various clauses. For example, the use of the word 'average' appeared, and employed as a technical term it meant 'partial loss' of the insured subject matter. For many years, therefore, exporters would have been familiar with such clauses as FPA (Free of Particular Average) not covering partial loss, and WA (With Particular Average) covering partial loss. Other clauses such as 'all risks' were also employed.

Over a period of time naturally these different types of terminology have become very complex and the whole subject was studied by UNCTAD (United Nations Conference on Trade and Development). The result of these deliberations was the introduction of the Marine All Risks Policy with a series of restructured risk clauses.

The use of the MAR policy has been obligatory from 1 April 1983, following UNCTAD *Report on Marine Insurance,* which was considered by the Institute of London Underwriters, after much detailed study of technicalities and various clauses by a special committee of ILU. The underlying purpose is to bring marine/ cargo insurance cover into line with the movement of goods by a variety of transport modes coming into common usage during the past few years – the main one being containerization, and to make sure the international trading community worldwide works to full-accepted standards and conduct in insurance, including, of course, countries of left and right political hues, COMECON, for example.

The new policy is dissimilar to its predecessors in that it is simply a document taking in ILU clauses which constitute the cover terms and conditions. All that is recorded on a MAR policy is: full name of assured, the place whence the insurance commences or attaches, the oversea vessel/or conveyance, ports or places of loading, ports and places of unloading, final destination, insured value, currency of cover, details of what is insured and its packing. There are spaces for ILU clauses incorporated in that particular policy, and instructions about procedures in the event of loss or damage, for which the underwriter has become liable.

There are five basic sets of ILU cargo clauses: Institute Cargo Clauses (A), (B) and (C), Institute War Clauses (Cargo) and Institute Strike Clauses (Cargo):

ILU CLAUSE (A): cover 'all risks of loss of or damage to the subject matter insured', subject to a general exclusions clause, exclusion of damage due to unseaworthiness of the vessel and to war risks and strikes. The duration is warehouse-to-warehouse and is defined specifically. Other sections deal with claims, the age-old duty of the assured to minimize losses and to avoid delay. The insurance is subject to English Law and practice. The point to remember here is that each member country of the EEC is bringing its statutes more and more into balance and tune with Community legislation, so insurance will doubtless be one of the first commercial activities to 'cross' or 'parallel' its legal obligations and liabilities, as insurance is so fundamental to any transaction, big or small

ILU CLAUSE (B): cover 'loss of or damage to the subject matter insured reasonably attributed to fire or explosion, vessel or craft being stranded, grounded, sunk or capsized, overturning or derailment of land conveyance, collision or contact of vessel, craft or conveyance with any external object other than water, discharge of cargo at a port of distress, earthquake, volcanic eruption by general average sacrifice, jettison or washing overboard, entry of sea, lake or river water into vessel, craft, hold, conveyance, container, lift van, or place of storage, and total loss of any package lost overboard or dropped whilst loading on to, or unloading from, vessel or craft. As with ILU Clause (A), there are exclusions and the other duties and paramount law.

ILU CLAUSE (C): cover provides basic standard protection against major casualties, but are not as comprehensive as ILU Clause (B) and are not as full as ILU Clause (A). (A useful way of rule of thumb memory when arranging insurance is that cover decreases in power or force as we go through the alphabet.) Clause (C) says loss of or damage to subject matter reasonably attributed to fire and explosion, vessel or craft being stranded, grounded, sunk or capsized, overturning or derailment of land conveyance, collision or contact of vessel, craft or conveyance with any external object other than water, discharge of cargo at a port of distress, loss of or damage to the subject matter insured causes by general average sacrifice or jettison. As with Clauses (A) and (B), there are exclusions, and the other duties and paramount law.

A very important fact to notice is that delay, inherent vice, or nature of the subject matter losses are excluded from clauses and need careful attention to avoid unpleasant results from wrong assumptions or ignorance.

ILU CLAUSES War Risks (Cargo) and Strike Risks (Cargo): losses by risks of war and strikes are incorporated in the MAR policy by adoption of the appropriate ILU clauses. War risk cover exists only whilst goods are on board and ceases upon discharge (or can be earlier in certain circumstances – underwriter and insured must be quite clear about start and finish of war cover, say, in the Middle East today).

MAR has been tailored to take in many of the older trade clauses appertaining to special interests, and once all have been accommodated satisfactorily the Lloyds policy would become superfluous.

As exporters and importers may, for a time, still come across a mixture of old and new terminology, as a guide we could bear in mind the approximate (not exact) equivalents:

Free of Particular Average (FPA)
   Now Institute Cargo Clause (C)
With Average (WA)
   Now Institute Cargo Clauses (B)
All Risks (AR)
   Now Institute Cargo Clauses (A)

Care should be taken when, for example, handling letters of credit, that there is no confusion between the old and new terminologies.

Air cargo

Air cargo is covered by ILU Air Cargo Clauses (All Risks)

The speed and ease of handling of air freight makes an insurance risk attractive to the underwriter/insurer, characteristics which are reflected in the lower rates charged generally. Whilst an air disaster is spectacular and concentrates the public attention exceptionally, it is true that air traffic is one of the safest methods of travel/moving goods and has been over many years. Statistically it is far removed in the safety factor league from street/pedestrian/road accident which is notoriously high!

By the nature of air movements, very short transit times, lighter packing required, quick clearance at destination points and, in most places, stricter theft-pilferage control, a significant number of export despatches go by air these days, and no longer is it only a service for smaller items, lighter weight and valuables. A typical aircraft manifest, or loading list, shows a wide variety of goods carried.

Though it is possible to arrange lesser cover, it is recommended that the all-risk ILU clauses be used since these give such good protection. Total loss, theft, pilferage and non-delivery are the main worries to be eliminated, if we are prudent.

In another chapter the carriage of dangerous or hazardous goods is mentioned and we refer again to this activity; for obvious reasons 'restricted articles' regulations bulk large in air freight handling and it is emphasized strongly that the description of what is offered to the airline must be precise. If it is found later, perhaps in less than a total 'casualty', that this was not done, the insurers will declare that cover null and void and cancelled. It is never worth while being less than completely frank and honest about our goods – you are not only endangering the passage of inanimate objects, you are endangering lives.

General average

The use of the term 'average' must be quite clearly distinguished from that so far considered. It is quite separate and distinct inasmuch as it envisages the sharing of a loss between shippers and ship-owners. First of all, 'general average' is based upon a relationship between the ship-owner and *all* the shippers who have cargo aboard the same vessel on a particular voyage. All these parties are said to be bound together in the 'adventure'. If, in order to save the ship and some of the cargo, a particular shipper's goods have to be sacrificed, then an act of general average is declared and the ship-owners and the other shippers, whose cargoes have arrived safely, are called upon to contribute towards the loss of the shipper whose cargo has been sacrificed. An example might be of a ship with a full load which takes fire in No. 5 Hold. Action is taken by hose and by throwing overboard burning cargo. The danger is averted and the ship makes port safely with the rest of the cargo intact. All the cargo in No. 5 Hold, however, has been sacrificed. In such a case a general average would be declared and the ship-owner and the owners of the remainder of the cargo would contribute towards the lost cargo in proportion to the value of the ship and freight.

The rule of maritime law relating to general average is extremely ancient. It can be found in the Digest of Justinian and has throughout the centuries become a part of the Common Law of England. There are in existence the York-Antwerp Rules which relate to general average. These rules, first formulated in 1877, have been revised several times, the present set dating from 1950 and 1974. They consist of a series of lettered and numbered rules, the following being two specimens:

Rule A   'There is a general average act when, and only when, any extraordinary sacrifice or expenditure is intentionally and reasonably made or incurred for the common safety for the purpose of preserving from peril the property involved in a common maritime adventure.'

Rule 2   'No jettison of cargo shall be made good as general average, unless such cargo is carried in accordance with the recognised custom of the trade.'

The rules are not a complete code of law but provide a framework and basis of reference and interpretation which can be modified or supplemented by different legislation and practices of individual ship-owners. The Carriage of Goods by Sea Act 1924/1971 allows for the insertion in a bill of lading of clauses covering any lawful provision regarding general average. The exporter would find such clauses printed amongst the terms and conditions on the back of the bill of lading which might contain the following type of wording:

'General Average, if required, according to York-Antwerp Rules 1950/1974. Adjustment shall be prepared at such port as shall be selected by the Ship-owners. Such deposits as the Ship-owners or their Agents may deem sufficient to cover the estimated General Average contribution and any salvage and special charges to be made by the Shipper, Consignee, Owner of the goods and/or Holder of this Bill of Lading before delivery.'

A general average loss, therefore, takes the form of a deliberate sacrifice of property or the incurring of expense. The following basic elements must be in existence before such a general average can be declared:

(1) The purpose of the act must be to preserve the whole maritime adventure. Any such expenditure or sacrifice of property merely to help preserve a part of the adventure would not constitute a general average loss.
(2) The particular act must be voluntary and deliberate. General average is a system of making good international losses, not those which happen by accident.
(3) The loss must be extraordinary.
(4) The loss must be reasonably and prudently incurred bearing in mind all the prevailing circumstances. Any hasty or panic action would not result in general average.
(5) The particular loss must be a direct result of the general average act. Indirect losses such as alternative opportunity costs, etc. would not be admitted.
(6) The exporter or shipper must study the appropriate clause on the back of the bill of lading which will show in detail the particular implications that arise between him and the ship-owner, should general average arise.

When a ship arrives 'under average' the ship-owner will appoint an 'average adjuster' whose task it is to arrive at an impartial assessment of the values involved and ensure an equitable apportionment of the sums of money due. This is a highly complex and exacting profession calling for a deep knowledge of maritime law and marine insurance. Basically, the contribution will be levied on the net values of the various interests at the point of destination, as follows:

Ship   Value at place where voyage ends. If the ship is damaged the cost of repairs is deducted from the estimated sound value.

Freight   Any freight earnings which accrue to the ship-owner which might not have done so if the ship had not made port. This might apply to consignments shipped on a freight forward basis.

Cargo   Market value of the cargo on arrival at destination.

Even a simple case of general average will often take a long time to assess completely. It may be necessary to examine and analyse many different cargoes in order to trace damage which is allowed in general average and that which is not. This, for example, could be a very complex affair if damage was by fire.

Owners of cargo will be called upon to produce declarations of value and to substantiate these with appropriate documentation. They will then be expected to sign an 'average bond' which represents an undertaking to pay any amounts which may become due. Sometimes deposits may be called for and these will be based on a rough estimate of the respective values involved. The shipowner has a lien on the goods until such deposits, if called for, are paid by the cargo owner.

The insured cargo owner will, of course, be covered for such general average amounts as may become due, and the following clause would be found in his cover:

'*GA Clause.* General Average and Salvage Charges payable according to Foreign Statement or to York-Antwerp Rules if in accordance with the contract of affreightment.'

If a GA Guarantee is called for by the ship-owner, this would be signed by the insurers of the cargo.

Such contributions calculations under general average can be very involved but the following simple example may at least enable the basic principles to be identified.

Assume a ship with a value of £400 000 which was saved owing to a general sacrifice of cargo. The cargo itself, if it had arrived, would have been valued at, say £120 000. Let us assume that the remainder of the cargo which was actually saved, amounted to £80 000 – all freight being paid in advance.

The *contributory values* of the property saved would be:

Ship	£400 000 — saved
Cargo	80 000 — saved
	£480 000

If the two interests had to pay towards the £120 000 in full they would each have to contributed 25 per cent of their value. However, the loser of the £120 000 cargo also has to make his general average contribution, so the calculation would appear as follows:

	Contributory value		Contribution
Ship	£400 000	pays	£ 80 000
Sound cargo	80 000	pays	16 000
Amount made good in respect of sacrificed cargo	120 000	pays	24 000
Total	£600 000		£120 000

In the above case, therefore, the percentage contributions in each instance amount to 20 per cent of the respective values.

Again, it should be emphasized that the provisions in the bill of lading and the type of contract affreightment will often specify the particular code which is going to condition the average adjustment. When no such code is specified, then the adjustment will usually be according to the law and practice in the port where the voyage ended.

Marine insurance procedure

Having considered the background of legal aspects of marine insurance affecting the policy, and the various types of risk cover available, we can now consider how the exporter will enter into the contract of marine insurance, obtain cover and the relevant types of policy.

Insurance will be arranged by the exporter approaching an insurance company having a department specializing in marine insurance. There are at least 100 such companies, many of them maintaining offices in the principal commercial cities, especially London and Liverpool which are the two main insurance centres.

The services of a broker may be utilized. His job is to 'shop around' for the right type of cover and, wherever possible, obtain competitive premium rates. Marine insurance brokers are highly skilled technicians and tend to specialize individually in specific commodity groups or market areas. Consequently, their assistance can be of enormous benefit. Their success will depend on their obtaining sound and reliable cover consistent with favourable premiums. It is of little use going for lowest premium rate if, in the event of a claim, the insuring company is slow, reluctant and unhelpful.

It is possibly true to say that the hub of marine insurance, certainly in the United Kingdom, and having an immense reputation throughout the world, is the Corporation of Lloyd's. This is in effect a market place for insurance where over £1560-million-worth of premium income p.a. is transacted, over half from abroad. There are some 26 000 'named' members of Lloyd's and insurance can only be placed with them through some 265 firms of approved brokers. Marine, motor and aviation business is conducted on the ground floor and general non-marine business on the gallery floor surrounding the Underwriting Room. Members have to deposit a substantial sum of money to act as security for their business; the standards which result are very

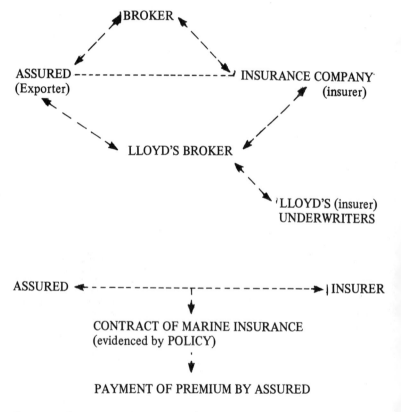

Figure 11.1 Relationship of parties in marine insurance

high. The members operate in groups known as 'syndicates' and there are some 380 syndicates currently in business. The whole principle of insurance can be seen to operate through the underwriting system as each syndicate, when presented with a 'slip' which sets out the details of the risk to be covered, can elect to accept a portion of the risk, which it does by 'writing a line'. The task of the broker, both at Lloyd's and with other insurance companies, is to obtain a series of 'names' so that all the risk is covered. He does this at the best premium rate which is consistent with the good cover and security. It should be stressed that the various syndicates are in competition with each other and that the Lloyd's brokers are not restricted and can approach other insurance companies for competitive conditions.

The broker acts as an agent of the assured, and yet he is remunerated by the insurer in the form of a commission which, while varying somewhat, in London is around 5 per cent. Usually, a 10 per cent discount is allowed originally as an incentive for the assured to pay the premiums promptly. When marine insurance has been effected, the broker is liable for the payment of premium but can exercise a lien on the policy for unpaid premiums. They may take care of the collection of claims, but only if specifically requested to do so and would normally be entitled to charge collection commission. It might be useful to trace the relationship of the various parties by means of *Figure 11.1*.

Some traders will ask their shipping and forwarding agent to take care of the insurance on their behalf. In this case, such agents would apply this against their own block policy cover.

Warranties

We have seen so far that the general terms of the insurance required are put forward by the broker on the 'slip'. At this stage it is necessary to remember that a fundamental principle of all insurance is utmost good faith, coupled with the disclosure of all relevant facts pertaining to nature of goods, destination, value and packing, etc. Sometimes it will be necessary for the cover to be based on the concept of a warranty which means in effect an undertaking that some particular condition will be observed. With delicate scientific equipment or aircraft parts, for example, it may be a condition of the terms of insurance that they should be 'warranted professionally packed'. Equally, the nature of the packing may require a warranty, such as

200 wooden cases of Carbon Black warranted packed in internal polythene bags.

A breach of such warranties could well discharge the insurer from liability. There may be a compromise made in the shape of a warranty such as 'packed in steel drums or held covered'. In this case, should the consignment be going forward not, in fact, packed in steel drums, then the insurer will require immediate notification in order to arrive at an additional premium although the consignment would in fact be covered for risks.

Type of insurance policy

The basic instrument in a marine insurance contract is the *policy*, essential features of which are

(1) Name of assured (or agent who effects insurance),
(2) *bearer* policies, although used in some countries, are not effective in the UK,
(3) subject matter designated with reasonable certainty and clarity,
(4) destination,
(5) name of vessel and/or steamer,
(6) types of risk covered,
(7) where claims are payable,
(8) sum insured, and
(9) dated and signed.

Against Item (5),when showing the name of the vessel, it is usual to indicate it in a general manner, such as

'mv HEINRICH and/or Steamers as per Institute Classification Clause attached and/or Conveyances.'

The reference above to the 'classification clause' might be encountered when the insurance cover requires the employment of a vessel of a particular standard, such as Lloyd's Register 100A1. When the policy has been prepared and received by the exporter he will usually (for example in a CIF transaction) 'assign' the policy to the buyer by stamping it on the back with the name of the company, together with a signature by an appropriate official of that company.

Open cover and the floating policy

From the standpoint of a busy exporter, it is not practicable for him to arrange individual insurance cover and obtain policies of insurance for each shipment of goods. We find, therefore, two basic types of mechanism which are designed to overcome this problem. They are 'open cover' and the 'floating policy'.

Open cover

These contracts may be run for a fixed period with automatic renewal, or may continue indefinitely until cancelled. They are represented by a written undertaking on behalf of the insurer that policies will be issued within the terms of a generally agreed form of insurance cover.

Floating policy

This type of policy describes the insurance in general terms, leaving the name of the ship and other particulars to be defined by subsequent declarations. An average premium is paid at the beginning of the period and if subsequent shipments are made with varying premium rates, there is a periodical adjustment. An example is shown below:

Floating policy for £50 000 at average premium £0.50%

1st shipment	£20 000.00	@	£0.50%	=	£100.00
2nd shipment	£10 000.00	@	£0.25%	=	£ 25.00
3rd shipment	£20 000.00	@	£0.375%	=	£ 75.00
	£50 000.00				£200.00

Total premium paid = £50 000.00 @ £0.50% = £250.00
Refund = £50
Total premium earned = £200.00

Floating policies operate in a manner very similar to the open cover, except that an actual policy is in existence. Each shipment is declared, written off the policy until the total coverage has been exhausted and then, in most cases, a new policy is issued. These policies are tending to decline since they are somewhat cumbersome to administer and premiums have usually to be paid in advance.

With both open cover and floating policies, the assured is required to make a series of declarations covering the individual shipments as they take place. Usually, these are done by filling in a particular type of declaration form similar to the following:

Please insure the following under the open policy in the name of

---

Messrs

Vessel

From	To	Via

Marks	Description of goods	*C & F value
		Insured value

Please send cover notes to *us

messrs

---

*Please delete as applicable

Another method which is now more usual among exporters is for them to complete an actual certificate of insurance which they are empowered to sign. This acts as a declaration of the details and value of the consignment for the insurer, and other copies can go to the customer as documentary proof that insurance has been effected. Although strictly speaking a CIF contract, for example, requires a *policy* of insurance, commercial practice has established internationally the tradition of providing certificates of insurance. Indeed, most letters of credit allow for the production of this type of document.

Because of the somewhat vague terms which operate under the open cover, and to a slightly lesser extent floating policies, a number of clauses have been developed to enable the insurers to maintain a degree of control over the various aspects of the risk cover. These can be outlined in the following manner:

(1) *Basis of Valuation Clause* indicates how the consignment is to be valued, e.g. CIF plus 15 per cent.
(2) *Declaration Clause* states the manner and the periods of time involved in declaring shipments to the underwriters.
(3) *Classification Clause* (example as above) relates to the requirements of vessels being up to a satisfactory standard and age.
(4) *Location Clause* specifies amount of insured risk at any single place on land such as a warehouse or shed at the dock.
(5) *Cancellation Clause* provides for an agreed period of notice required for the cancellation of a cover.
(6) *Limit per Consignment Clause* means that an individual shipment may operate only up to a specified value.
(7) *Advice Clause*: provisional advice may only be required if the shipment value exceeds an agreed level.

The Marine Insurance Act makes provisions for 'valued' and 'unvalued' policies. The former is self-explanatory in the light of earlier comments on insurable value. The unvalued policy does not specify the value of the subject matter insured. This might be applicable to products and commodities whose market value fluctuates markedly. In such a case as this, the basis of valuation clause may operate.

Premiums

So far it has emerged that there is a wide variety of risks for marine insurance cover and a number of ways in which they can be covered by the insertion of the appropriate set of clauses. Naturally, the premium to be paid will be relative to the risk, and the skill of the underwriter will be directed towards all the various factors that together will give rise to the cost of the insurance of a commodity or a market. Any attempt to be very precise would be misleading as there are enormous variations in premium rates. These are often set for each policy on an individual basis. In many cases, large international trading organizations would receive preferential rates becuse the large volume of business enables the underwriter to spread the risk element. Again, rates must vary widely with different product categories and market areas.

A selection of typical rates is set out below, which will attempt to provide a comparison resulting from

(1) Different product categories,
(2) type of risk covered, e.g. ILU(C), ILU(B) etc.,
(3) geographical areas involved.

General cargo–machinery, paper goods, etc.	ILU(A)		
France, Holland, Denmark	£0.20%	+ £0.05	War Risk
Germany	£0.25%	+	"
South America (East Coast)	£0.375%	+	"
South America (West Coast)	£1.00%	+	"
Malaysia	£0.50%	+	"
Cyprus (ports)	£0.50%	+ £0.075	"
Cyprus (inland)	£0.50%	+ £0.20	"
Chinaware			
Aden	£5.25%	+ £0.05	War Risk
Hamburg	£4.00%	+	"
New York	£5.00%	+	"
Candles			
Australia	£1.00%	+ £0.05	War Risk
Ghana	£2.00%	+	"

The above examples give some idea of magnitude and comparison between the different product categories and geographical areas and assume the same type of risk, namely 'all risks' plus war risks.

Another set of figures was obtained but this time with the main object of obtaining some idea of the possible rates that would result from different risk cover. These are set out as follows:

Machinery	*Malaysia*	*Near Continent*
ILU(C)	£0.20%	£0.10%
ILU(B)	£0.31%	£0.15%
ILU(A)	£0.625%	£0.20%
China and earthenware		
ILU(C)	£0.25%	£0.12½%
ILU(B)	£0.44%	£0.20%
ILU(A)	£6.00%	£4.00%

It is interesting to note the big jump in premiums for China between ILU(B) and ILU(A). Again, it must be stressed that the premium rates themselves should not be taken as being precise because of the possibility of their variation from company to company and between different insurance companies and brokers. Many other factors will enter into an underwriter's calculations and it might be of value to consider a most exhaustive list of such factors which has been prepared by the Insurance Company of North America. They list 14 specific factors which will be considered when the underwriter calculates a rate of premium for a policy. They are:

(1) Type of coverage (risk, etc.).
(2) Commodity characteristics.
(3) Origin, destination and voyage.
(4) Carriers used.
(5) Any warehousing or transhipment during voyage.
(6) Possible effect of shrinkage, loss of weight, etc.
(7) Seasonal character of shipments.
(8) Type of packing.
(9) Relationship of value to packing, susceptibility to pilferage.
(10) The experience of the assured as an exporter.
(11) Normal shipping and handling practices appropriate to the particular trade involved.
(12) Relationship of assured to consignee and his outlook towards claims.
(13) Efficiency and attitude towards third party claims and recoveries.
(14) Possible salvages applicable to the type of product and market.

It will be seen from the above that a prudent exporter, acting in an efficient manner, can in some respects conduct his business in a way which will enable him to obtain good premium rates. If his record is good with regard to his action against third parties, packing, steps taken to prevent pilferage and efficient handling of his insurance business, this will naturally place him in a beneficial position.

The premiums shown above are, of course, based on value for insurance declared by the exporter.

Example: 1 case of machinery valued at £1000.00
Premium rate £0.225% *Marine* subject to Institute Cargo Clauses

FPA *Institute War Clauses* £0.05%. Warranted no risk to attach this policy on the expiry of fifteen days after discharge of goods at destination port.

Therefore £1000.00 @ £0.225% Marine, £0.05% War = Premium of £2.75
(Note in above example a type of time-limitation warranty, i.e. 15 days after goods arrive at destination port.)

It has already been stated that the assured will normally declare values of at least CIF plus 10 per cent and often much higher, owing to inland journey cover and possible loss of duty. There are two points to be borne in mind with regard to these possible 'uplifts'. First, if in doubt, the assured should always give details of large uplift figures to the insurer who may desire to check the position in order to ascertain if there is in effect valid insurable interest. Secondly, where high duty figures are involved, they should be shown separately as often the premium on the actual duty component can be lowered if assessed separately rather than simply lumped together in a total CIF value.

The following is an example of a typical breakdown figure which might be found on an insurance certificate.

'£2200.00 + £500.00 Stg. to cover Duties from time of arrival in New York, USA. We hereby declare for Insurance under the said Cover Two thousand seven hundred Pounds Sterling on interest as specified hereon so valued per TRIAS TRADER at and from Works UK via London to Works New York, USA, subject to the terms of the Standard Form of Lloyd's Marine Policy and the special conditions stated below and on back hereof.'

Franchise and excess

A 'franchise' refers to a percentage of the loss or damage which it is agreed will not be covered by the underwriter. An ILU Clause (B), for example, may incorporate a franchise of say, 5 per cent. Let us assume this applies to a cargo of cartons of books. Assuming the cartons arrive and on outturn it is found that 2 per cent of the value of the books were damaged; in this case no claim would be payable. If the value lost was above the 5 per cent figure, then a claim would be payable.

An 'excess' is where the exporter would undertake to be responsible for a certain percentage of any loss himself.

Claims

When considering a CIF contract, one would expect the exporter to arrange insurance, procure the appropriate policy or certificate and send it to his customer with other relevant documents such as bill of lading and the invoice. The policy or certificate would be *assigned* accordingly to the customer who, in the event of loss, would normally be responsible for actually carrying out the claim procedure. However, in many cases it will be necessary in the interest of good customer relations to assist the buyer in his claim. It is interesting at this point to remember the 'ex ship' type of contract which, as distinct from CIF, is an obligation actually to effect physical delivery of the goods. In a case such as this, the obligations would probably rest upon the exporter's shoulders to lodge a claim for any loss.

As has been seen when analysing the structure of the marine insurance policy, it is incumbent upon the assured to take all appropriate steps to minimize damage, and the *Sue and Labour Clause* may, in certain circumstances, entitle him to payment for any expenses involved in carrying out such operations, although he would be wise to check with the insurer's agent and representative first.

A typical declaration of the action that the assured is required to take is represented by the following instructions that might well be attached to a policy:

Important notice to assured concerning liability of carriers, bailees or other third parties.

'It is the duty of the Assured and their Agents, in all cases, to take such measures as may be reasonable for the purposes of avoiding or minimizing a loss and to ensure that all rights against Carriers, Bailees or other third parties are properly preserved and exercised. In particular, the Assured or their Agents are required:

(1) To claim immediately on the Carriers and on the Port Authorities for any missing packages.
(2) To apply immediately for survey in the docks by Carriers' representative if any loss or damage be apparent and claim on the Carriers for any actual loss or damage found at such survey.
(3) In no circumstances except under written protest, to give clean receipts where goods are in doubtful condition.
(4) To give notice in writing to the carriers' representative within three days of delivery if the loss or damage was not apparent at the time of taking delivery.

Note: The Consignees or their Agents are recommended to make themselves familiar with the Regulations of the Port Authorities at the port of discharge.

The assured, as soon as he becomes aware of loss or damage, should send written notice to the insurance company or their agent in order to arrange a survey and obtain the necessary survey report. The Corporation of Lloyd's, for instance, has some 1500 agents throughout the world and it is often the practice for policies to state that, in the event of loss or damage, settlement of claims will be facilitated if Lloyd's agents are called in to hold survey.

It is customary for the maritime insurance company groups to issue handbooks covering the marine claims settling agencies which they utilize throughout the world. We might find for example that in Paris the Agent representing the Royal Insurance Co. Ltd., might be given as J. Robida et Cie. Similarly, the same company might be represented in Naples by Mario Erra. It should also be noted that sometimes the appropriate agents might only arrange surveys while another centre would have to be used for making claims.

The exporter will be concerned with claiming for the loss under one of three basic headings, namely 'partial loss', 'total loss' or 'constructive total loss'. The first two are self-explanatory. Constructive total loss applies, for example, when the consignment may not be 100 per cent damaged, but is in such a state that it would cost more money to put it back in its original form and it might therefore have to be sold for scrap.

For total loss of part of the cargo, the claim calculation would be simple, following the lines of the following example:

10-cartons of Carbon Black, which should have a gross arrived value of	£2000.00
Actual consignment arriving has a value of (owing to loss of one case)	£1800.00
Amount of loss	£ 200.00

Loss = £200 or 10%
Therefore claim based upon 10% of insured value, say 10% of £2200 = £220.00

An example of partial loss if, say, 1 carton was not lost but was only damaged, might be as follows:

Gross arrival value should be	£2000.00
Less damaged carton	£ 200.00
Actual arrival value, 9 cartons sound	£1800.00
Damaged carton realises	£ 150.00
	£1950.00

Amount of loss = £50.00 or 2.5% of gross arrived value

The claim should be filed with the insurance company as soon as possible. The assured should check the policy or certificate to see if any express instructions pertaining to claims are contained therein but he would normally expect to send the following documents:

(1) Insurance policy or certificate suitably endorsed.
(2) Survey report.
(3) Possibly an Outturn Report.
(4) Master's Protest – usually a formal statement commenting on the conditions and causes relating to the loss.
(5) Bill of lading.
(6) Invoice.
(7) Accounts sales if there are proceeds of sales.
(8) Any correspondence with shipowner or other third parties.
(9) Letter of Subrogation which transfers any rights of claimant against carriers to the insurer (see Appendix B).

The number and type of documents will to some extent depend upon the type of loss. In the case of total loss, a full set of bills of lading would normally be expected. For partial losses, additional weight notes or packing lists would have to be produced.

Care should be taken with regard to actual place where the claims are payable. This should normally be covered in the original contract, when we would expect to find perhaps 'Claims Payable Abroad' (CPA) inserted in the policy. At all times it must be ensured that any settlement of claims at destination does not conflict with existing laws or financial regulations.

12 The simplification of documentation

Most exporters, be they new to the field or experienced practitioners, are to some extent bound to be frustrated by the various documentary processes to which they have to conform. Even if they have mastered all the technical details and have become experts in preparing and processing documents with complete success, there is still the feeling that much of the work is really fruitless and that if one country can accept goods without a lot of complicated documentation why cannot other countries? The very wide variations themselves also contribute to the great difficulty in training new personnel: there seems at first glance to be little uniformity.

Our preceding consideration of export practice will have made us realize that there are so many functions in an export transaction that there will be a stream of documents from different sources. Equally, we must be realistic and accept the fact that a large number of these will almost always be essential. If we insist on a letter of credit in order to enjoy a great degree of security, then this will impose certain documentary demands. If we ship goods, we shall in many cases want a receipt and title to ownership; this will mean a bill of lading. In order to ensure risk cover, combinations of insurance policy or certificates will have to be arranged.

Equally, we must see the whole process as a dynamic one and be prepared for a constant state of flux. Trading agreements may arise between countries which allow for some documentary relaxation but, at the same time, new sovereign nations are emerging which may call for new documentary systems and obligations. The conclusion of some preferential tariff arrangement between countries will be enthusiastically welcomed by international traders, but will at the same time, inevitably lead to the necessity of some type of documentation to substantiate the origin of the goods in order that they should qualify; examples of EUR 1, T2L forms and other types of certificates of origin illustrate this point. Similarly, even if the actual forms themselves could be eliminated, there would still be the necessity to provide some form of input data for statistical and other purposes.

These remarks are not intended to be a form of apology for documentation but simply to remind ourselves that when we look at the export order and its various stages, we are bound to accept the fact that there must always be a fair measure of documentary procedure involved. Our task at this stage is to examine the efforts that have been made to improve the position and the very substantial improvements that have, in fact, already been achieved.

The process of simplification

It might be fruitful at this stage to consider the concept of simplification under three main headings:

(1) *The technical production process.* Under this heading, we consider the actual production and typing of the individual documents themselves. How can the forms be so designed that a number of different documents can be produced at one typing? How can devices such as photo-copying processes and computerised systems or word processing be brought to bear upon the problem?

(2) *The simplification of the actual export transaction itself,* which automatically brings about a reduction of documentary requirements. An example of this is the growth of the container system which means that a number of individual organisations previously handling the transaction can be concentrated into one organisation and can issue one document covering a series of hitherto separate functions.

(3) *An examination by different governments of possibilities of reducing their actual demand for certain documents.* It might be possible, shall we say, for consular invoice requirements to be relaxed or customs entry procedures to call for less, or at least simpler, documentary procedures.

It is possibly fair to say that up to now the greatest progress has been made in category (1), the streamlining of document production. The first move in this field must of necessity be an attempt to achieve some form of international understanding with regard to the shape, size and layout of the documents themselves. The concept is, of course, not new. As far back as 1874, the Universal Postal Union introduced standardized forms for international postal traffic. The Berne Convention (CIM) similarly achieved the standardization of forms for international rail carriage. In 1953, the French delegation to the Customs Co-operation Council proposed that a technical committee should examine the possibility of reducing the number of documents used in international trade and to see if the remaining indispensable documents could be standardized in design and format. As a basis of study, the documents required by the Customs officials of member countries were collected and examined. This revealed the fact that there would be considerable difficulty involved in the standardization of all these documents because of the variety of legislative requirements of the countries concerned.

The credit must go to Sweden as the country which, starting in 1955, was the first to achieve a standard layout of international trade documents with particular reference to seaborne trade. Later, Denmark, Finland and Norway adopted an aligned series of commercial and official documents. It was soon apparent that extremely worthwhile savings could be achieved. Scandinavian companies were reporting cost savings on documentation of up to 70 per cent, and cuts of up to 20 per cent were being made in some export administration departments.

Work in this field was extended internationally when Sweden brought the matter before the United Nations Economic Commission for Europe (ECE) and in 1960 a working party was set up to investigate systematically the various possibilities of standardizing and simplifying export documentation. Meeting in 1961, the working party invited each country to set up its own national committee. Governments and international organisations, particularly the International Chamber of Shipping and the International Chamber of Commerce, aimed at an agreed standard size and layout which could become the basis of a simplified system for all the main export documents. The result came to be known as the 'ECE layout key' now known as 'UN layout key', and was based upon a standard bill of lading Model B which was on international A4 size paper (297 mm × 210 mm), a size which was already finding favour on an international level.

One of the results of the working party was the formation in the United Kingdom of the Joint Liaison Committee on Documents used in the International Carriage of Goods (JLCD). This committee was formed in 1962 and later developed into the very important body known as The Simplification of International Procedures Board (SITPRO). This body, formed in 1970, is an independent organization set up by the Department of Trade. Its board and specialist working groups draw on a wide range of interests, including exporters, carriers of all modes, freight forwarders, bankers and government departments. SITPRO staff are recruited by the Board itself with an eye to practical experience of international trade and information systems. Work is carried out in the closest possible consultation with British interests likely to be affected by, and benefit from, the results. About 200 people from business and relevant government departments help directly in the practical work. In this way any product, solution or service marketed by SITPRO is moulded to the needs of British international trade.

SITPRO master systems

The terms of reference are to survey the whole range of existing documents needed for the international carriage of goods with reference to simplification methods. It was also essential that any investigations should consider the problems of all parties concerned including exporters, shipping and forwarding agents, port authorities, insurance companies, shipowners and government departments.

It soon became apparent that, as has already been implied, the greatest obstacle to streamlining was the variety of sizes, shapes and designs of the relevant documents currently in use in export transactions. Their standardization and layout were, therefore, the first step towards an all-round improvement. As a large proportion of international trade is still seaborne, most governments, including the United Kingdom SITPRO, tended to concentrate first of all quite naturally on maritime documentation, although it was always invisaged that ultimate application would be extended to other forms of transportation. This was illustrated by the emergence, in 1982, of the new UN-aligned air waybill.

Although the very term 'export documentation' can be applied to all documents associated with the export transaction, from the stage at which the order is received and acknowledged right through to the delivery of the goods to the dock and ultimate loading on board ship and then extended to the ultimate receipt of payment, it was felt initially that certain of these stages could not be effectively covered. The many invoice-based forms and financial documents had obviously been designed to meet the special commercial requirements of individual exporters and indeed many of them were designed to meet the statutory requirements of overseas governments such as consular invoice forms, preferential certificates of value and origin and straight certificates of origin. Consequently, committees like SITPRO have concentrated on the 'consignment-based forms' which are controlled and issued by ship-owners, chambers of commerce and government departments. However, over the past few years great strides have been made in extending the master layout schemes to a wider range of documents such as invoices etc., as will be seen later. Incidentally, it is of interest to note that, quite apart from any other consideration, the move towards a standardization of shape, size and layout by itself makes it easier for an exporter to look at the various forms and understand them and to complete them with the relevant data. One has only to look back over a short period of time to remember the many shapes and sizes of bills of lading and how difficult it was to remember where particular details had to be inserted. To anybody but an experienced practitioner, it was difficult to believe that the many types of bill of lading from different shipping companies were in fact the same basic document and fulfilling the same purpose.

Consequently, the first stages of simplification usually take the shape of a basic standardized key layout which can then be used with a number of prime documents which have in turn to be modified in shape and size to enable them to be used with the master key. Usually, the first phases concentrate on the 'consignment-based forms', over which government committees can, in fact, exert some control or influence. Following upon this it has become increasingly feasible for the individual exporters to modify many of their own office produced documentation

It is evident, therefore, that the design of the UN key layout has to be very precise, with its objective nothing less than a concentration of all the essential information required for various trade documents in an export transaction. This information includes:

Name and address of buyer and/or consignee or order
Notify address
Name and address of exporter or shipper
Name and address of forwarding agent (if applicable)
Country of origin
Country of destination
Trading country
Method of transport
Marks and numbers of packages
Gross and net weight
Quantity and specification
Value of goods
Appropriate statistical code number

Date and place of issue of documents
Appropriate reference numbers
Insurance value
Terms of sale
Method and terms of payment
Currency involved
Appropriate signature

Some degree of flexibility must always be allowed for by designing a blank space within the layout key which can be utilized for unusual or infrequent requirements.

From the concept of the 'master copy' certain principles emerge which apply to the design and co-ordination of a documentary system.

The standardization is aimed at questions of size and layout only. The object should be to provide standard positioning of the data which is actually included on the form.

Very careful initial measurement is required pertaining to the spacings used in order to correspond with a wide variety of office machines in use, dimensions of vertical columns, etc.

There should, wherever possible, be a natural sequence to the various groups of information.

Spaces reserved for addresses should be standardized and placed in positions suitable for use with window envelopes.

The system is intended to assist many different categories of exporter, operating under diverse circumstances, and utilizing a wide variety of office equipment. Any new system must be flexible enough to be a practicable proposition in small offices on simple equipment as well as in the offices of large organizations complete with elaborate reproduction equipment and technical expertise to operate them.

So far we have arrived at the concept of a master copy on which all possible information is placed, plus the fact that all the main documents have been brought into line as far as shape, size and layout are concerned. It should be possible to complete the master and then, by various reproduction methods, using an appropriate masking system, to produce at one run a set of shipping documents. This is known as the aligned 'one-run' system. During the design stages of this system, SITPRO surveyed thousands of consignments shipped to all parts of the world and came to the conclusions that this master/aligned series method should prove capable of accommodating the details of 80 per cent of the consignments examined.

Range of documentary simplification

This method of completing a set of shipping documents has the obvious advantage that only one document actually needs typing and, equally important, that once it has been checked, the accuracy of all the other forms is assured. Once the concept has been accepted, it is really most gratifying how many individual documents can be brought into line with the aligned series system. The main categories of document conforming to the SITPRO aligned systems include

(1) Bill of lading
(2) Customs Entry C273
(3) Customs Entry C63A
(4) Standard shipping note
(5) Invoices/certificates of value and origin
(6) Certificates of insurance
(7) Application forms for special stowage (hazardous goods, etc.)
(8) Movement certificates
(9) Bank Instruction Forms
(10) Export cargo shipping instructions

This range is already quite extensive; a surprising number of functions which form part of the overall export transaction are covered. We can expect the range to be extended considerably in the non-to-distant future. There must, of course, be some limiting factors on the amount of information which can be contained on a master key. Companies exporting very complicated items such as machinery or prefabricated buildings are often called upon to provide on their bills of lading and invoices, etc., very long and detailed specifications which in many cases could not be incorporated in a master copy system.

There are, of course, problems in the sense that if we look at the types of form which can be used with the aligned series system, a number of these, such as the Customs entry form and standard shipping note, together with bills of lading, might very well be handled by the exporter's shipping and forwarding agent or loading broker. Nevertheless, all exporters should consider carefully the use to some extent of the master key/aligned series system. There is no reason why internal paperwork systems should not be adapted so as to dovetail with the streamlined system. For example, quotation layouts, stock letters, acknowledgements of orders, despatch notes, pro forma invoices and other domestic documents are in many ways capable of modification. Nor should it be overlooked, where space limitations restrict the amount of data which can be contained on a master copy, that considerable savings can still be achieved if only a portion of the data is reproduced, as the time needed in a separate operation to complete the required details might still be less and therefore bring about staff economies. Considerable work is being done in this field by specialists in organizations and methods, office managers and manufacturers of reproducing equipment. In short, the whole area is capable of much development.

Many exporters are inhibited from attempting to develop such systems because they feel that they are appropriate only to the large, heavily mechanized organization handling a very large volume of export orders. This is a pity, because although there are limiting factors to all systems, it is very often worthwhile to use the aligned system even if the documents are being produced manually and no mechanical forms of reproduction are used. Suitable masking sheets can be interleaved between carbon papers and there are the peripheral benefits of uniform-sized documents which make filing and storage easier. Also, as has already been implied, documents will be easier to identify and understand. It will also be easier to train staff if the same information always appears in the same relative position on each form.

Types of copying process

The greatest economies will tend to flow from high-volume documentary production, coupled with some type of reproducing equipment. Although this would not be the appropriate place to go into the technical details of the various processes available, perhaps brief mention could be made of the basic types.

Spirit duplicating

The master is produced by typing or photocopying and utilizing hectographic carbon. This is placed in contact with paper which has been dampened by spirit solution. The spirit softens the carbon deposit on the master and allows an impression to be transferred to blank copies of printed forms. The type of registration achieved is good and both manually and electrically-operated models are available. Pre-cut masks are placed between the master and the copies; this allows the various details to appear as appropriate on the particular form.

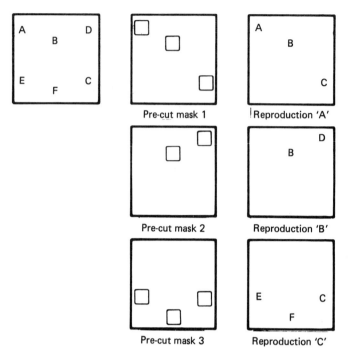

Figure 12.1 Masking a master key layout to obtain different combinations of details

Dyeline process

The original master is translucent and exposed to ultra-violet light over a sheet of copy paper whose light-sensitive coating is destroyed except where protected by liquid or heat. A double-exposure is involved, the first reproducing the outline and basic static information of the particular form. The second superimposes the selected information appearing on the master. This is achieved by using two specially prepared translucent plastic folders.

Photocopier systems

This method is probably at present the most popular, since it employs equipment which is often already installed in the office and could be applied to many different areas of a company's business operations. It fits in ideally with the master/overlay system and a wide range of overlays is available from SITPRO. For companies processing a large volume of export orders the manipulation of individual overlays on small photocopiers might prove a little cumbersome, and in this case more sophisticated systems employing a 'web' or 'reel' system (such as produced by Rank Xerox) can be pre-set and operated, say, under micro-processor control. Mr. Charles Freebury, a director of SITPRO, estimates that some 4000 export companies employ photocopier methods.

Computers

The use of these is continually growing and many applications are now possible. For example, they can be made to link up to the company's internal operations via, say, photocopiers and word processors.

The computer could be used to produce a pro forma invoice for the customer to obtain an import licence, and a word processor to write the letter giving details of the potential order.

The letter of credit arrives. The system is set to produce banking documentation requirements, having processed the factory instructions and despatch instructions to vessel, perhaps through a freight forwarder. An interesting fact is the possibility of direct connection between Customs and private entities for computer import entries, and this is likely to become commonplace for both imports and exports.

This direct connection is used extensively by freight agents, and the trend will be to encourage links between Customs and private authorized despatch points, or through inland container facilities, for example. For speeding paperwork and to save costs by simplification of method, computer use on the physical distribution side of exports – say, assembly of goods, handling, packing and exit overseas of an order – shows significant benefits, which will grow.

Whatever system is being operated, of crucial choice is of course the appropriate 'software'. This must be researched carefully in the light of the individual exporter's requirements. Lack of planning and research in this area can lead to disappointment and represent a very costly mistake. There are today many specialist consultancy companies who can help to advise and select a suitable hardware/software system consistent with the exporter's needs and resources.

One of the most world-wide in operation is the SITPRO Spex 2, a leader in the field of micro-computer packages. This system can store large amounts of data drawn from the company's mainframe computer and prepare a wide range of documents for many overseas markets and also produce the appropriate calculations. The current outlay is in the neighbourhood of £7000 for a single micro-computer installation, and Mr. Freebury estimates that most exporters can look for a 'pay back' in as short a time as six months.

The above is intended to give only an outline of some of the methods available and a sample of the appropriate terminology. It will, however, be realized that ranging from the smallest exporting organization to a sophisticated office system, there will be available some form of process which can be adapted to meet specific requirements.

The other move towards documentary streamlining and simplification will obviously proceed hand-in-hand with improved systems of transportation. It has long been accepted that large segments of the overseas transaction are much simpler when air transport is used. A substantial proportion of air-carriers actually handle clearing and customs, etc., facilities and, as they concentrate a number of activities into their hands, there is a diminution of documentary requirement. By tradition the air waybill is not employed so often as a transferable document of title and therefore the documents go forward by air to the consignee. The fact that airlines, by their very nature, have built up more closely-woven international organizations also enables them to incorporate many functions in the overseas country.

We now see changing sea and land transportation methods play their part in simplifying documentation. We may consider, for example, a container transaction where the shipping company will often arrange to collect from an inland factory or clearing depot and issue a 'received for shipment' bill of lading, thus removing many of the intermediary stages. Some shipping lines can now issue 'non-negotiable' sea waybills which if suitable for the exporter's financial arrangement can often streamline documentary operations and assist in avoiding demurrage charges. This type of waybill has, in effect, brought sea transport operations into line with air transport from the point of view of paperwork. In some instances container companies have taken it upon themselves block insurance cover enabling them to issue combined bills of lading and certificates of insurance. It is true that there are many genuine difficulties associated with traditional insurance cover and risk-spreading, but these are all pointers to the future and indicate the areas where we can look for improvements.

It was seen earlier that a segment of documentation falls under what we have chosen to call the 'regulations' heading and this has always proved something of a stumbling block to documentary simplification efforts. The International Chamber of Commerce has pointed out that there are still major difficulties arising out of consular requirements and formalities and Customs requirements. Although much progress has been made towards reducing the demand by various countries for consular invoices/consular legalization or chamber of commerce certification, there are still some countries, particularly in Latin America, who require these types of documentary process. Sometimes, these requirements are also linked with unreasonable demands regarding documentation, with unnecessary rules with which it is often almost impossible to comply, and with the ultimate outcome of heavy fines.

The number of Customs requirements calling for special invoices and valuation amount to what is often a very severe trade barrier. In many cases, countries are being asked to look at their requirements to see if irrelevant data can be omitted and if certain declarations can be combined on one document such as value and origin. The widespread adoption of uniform Customs description in the shape of the Tariff/Trade Classifications such as the CCCN has also been a step forward and is, as we have seen in an earlier chapter, itself undergoing further modification and development. It is a salutary thought, and one on which the exporter might dwell when he considers all the various organizations, many of which we have mentioned above, who are constantly working in an untiring effort to smooth the path of the international trader.

13 Customs 88 project

In previous parts of this book reference has been made, particularly in Chapter 7, to impending changes mainly in the sphere of Customs procedures due for promulgation in 1988. The result will be major innovations in Tariff classifications and structure and EEC documentation and procedures.

Originally, when revising this edition, many of the proposals and plans being formulated were still largely in a planning and tentative situation. Since the completion of the manuscript, however, most of the agreements and discussions have been finalized and the position has consequently become much clearer. In the UK, HM Customs and Excise have begun to release an excellent series of *Information Notes* charting progress and outlining the new procedures.

In these circumstances therefore it was felt that it would be beneficial to add a short final chapter outlining some of the main aspects of the changes and how they will impinge upon present documentary procedures.

Basically these changes will influence the following segments of the export transaction:

(1) The introduction of a new, more detailed system of Tariff classification and commodity description.
(2) Changes in documentary procedures and Customs requirements for imports/exports with particular reference to EEC operations.
(3) A new range of Customs Procedure Codes (CPCs) replacing the existing Customs Transaction Codes.
(4) The emergence of a brand new form, the Single Administrative Document (SAD), which will embrace many of the procedures outlined in (2) above and will markedly transform much of the EEC documentation currently operated through T2, T2L forms, etc.

The above must therefore be carefully studied by both practitioner and student alike but they must also be kept in perspective. If reference is made to the four-fold classification of the export order in Chapter 2 (p.31) it will be seen that the changes will mainly impact upon the Regulations section. Whole areas of export documentation embracing bills of lading, waybills, carnets, invoices, certificates of origin, etc., will obviously remain in operation in their present mode.

Tariff classification developments

It must be kept clearly in mind that tariff classification systems have evolved in order to fulfil two main requirements, namely:

- (a) To provide a statistical classification tool to enable the measurement and identification of the import and export of an increasingly wide range of products.
- (b) To relate particular categories of products to possible import duty or tax rates, or to other forms of possible control such as 'end-use', quotas, etc.

On many types of export/import customs form, plus in many cases invoices, there will often be the requirement for the insertion of various tariff numbers. As these activities are viewed against the background of international trade it will also be obvious that there has always been the need to try to make classification systems and numbers as international as possible so that a wide range of countries could employ the same systems. Consequently the history of international trade abounds with activities in this direction.

As has been seen earlier in the book the present major international tariff classification numbers are based upon the CCCN (which is still not universally employed). As the new tariff classification systems will follow the pattern (though not necessarily the same numbers) as the CCCN we can consider this in more detail.

The basic CCCN approach is based upon chapters, headings and subdivisions. Thus:

Men's and boys outer garments	61.06
Coats	61.06 0100

It will be seen that the normal current pattern is one of eight digits and, of these, digits 5–6 relate to certain statistical classifications required by the Statistical Office of the European Community (SOEC) as well as duty relationships of the Common Customs Tariff (CCT). This number is known as the CCN/NIMEXE Code

(Nomenclature for the Foreign Trade Statistics of the EEC). Digits 7–8 incorporate certain UK statistical subdivisions. The point to be stressed here is the manner in which tariff classification systems generally have to cope with the requirements of both international community and national components.

Since the initial work of the CCC in 1950 leading up to the adoption of the CCN by a large number of countries, there has naturally been a growing need for further classification development and refinement. Work therefore began in 1973 on a new system which has now emerged as the Harmonized Commodity Description and Coding System, known as HS, which will supplant the existing CCCN system by 1 January 1988. It is hoped that it will also be embraced by countries such as the USA, China and Canada whom do not at the moment employ the CCN system, and that the HS will therefore represent amongst other things a major step forward in the field of internationally accepted classification systems.

Although, as already mentioned, the HS will follow the structural lines of the CCN (namely based upon chapter and heading numbers), there will be additional subheadings and extended statistical classifications for freight tariffs and production statistics. There will of course be extensive renumbering as the HS nomenclature is expected to be expanded to cover some 5000 descriptions compared to the current 1000 of the CCN. New tariffs will be published (in the UK through HMSO) and of course it is expected that certain correlation tables will become available to assist in reclassification. However, it must be stressed that, owing to the considerable expansion of the tariff, simple direct core correlation will not be possible because as already mentioned extensive renumbering is taking place.

The new tariff classification numbers will also impinge upon other procedures such as their relationship to the rules of origin for FTA treatment as set out in HM Customs Notice No.828 (pp.148–149). Revision of these rules must therefore be expected.

With the implementation of the HS the EEC is taking the opportunity to link the change with the introduction of an EEC form of integrated tariff known as TARIC. This of course will be based upon and fused into the HS but the systems at time will be considered as entities in their own right. The normal type of intracommunity trade classification will consist of a nine-digit system with possibly up to 11 digits (and sometimes additional numbers) for certain third country transactions or perhaps specialized situations such as CAP exports and imports.

Bearing in mind what has already been written in this chapter regarding the number of digits, the Community Integrated Tariff (TARIC) is expected to shape up as follows:

Digits	1–6	HS code
	7–8	CCT/NIMEXE code
	9	National statistical subdivision for member states
	10–11	To identify certain aspects such as quotas, licensing or other community measures on imports from third countries and possibly some intra-EEC trade re end-use, etc.
	12 and above	Might be utilized by individual countries for, say, specialized excise or VAT identification.

It can be seen therefore that exporters/importers might find themselves referring to:

Short code	9 digits
Long code	11
Additional codes	possible extra numeric or alphanumeric characters

With regard to the impact of HS on duty rates, GATT will apply the criteria for the transposition in terms of concessions, etc., and it is expected that during this process there will be some amendment in duty rates applied between trading partners. Negotiations are proceeding in Geneva at present. This will mean that from the export marketing point of view many exporters will be scrutinizing some of their overseas markets to see if there will be any change in duties applied to their particular products and this will naturally go hand in hand with their work of reclassification.

Procedural and documentary changes

The other major innovation in 1988 will be the introduction of a multi-page, multi-functional document, the Single Administrative Document (SAD). In essence, this will provide a system whereby, during the course of an export consignment movement, various pages of the SAD will be utilized to satisfy the various requirements at the different stages of export entry, transit in EEC and import clearance. Considerable discussion and experimentation has taken place but the final version of the SAD was adopted

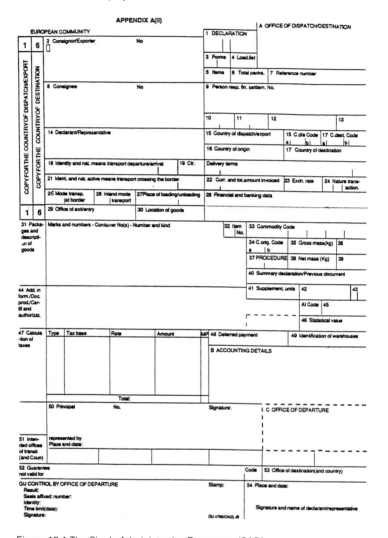

Figure 13.1 The Single Administrative Document (SAD)

in Brussels on 27 June 1986. *Figure 13.1* illustrates a page from this new document which is normally expected to be an eight-page set. A breakdown of the utilization of the various pages is set out below (HM Customs *Information Note* No. 3):

Copy 1   replaces copy 1 of full procedure T form (T1 or T2)
Copy 2   Export Declaration for statistical purposes

Copy 3   Exporter's/Agent's copy
Copy 4   Replaces T2L or copy 2 of full procedure T form
Copy 5   Replaces copy 3 of full T form
Copy 6   Customs declaration at country of destination
Copy 7   Statistical declaration for country of destination
Copy 8   Importer's copy

The above disposition is obviously based upon an intra-community operation and can be seen essentially as a form of 'sandwich'. Copies 1–3 would take care of procedural requirements in the exporter's country, for example copy 2 will replace the C.273 or other similar types of customs entry form. Copies 4–5 are essentially taking care of the transit operations and replacing certain types of T form. Copies 6–8 will be employed at the receiving end and will of course replace appropriate customs import entry forms.

A special version of the SAD can be provided for companies operating computerized documentation who may be using printers not capable of accommodating eight copies in a single set. This version will be a four-page set, each copy having a dual purpose, thus:

Copy 1 or copy 6
     2 or   7
     3 or   8
     4 or   5

Exporters could, if they wished to provide an eight-copy set, print two sets and simply delete copy numbers. *Figure 13.1* illustrates the dual numbered copy 1.

Naturally the system has mainly envisaged intra-community practices and the operation of the sandwich will of course vary with this type compared, say, with EEC/EFTA or third country transactions. Much will naturally depend upon other third countries and their willingness to accept SAD pages or their equivalent in place of their own particular types of import form and procedure.

In order to maximize the benefits of the new form the designers of the SAD have made provision for a 'split use option' so that the various functions can be separated, e.g. to enable the form to be used only as an import declaration (in order perhaps to preserve and allow pre-lodgement facilities already being used by an importer at the receiving end). Hand in hand with the employment of the SAD will go a degree of redesign of other customs forms so that an exporter engaged in third country trade may be able to utilize documentation compatible with SAD layout but perhaps with provision for extra Customs information.

Naturally no one document can be expected to carry all burdens, but it is encouraging to know that it is claimed that some 70 existing documents within the EEC will be replaced by the new system. Inevitably some existing forms are expected to be retained, such as the C1220 employed with CAP transactions. Some other existing forms may be retained in a redesigned format. Equally it is felt that the EUR1 document for EEC/EFTA trade is likely to continue in use. There can be little doubt, however, that 1988 is to be a year in which the most major step forward in improved documentary practices will be achieved.

Appendix A
Incoterms. Abbreviations for export clauses. A three-letter system to enable automatic data processing developed by ICC in conjunction with UNEC

1. ex works = EXW
2. FRee Carrier (named point) = FRC
3. Free On Rail/Free On Truck = FOR/FOT
4. Free On board Airport = FOA
5. Free Alongside Ship = FAS
6. Free On Board = FOB
7. Cost and FReight = CFR. Until lately, this has been known as C & F
8. Cost, Insurance and Freight = CIF
9. Freight or carriage paid to (named point) = DCP. This is the container equivalent of Cost and FReight (CFR)
10. Freight or carriage and insurance paid to (named point) = CIP. This is the container equivalent of Cost, Insurance and Freight, CIF
11. ex ship = EXS
12. ex quay = EXQ
13. Delivered At Frontier = DAF
14. Delivered Duty Paid = DDP

Appendix B: Export credit insurance compared

	Insurer	Types of Organisation	Maximum percentage of cover on risks			Other	Main Risks Excluded	Max. Length of Credits (years)
			Commercial	Political	Economic			
Britain	Export Credits Guarantee Dept.	Government Department	90	95	95	50% of losses on export promotion	Losses on exchange fluctuation	5 (occas. 7, or more to 'match' competitors)
United States	Eximbank; Foreign Credit Insurance Assoc. (F.C.I.A.)	Autonomous govt. agency; assoc. of private insurance cos.	90	short-term 95 medium-term 85	short-term 95 medium-term 85	–	–	5 (occas. 15)
W. Germany	Hermes Versicherung A.G. Deutsche Revision und Treuband A.G.	Private corps acting on government's behalf	Private 80 Public 80	90	85	Preshipment manufacturing risks (85% of cost)	Default of private buyers	5 (occas. 12: up to 20 on investments)
France	Compagnie Francaise d'Assurance pour le Commerce Extérieur (C.O.F.A.C.E.)	Private corp. but government's agent for political risks	Private 80 Public 90	Private 90 Public 95	Private 80 Public 90	50% of loss on market exploration 100% on losses on cost rises above 20%	Default of private buyers	5 (occas. 7–10)
Italy	Instituto Nazionale delle Assicurazioni (I.N.A.)	Govt. agency	Public 85	85	85	60% of losses on cost increases or planning studies	Private insolvency or default	5 (more for major products)
Belgium	Office National du Ducroise (O.N.D.)	Public organ. with govt. guarantee	75 (exceptionally 80–85)	90	90	–	Default of private buyers: exchange fluctuations	5 (more for major products)
Netherlands	Nederlandse Crediet verzekering Maatschappij N.V.	Private co. but state reinsures some risks	90	90	90	90% on non-acceptance of goods	–	5
Japan	Ministry of Trade and Industry (M.I.T.I.)	Government Department	90	90	90	–	–	10

There are very broad and general comparisons and are intended only to give an outline of some of the many international institutions. The reader should refer to the more detailed matter available for a more comprehensive comparison.

Appendix C:
Letter of subrogation

Vessel ....

Voyage ....

Sum Insured ....

In consideration of your paying us for a total loss on the undermentioned goods insured with you (in virtue of which payment you will become subrogated to all our property, rights and interests in the said goods and in any monies payable or recoverable in respect thereof on account of general average, salvage, or other wise howsoever) we hereby authorise you to make use of our name for the purpose of any proceedings or measures, legal or otherwise, which you may think fit to take in respect of the said goods, and we declare that we were the owners thereof at the time of the loss, and we undertake to furnish you with all the papers and correspondence in our possession or control relating thereto, and to make any affidavits and to give any oral evidence which we can properly make or give, and generally to render to you any such assistance as you may from time to time reasonably require, in connection with any such proceedings or measure, you indemnifying us against all liability costs charges and expenses incurred in connection therewith and with the use of our name therein.

Dated .... day of 19

Description of Goods.......

Bibliography

Colin Barnes, *Metric Conversion Manual*, Croner Publications, New Malden, Surrey

Don Benson and G. Whitehead, *Transportation and Distribution Made Simple*, W. H. Allen, London

David Cox, *Elements of Banking*, John Murray

Arthur J. Day and colleagues, *The Freight Forwarders' and Export Managers' Handbook*, Cornhill, London

D. M. Day, *The Law of International Trade*, Butterworths, London

E. R. Hardy Ivamy, *Casebook on Carriage by Sea*, Lloyd's of London Press

J. McLoughlin, *Introduction to Negotiable Instruments*, Butterworths, London

Alan Mitchell, *Bills of Lading – Law and Practice*, Chapman & Hall, London

D. Prag and E. D. Nicholson, *Businessman's Guide to the Common Market*, Pall Mall

Clive M. Schmitthoff, *The Export Trade – a Manual of Law and Practice*, Stevens, London

Eric Swift, *Managing Your Export Office*, Business Books Communica-Europa

Michael J. Thomas, *International Marketing Management*, Houghton Mifflin, New York

F. M. Ventris, *Bankers' Documentary Credits*, Lloyd's of London Press

Regular publications and reference sources

British Overseas Trade Board, London and branches: Various publications and guides for exporters

Croner Publications, New Malden, Surrey: Reference books for exporters, air transportation and conference lines, etc. Very valuable documentation reference

Export Credits Guarantee Dept., London and branches: A range of booklets and leaflets

GATT, Geneva: *Forum* publication

HM Custom and Excise, London and branches: A wide range of notices and explanatory booklets

Institute of Export Journal, 64 Clifton Street, London EC2: A wide range of data and articles

International Air Transport Association (IATA), Geneva: Traffic publications

International Chamber of Commerce, London and overseas: A wide range of brochures and publications

Lloyd's of London, London: *Loading Lists* and various *Supplements,* and other publications

National Westminster Bank, London and branches: Monthly *Exporters' Bulletin* and a range of export/finance publications

Documentation Guide, Tate, Milton Keynes, Bucks

Index